Revolution and Reaction in Cuba, 1933–1960

A Political Sociology from Machado to Castro
by Samuel Farber

Wesleyan University Press
Middletown, Connecticut

The publishers gratefully acknowledge the support of the Andrew W. Mellon Foundation toward the publication of this book.

Library of Congress Cataloging in Publication Data
Farber, Samuel, 1939–
   Revolution and reaction in Cuba, 1933–1960.
   Bibliography: p.
   Includes index.
   1. Cuba—Politics and government—1933–1959.
2. Communism—Cuba. I. Title.
F1787.5.F37   320.9'7291'063   76-7190
ISBN 0–8195–4099–4

Book design by Jorgen G. Hansen
Manufactured in the United States of America
First edition

*To Jacek Kuron
and
Karol Modzelewski*

Contents

Acknowledgments   ix

Preface   xi

Major Events in Cuban History, 1868–1960   xvii

Chapter 1. Toward a Theory of
the Cuban Revolution   3

2. The Revolution of 1933   28

3. The Social Context
of Revolutionary Failure   52

4. The Counterrevolution of 1935   78

5. The Constitutional Period
of the Forties   93

6. The Failure of Constitutional
Politics and Its Consequences   117

7. The Second Batista Dictatorship   145

8. The Rise of Revolutionary Politics   176

9. The Early Development of
the Revolutionary Regime   202

Notes   239

Selected Bibliography   261

Index   271

Acknowledgments

PART OF THE editing necessary to prepare this study for publication was underwritten by a grant from the Committee on Research of the Academic Senate of the University of California, Los Angeles, for which I am grateful.

The research for this book would not have been possible without the assistance of the staff of the Inter-Library Borrowing Department of the Library of the University of California, Berkeley, and that of various individual librarians at the New York Public Library, the Library of Congress in Washington, D.C., the Hoover Institute Library at Stanford University, the Library of the University of Miami at Coral Gables, Florida, and the Library of the University of California, Los Angeles.

Numerous people have read and commented on partial and complete drafts of the manuscript while it was in preparation. I want to thank all of these friends and to give special thanks to four people whose editorial and intellectual advice was truly invaluable — Sherri Butterfield, Elizabeth Kodama, William Kornhauser, and Michael Rogin.

Preface

ALTHOUGH THE Cuban Revolution of 1959 has aroused much interest throughout the world, most analyses of it have been inadequate in that they have oversimplified its causes or labeled it rather than explained its character. This failure to deal adequately with the nature of the Cuban Revolution is perhaps a reflection of a greater one, the failure of historians and social scientists in particular and authors in general to deal adequately with Cuban society and politics before the 1959 revolution, which thrust international political significance upon a rather small and often unnoticed island.

Whatever the cause, this scholarly neglect both in and out of Cuba has resulted in a scarcity of primary research on a wide array of questions, the answers to which are indispensable as background information. There are, however, a variety of studies made at various times in the past by both Cubans and foreigners with which one can begin to reconstruct a picture of the political and social conditions that made Cuba ripe for revolution in the fifties.

After going through most of this varied literature and doing a significant amount of primary research in Cuban periodicals and similar sources, I believe that I have succeeded in assembling enough reliable evidence to support my interpretation of Cuban society in the period between the Revolution of 1933 and that of 1959 and of the way in which that society influenced the course of Cuban political history.

Unless otherwise noted, translations from Spanish are my own. I have tried to avoid political jargon and obscure technical terms.

Thus, for example, I use the familiar term Communism instead of Stalinism, without linking it with the communism of Marx, Engels, Lenin, Luxemburg, and Trotsky, however.*

I have been selective in my treatment of the period 1933–59 in Cuba. I did not intend to write a full, detailed history, but to focus upon various crucial aspects of the political history of this period. Many important issues are not analyzed: the specific economic nature of imperialist domination, and the nature of race relations, among others. These questions, though extremely important in their own right, are not directly relevant in proving the validity of my main theses. Such a process of selection entails dangers, but inevitably one must make such choices.

II

I owe it to my readers, I feel, to state as clearly as possible the political standpoint from which I have examined and analyzed the data. I was born in Cuba and lived there until the age of eighteen. During my teen-age years, I was involved in student politics at a public high school. At that time I could have been described as a "democratic populist." High school politics were, to a large degree, an extension of the national oppositionist politics that had their origin among the militant student body at the University of Havana. I left Cuba before the advent of Castro; since then I have experienced new and different political situations, and my views have evolved. Today my politics could best be described as revolutionary democratic socialist. I see the working class, internationally, as the key agency for revolutionary socialist change; and I unconditionally support all anti-imperialist struggles as well as the struggles of all oppressed groups in the United States and elsewhere. From my point of view, the nationalization of the means of production is a

*To clarify this distinction between the original meaning of the word communism and the Stalinist appropriation of the term, I have capitalized all uses in the latter case.

necessary but insufficient condition for the attainment of a qualitatively better society; nationalization must be accompanied by democratic control from below.

These are some of the fundamental premises that guide my political judgments and daily political activity. It goes without saying that my revolutionary opposition to the regime now in power in Cuba is inextricably linked with my revolutionary opposition to capitalist restoration and to imperialist intervention (whether American or Russian) in that country.

It is high time to acknowledge that Cuba is now a totalitarian and bureaucratic state in which one man, with the aid of a small group of associates, controls the economic, social, and political life in the country. The Communist party of Cuba is organized on the principle of elite membership and forbids any internal factions or deviations. The powerful armed forces are organized in an even more authoritarian fashion. As Fidel Castro has explained, "Educating and orienting the revolutionary masses is an unrenounceable prerogative of our party, and we shall be very jealous defenders of that right. And on ideological matters it will be the party that dictates what ought to be said. . . . All material about politics can come to the people only through our party, at the time and the place that our party determines."[1]

Castro has left no doubt that he considers this the desirable and appropriate form of political organization not only for Cuba and other less economically developed countries but for any "socialist" country, regardless of its degree of economic development. In his indictment of the Czechoslovakian reformers he clearly stated this:

> A real liberal fury was unleashed; a whole series of political slogans in favor of the formation of opposition parties began to develop, in favor of openly anti-Marxist and anti-Leninist theses, such as the thesis that the Party should cease to play the role there of a guide, supervising some things, but, above all, exerting a sort of spiritual leadership — in short, that the reins of power should cease to be in the hands of the Communist party. . . . A series of slogans began to be put forward, and in fact certain measures were taken such as the establishment of a bourgeois form of "freedom" of the press. This means that the

counterrevolution and the exploiters, the very enemies of socialism, were granted the right to speak and write freely against socialism.[2]

Even Castro's self-critical speech of July 26, 1970, while acknowledging many mistakes and promising as many changes, failed to deal with the crucial question of his own personal rule and the corresponding lack of popular control independent of Castro and his close associates. It is only logical and natural that a governmental system which does not allow *independent* feedback from the Cuban masses should not only encourage but in fact inevitably produce arbitrary and bureaucratic behavior on the part of officials at all levels.

A democratic revolutionary socialist alternative was possible in Cuba in 1959. The urban and rural working class and the peasantry could have been politically organized and led toward taking power into their own hands instead of being cast in the role of providing plebiscitarian approval for the revolutionary elite at mammoth rallies. That would have required a political program, organization, and leadership aimed at making the masses more politically self-reliant. Far from this, however, the Fidelista leadership has preserved unaltered the most fundamental elitist and undemocratic concepts of contemporary Communism. This has been true also of the most radical Fidelistas such as Ché Guevara. As the socialist author K. S. Karol has explained, "Che preferred to take shelter behind two myths, both of them imported from the U.S.S.R. First, after the Revolution, the workers should have no interests other than the acceleration of production in accordance with the overall economic plan; and second, the revolutionary leaders know best how to interpret the thoughts and needs of the working class, from which they themselves have sprung."[3]

It is quite true that a revolution in which the workers and peasants took power in Cuba would have provoked no less domestic and foreign resistance than did Castro's revolution. It is also clear that a revolutionary socialist Cuba could survive by itself in a hostile imperialist world no more easily than a Communist Cuba can. A revolutionary socialist Cuba could have been defeated if it had failed to obtain sufficient international support to withstand imperialist hostility. However, revolutionary socialism was no less defeated when Communism triumphed in Cuba. For Communism is not a "second best" choice if it prevents a people from democratically controlling the economic and political life of their country. Rather, it is as much the enemy of such democratic control as capitalism is. In any case, it is not for students of the Cuban Revolution nor for the revolutionary leaders to make such a choice — it is the Cuban people themselves who must make such a truly free decision, and they have not yet done so.

I have made this political statement because students of society do not approach their material with empty minds to which each datum seems as good as any other. We select data out of a rather large universe of facts, and we do so at least partly on the basis of our own predispositions. As a matter of elementary honesty, an author should, therefore, make clear his or her own predispositions so the reader can bear these in mind when evaluating the author's work.

Major Events in Cuban History, 1868–1960

1868–98	Cubans wage war against Spain during most of this period.
1898	Battleship *Maine* explodes in Havana harbor, and the United States declares war on Spain. A peace treaty is later signed, making Cuba a protectorate of the United States.
1901	Platt Amendment is attached to the Cuban Constitution granting the United States the right to intervene in Cuban affairs.
1902	Cuba is officially declared independent with Platt Amendment restrictions on its sovereignty.
1906–09	The United States intervenes in Cuba again.
1917–22	The United States intervenes in Cuba a third time.
1925–33	Gerardo Machado rules as dictator.
1933	United States Ambassador Benjamin Sumner Welles mediates between Machado dictatorship and part of the opposition. Machado abandons power on August 12. On September 4, 1933, Sergeant Fulgencio Batista leads revolt with the support of civilian revolutionaries. Ramón Grau San Martín becomes provi-

	sional president. Grau government is not recognized by the United States.
1934	Batista removes nationalist government of Grau San Martín. Platt Amendment is officially abolished but the United States retains a naval base in Guantánamo Bay. Reciprocal Trade Agreement between Cuba and the United States is signed.
1934–40	Batista controls Cuba through puppet governments.
1940	New Cuban Constitution is established.
1940–44	Batista rules Cuba as constitutional president.
1944–48	Ramón Grau San Martín is president.
1948–52	Carlos Prío Socarrás is president.
March 10, 1952	Batista overthrows Prío in military coup.
July 26, 1953	Attack on Moncada barracks fails and the Castro brothers and followers are captured.
May 15, 1955	Batista decrees political amnesty and the Castro brothers, their followers, and other political prisoners are released from prison.
December 2, 1956	The *Granma* lands in Oriente Province, bringing Castro and his followers from Mexico.
March 13, 1957	Presidential Palace is assaulted by Directorio Revolucionario.
April 9, 1958	General strike fails.
January 1, 1959	Fulgencio Batista leaves Cuba and rebels take over.
May 1959	Agrarian Reform Law is enacted.
May 1960	Fidel Castro achieves complete control of Cuban press and mass media.

June–July 1960

United States–owned oil companies refuse to process Russian oil and are then expropriated by Cuban government. Eisenhower abrogates Cuban sugar quota.

August 1960

Large-scale expropriation of United States–owned property in Cuba is undertaken by Castro.

October 1960

Full-scale United States economic blockade of Cuba begins. Large-scale expropriation of property owned by Cuban capitalists is undertaken.

Revolution and Reaction
in Cuba, 1933–1960

1 | Toward a Theory of the Cuban Revolution

IN 1959 a revolution took place in Cuba which resulted in the eventual establishment there of a Communist regime, the first in Latin America. Knowing the conditions of poverty, under-development, and oppression that have been characteristic of Latin America, one might well ask why this revolution took place in Cuba and not in some neighboring country. The failure of later guerrilla movements ostensibly modeled on the Cuban experience suggests that generalizations about underdevelopment, dictatorship, and imperialism in Latin America as a whole are necessary but in-adequate for an understanding of the peculiar nature of the Cuban revolutionary process. The early insistence of the Fidelista leader-ship that there were no major differences between Cuba and the rest of Latin America and that the guerrilla warfare road was essen-tially the same for all these countries has become increasingly un-convincing.[1]

Cuban Communism was established under exceptional cir-cumstances, as the eventual outcome of an ostensibly liberal revolu-tion against a rather typical Latin American dictatorship. Although distinctive in some ways, the initial revolutionary struggle against the Batista regime did not appear to be much different from count-less other movements against dictatorial Latin American regimes. In this light, the very rapid and unusual social upheavals that shortly followed the overthrow of the Batista regime demand serious study. Furthermore, it is essential to analyze the connection between these dramatic changes and various aspects of prerevolutionary

Cuban society, for this is the only way to understand the uniquely Cuban, and not simply Latin American, aspects of the revolutionary process. Such an investigation might clarify the reasons for the complete collapse of the traditional army, for Castro's ease in controlling and defeating the Cuban upper and middle classes, and for other special traits of the Cuban Revolution.

Interpreting the Cuban Revolution

Recent literature on the Cuban Revolution is somewhat more penetrating than earlier impressionistic accounts. For some time, many authors apparently deemed it sufficient merely to sketch the nature of a satellite economy based on sugar monoculture, and an unstable political system. To be sure, prerevolutionary Cuba was part of a system of United States imperialist dominance which included the rest of Latin America, and this dominance was reflected in the reign of sugar monoculture. While Cuba was among the more prosperous countries in Latin America, extensive poverty did exist on the island.[2] It is necessary, however, to go beyond this point in order to analyze the causes of a major revolution. Different authors have tried to do so, interpreting the Cuban Revolution variously as a "bourgeois," "peasant," "working-class," or "middle-class" revolution. The use of such diverse classifications to describe one and the same phenomenon is puzzling and further demonstrates the need for a more detailed examination of the various components of Cuban society, particularly its social classes. However, the effort to provide a class interpretation of the Cuban Revolution leads to difficulties of at least two kinds.

In the first place, there are serious methodological difficulties in the class interpretation of any revolution. One must distinguish among criteria that are often entangled, such as the respective social compositions of the leadership, the active followers, and the inactive sympathizers. Further, social composition includes not only the social origins of the members of a group but also their later social class and status, which may well differ from their origins. All of these considerations must in turn be distinguished from a determination of whose interests are supposedly served by the policies of the revolutionary leadership. Above all, one must carefully analyze the nature of the relationships between leaders and followers, as well as the social and political consciousness of both.[3]

The other major difficulty is closely related to the first: the usual methodological problems involved in class analyses of revolutions become far more serious in the Cuban case, where social classes were relatively weak and fragmented, and the relationship between the class structure and political events was consequently even more complex.

The Cuban Revolution as a Peasant and as a Working-Class Revolution

One of the earliest class interpretations of the Cuban Revolution was published in 1960 by Leo Huberman and Paul M. Sweezy.[4] The very crudity of many of its theoretical formulations illuminates the serious problems faced by any who would apply to the Cuban Revolution a schematic class interpretation. These authors interpreted the Cuban Revolution as the work of a peasantry with collectivist inclinations, under the leadership of Fidel Castro. Only a few peasants, however — one or two thousand at the most — ever participated in the revolutionary struggle against Batista. There is real doubt, moreover, whether the rural elements that actively supported Castro were in any way collectivist. As Ché Guevara himself stated:

> We ought to mention, out of respect for the truth, that the first territory occupied by the Rebel Army, made up of survivors of the defeated column that had arrived aboard the Granma, was inhabited by a class of peasants different in its cultural and social roots from those that dwell in the regions of extensive, semi-mechanized Cuban agriculture. In fact, the Sierra Maestra locale of the first revolutionary hive, is a section that serves as a refuge to all those country workers who struggle daily against the landlords. They go there as squatters on land belonging to the state or some rapacious landowner, searching for a

> piece of land that will yield them some small wealth. They must fight
> continuously against the exactions of the soldiers, always allied with
> the landowning power; their horizon does not go beyond a document
> of title to their land. The soldiers that made up our first guerrilla army
> of country people came from the part of this social class which shows
> its love for the possession of land most aggressively, which expresses
> most perfectly the spirit catalogued as petty bourgeois; the *campesino*
> fights because he wants land for himself, for his children; he wants to
> manage it, sell it and make himself rich through his work.[5]

Contrary to common stereotypes, in the 1950s a majority of the rural
Cubans engaged in agricultural work were wage laborers, while
only about a third could be more appropriately considered peasants.
It happened that the rebels came into contact mostly with the latter
rather than with the presumably more collectivist agricultural
laborers.

A second problem is that Huberman and Sweezy seem to attribute a given class character to a revolution on the basis of their
own interpretation of who has benefited from it, rather than what
social groups exercised power and through what organizational
forms during that revolution. Thus they labeled the Cuban Revolution "peasant" because, up to the time of the publication of their
book, the central policies of the Castro regime revolved around a
drastic agrarian transformation. While there was good reason to
believe that the overwhelming majority of peasants and agricultural
workers did support the agrarian reform program at this time, they
had little or no role in the formulation and implementation of the
program, or in the creation of an agrarian movement which would
represent or at least echo the aspirations of that class. The revolutionary movement and regime were always controlled by urban
elements which at various points obtained nonurban support.

The weakness of Huberman and Sweezy's methodology became apparent as soon as the focus of Castro's regime moved from
the agrarian to the industrial sector through his program of nationalization. These writers were then compelled to revise their
earlier theory and to conclude that the Cuban Revolution was now a
working-class revolution. In effect, a change of policy by the revolu-

tionary leaders was presumed to be the same as a change in the class composition and nature of the revolution. In addition, Huberman and Sweezy seemed to believe that seizure of industry by the state was equivalent to a seizure of power by the working class. Because the government owned industry, workers were presumed to be in possession and control of their own establishments; however, the presumably autonomous power of the militia was the only evidence they could cite to support their belief that the government was in the service of the working class rather than vice versa.[6] This working-class interpretation, even more than the earlier peasant interpretation, illustrates the inadequacy of a theory that fails to address itself seriously to the power, organization, consciousness, and leadership of a class in order to discern whether it has led or actively participated in a revolution.

The Theory of "the Mountains and the Plain" (*La Sierra y el Llano*)

A more plausible but also misleading interpretation which strongly emphasizes the rural character of the Cuban upheaval contends that those rebels who fought in the mountains were strongly influenced by their direct contact with the peasants and were radicalized by that experience. This interpretation stops short of stating that the peasantry itself made the revolution but contrasts the fighters in the mountains with the fighters in the urban underground, who are described as being less radical, having been influenced by the petty bourgeoisie. This theory has been formulated in its crudest fashion by Régis Debray in *Revolution in the Revolution?*[7] However, Debray was simply echoing a theory that had previously been put forward by the Cuban leaders. Guevara, for example, had asserted that there were two competing views among the revolutionaries: that of the *Sierra* ("mountains"), which urged encirclement of the cities by the guerrillas; and that of the *Llano* ("plain"), which called for a general strike and armed struggle in the towns. According to Guevara, the latter was a less desirable strategy because "in that period the political development of the Llano comrades was incomplete and their conception of the general strike was too narrow. A general strike was called on April 9 of the following year [1958], secretly, without warning, without prior political preparation or mass action. It ended in defeat."[8]

This thesis is not in full accord with the facts. One of the reasons for the failure of the general strike was the exclusion of the Communist party from its leadership, a decision made by the Llano leadership appointed by Fidel Castro. Guevara and some of his Sierra associates did object to this decision, but it was criticized by even more of the Llano activists. After all, the Communist party and its political periphery were heavily concentrated in the Llano. Also, the fact remains that, up until the failure of the April 1958 strike (less than nine months before the overthrow of Batista), the Fidelista leadership in the Sierra was in agreement that the general strike was the decisive weapon of struggle. This was clearly stated in a manifesto issued by Castro in the Sierra Maestra on March 12, 1958.[9] In fact, the Sierra headquarters itself issued the orders that eventually led to the unsuccessful strike of April 1958 (for details, see Chapter 7). By this time, Radio Rebelde was in full operation, and it was often used to transmit orders to rebel units operating throughout the country.

The Sierra-Llano theory was formulated primarily *after* the revolution had proved victorious, when Castro and his supporters were searching for some social explanation and justification for his regime's having become far more radical than anyone had expected. It is interesting to note, however, that until Castro's final seizure of power none of the social measures adopted in the occupied territories under rebel army jurisdiction were in any way radical. None of these measures disturbed the large number of moderates who were then supporting Castro and who broke with him several months after he seized full power. Presumably, the radicalizing influence of the peasantry would have been strongest at this time of closest proximity to and reliance on the peasantry; instead, it was not until several months after Castro's victorious arrival in Havana that he began to implement his more radical measures.

Some tactical differences over the use of resources did develop between the Sierra and the Llano, but these differences did not correspond to an ideological dispute between moderates and radicals, both of whom could have been found within either the Sierra or the Llano. As I have pointed out, the Llano contained most of the Communist party members, who at this time were to the left of Castro on social and economic matters, and many activists and leaders who would become supporters of the Guevara-Raúl Castro wing of the revolutionary government, as well as many moderate activists and leaders. At the same time, there were plenty of moderates in the Sierra Maestra such as Majors Hubert Matos and Humberto Sorí Marín (Matos was later jailed and Sorí Marín was executed by the Castro regime); and, as we have already learned from Guevara, the peasants of the Sierra themselves were full of the "petty bourgeois" spirit.

The distinction between the Sierra and the Llano in fact obscured a more significant division among revolutionary leaders. Some were Castro's personal and political associates from the beginning of the struggle against the Batista dictatorship and remained loyal to him through all the stages of the revolution. Others, whether from a middle-class or any other background, joined Castro on the basis of the policies of a given period and later differed or broke with him. Among the former are Haydée Santamaria, Armando Hart, Juan Almeida, Raúl Castro, and Ramiro Valdés (for a long time head of the secret police and interior minister). This group of early associates constitutes a kind of inner circle around Castro, aptly described by Hugh Thomas:

> These early followers of Castro were the people who generally held to him thereafter as bodyguards, special assistants, chief assistants, chief confidants, men of all work and for all seasons. Not that all did so. One or two of the Moncada or *Granma* men[10] are in exile. One of the 19 (or 12, as it is now known) was shot as a traitor (Moran). Nevertheless,

> early in his revolutionary career Castro became surrounded by a
> number of close followers, mostly with no political views (except a
> general social conscience and resentment deriving from memories of
> childhood misery or absence of education), devoted to him as a leader
> rather than as an ideologue, who would have thoughtlessly followed
> him over any precipice, and indeed did over the icy one of com-
> munism.[11]

Most of these early associates remained close to Castro in the Sierra
and as a result this group became somewhat distinctive. Although
the human and physical environment most probably had a strong
influence on these men and women, the crucial factor was not their
physical presence in the Sierra but their constant close personal and
political proximity to Castro. In sum, the evidence seems to indicate
that the differences between the Sierra and the Llano were less
consequential than intra-Sierra and intra-Llano political differences,
and that loyalty to Castro was a crucial factor.

Maurice Zeitlin's Theory of a Working-Class Revolution

Another interpretation of the Cuban Revolution has been put forward by Maurice Zeitlin, who implies that it has been a working-
class revolution, at least since shortly after the establishment of the
Castro regime. The workers' role, he contends, has been "strategic"
because of "their mass, organized support for the defense of revolutionary measures put through by the revolutionary government."[12]
Unlike other proponents of a working-class theory, Zeitlin is aware
of some of its problems; he acknowledges that it was not a workers'
revolution in the "classical Marxian sense" because the workers did
not initiate the struggle for power. However, he fails to confront
fully the crucial questions of leadership: Who did lead the revolution, and who leads it now? What is the connection between that
leadership and the working class? Since Zeitlin claims that there is
organized, mass, working-class support for the Castro regime, an
analysis of the form, content, and leadership of these organizations
is essential to understanding the nature of the revolutionary process.

Zeitlin's interpretation of the Cuban Revolution is intimately tied to his basically misleading approach to the history of the Cuban working class; he identifies the following as the key points in Cuban working-class history before the Castro revolution: (1) The Communist party had been the predominant political influence among Cuban workers at least until the beginning of the Cold War. (2) Communists had led the Cuban working class not only in trade-union activities but also in the working-class revolutionary waves of the thirties. (3) There was no separation between the role played by Communists as trade unionists and their role as socialist agitators. (4) Socialist ideology thus had a significant base in the working class. The content of Communist "education, indoctrination, and agitation among the workers was anti-imperialist, anti-capitalist and revolutionary socialist," he claims. [13]

However, while the Communist party was at one time influential among Cuban workers, this influence declined sharply after 1947. Furthermore, even at the time of its greatest influence, the Communist party was in close competition with various "populist" parties. "Pro-Communist" workers often supported Communist trade-union leaders in union affairs but supported one of the various populist parties in national politics. In fact, one of the most significant traits of Cuban Communists after 1938 was the very separation between their roles as trade unionists and as "revolutionary socialist agitators," as Zeitlin calls them. Many of the "pro-Communist" workers were influenced not by Communist political education or indoctrination but by the fact that they viewed Communist leaders as more *personally* honest and dedicated, an important trait in a country rife with corruption. Yet this personal respect was often accompanied by political suspicion.

In addition, there was a substantial difference between the nature of Communist influence in the early, revolutionary 1930s, when politics and trade unionism were tied closely together, and in the years after 1938, when the party became very reformist and, for a time, openly class collaborationist. In this later period, the Communists gained official control of the trade-union movement. This was achieved, however, in exchange for political support for the

Batista regime. Even when the Communists strongly discouraged militant action in the shops, many workers continued to support them on the grounds that they were less likely to steal the union and retirement funds. At the same time, these very workers voted for and supported the anti-Batista and anti-Communist parties. Only the relatively few workers who were active (*militantes*) Communist party members, and not simply members of Communist-led unions or registered as Communists in the official electoral lists, were actually educated or indoctrinated in hard Communist party politics.

Finally, in spite of Zeitlin's claims, the Cuban working class was not "socialist" in any meaningful sense of that term, nor did it "make" or give its own distinctive character to the Cuban Revolution led by Fidel Castro. It is true that at many points most workers supported the Castro-led revolution and that most individual workers were hostile to the Batista dictatorship and to the prerevolutionary status quo, but this opposition was not expressed in active and organized class terms. As Castro himself pointed out in his unusually frank speech of July 26, 1970, "In 1959 the majority of our people weren't even anti-imperialists. There was no class consciousness. Only class instinct, which isn't the same."[14] This "class instinct" had been developed in a class with a history of nonsocialist but militant struggles for trade-union goals and social reforms. Its pattern of struggle could be described as "trench-class warfare." The working class would struggle to push back whatever advances the enemy made, and it would even make occasional inroads into enemy territory; but it had no strategy, even on a theoretical level, for taking state power and reshaping society on behalf of the interests of the class as a whole. As we shall see, this class never developed a crystallized ideology nor a mass political party. Its ideology was neither social revolution nor business unionism. Its militant reformism, particularly in the forties and early fifties, was the result of a long line of historical events and ideological influences which included Spanish anarchism, American business-unionism, and the Communist party in both its Third and Popular Front periods.

Yet the Cuban working class was an important — potentially

decisive — sector of the population. Cuba was not primarily a peasant country, and in a predominantly urban country (57 per cent urban according to the 1953 census) this class wielded much more social influence than do working classes in most less developed countries. In addition, the sugar industry with its "factories in the fields" strongly reinforced the proletarian character of Cuban society as a whole, and large numbers of agricultural wage workers belonged to trade unions. However, union membership was often meaningless to these workers; many of them were temporary and seasonal workers in the sugar plantations who moved to the cities during the off-season and were frequently forced to engage in very poorly paid occupations such as selling lottery tickets. In 1946, for example, only 53,693 out of 423,690 agricultural workers were permanently employed.[15] Many of the industrial workers were employed in small plants which were difficult to organize and which tended to hinder the development of militancy.[16] Also, there was a fairly high number of clerical, sales, and service workers, who are not easily incorporated into trade unions.[17] In spite of these and other undeniable weaknesses of the Cuban trade-union and working-class movements, the fact remains that, on balance, there was a fairly strong tradition of organization in the Cuban working class. The following summary description of the Cuban trade-union movement in the fifties would compare favorably with that of many other countries:

> More than half of Cuba's 2 million workers are claimed as members of 1,641 trade unions. The organized sectors of the economy include the extremely important sugar industry where virtually all the agricultural workers as well as the mill and office workers are unionized; practically all of the manufacturing industries; transportation (railroads, port operations, buses, etc.); communications; electric power; hotel and restaurant operations; banking; and some of the larger retail stores. Union organization is weak or non-existent in the multitude of smaller commercial enterprises which together comprise an important segment of the Cuban economy; in cattle raising; in coffee growing and on small farms other than those attached to the sugar industry.[18]

A relatively extensive system of communications and transportation, close proximity to the North American market and media influences, and urbanization helped to produce a working class that was restless and alert. The desire to achieve a standard of living comparable to that of workers in the United States encouraged both militancy and frustration. But all of this was not sufficient to produce a revolutionary class.

The Cuban Revolution as a Middle-Class Revolution

Taking a different line, Theodore Draper sharply criticized many interpretations of the Cuban Revolution and initially argued that "the Cuban revolution was essentially a middle-class revolution that has been used to destroy the middle class."[19] Draper emphasized the "coalitionist" period of 1956–58 and was able to make a seemingly plausible case for a middle-class interpretation of the revolution. On closer inspection, however, one finds a remarkable methodological similarity between Draper's interpretation and those of Huberman, Sweezy, and Zeitlin. All of these interpretations use the policies of the revolutionary leadership as the main criterion for determining the class character of the Cuban Revolution. If certain policies are seen by the author as benefiting or eliciting support from a given class, the revolution is then attributed to that class. Again, the whole question of the kind and degree of participation of the class in making those policies is ignored.

Because the revolutionary leadership advocated a wide range of policies at various times, different authors have chosen to concentrate on the policies of different periods to find support for their interpretations. While Draper concentrated on the "coalitionist" stage of the revolutionary process, other authors, particularly those sympathetic to Castro, tended to concentrate either on the earlier period of Castro's more radical pronouncements, such as the 1953 speech *History Will Absolve Me,* or on the even more radical post-1959 period. Draper's correct contention that at various crucial points the middle classes supported the Cuban Revolution does not prove the middle-class character of that revolution any more than

Huberman, Sweezy, and Zeitlin's correct contentions that the peasantry and working class supported the revolution at other points prove the working-class or peasant character of that revolution. All of these partial analyses obscure rather than clarify key aspects of the revolution, in particular the remarkable continuity of the revolutionary leadership throughout all of these radically different stages. The top leadership was able to maintain itself almost completely intact because it enjoyed an unusual degree of freedom of action; as we shall see, there were no revolutionary or class institutions that could hold the revolutionary leaders responsible for their policies and actions.

In arguing for the middle-class character of the revolution, Draper must get around the apparent paradox of Castro's later hostility to the middle class. His solution is to claim that Castro "betrayed" the revolution. Now, there are very serious problems in employing the concept of "betrayal" in an account of a rapidly evolving revolutionary process. Even leaving these problems aside, however, the Cuban Revolution is a singularly inappropriate case to which to apply the concept. Trotsky, for example, was justified in raising the issue of betrayal of the Russian Revolution in the 1920s, since he was a leading member of a well-organized political party with a set of principles and programs, and presumably an irrevocable class commitment. In Cuba, however, the leadership of a revolutionary elite was accepted as such by its supporters without even the pretense of programmatic or institutional controls over leadership by the ranks. The heterogeneity of the sources of support for the revolution freed the leadership from many responsibilities and restraints. After it came to power, the revolutionary leadership was thus in a position to alienate some sources of support and retain and encourage others. Draper himself described this revolutionary heterogeneity in an article written before he developed his thesis of the middle-class revolution betrayed: "Batista's coup made a revolutionary nationalist out of Castro and others like him. They abandoned the democratic path and have never found their way back. . . . Long after the rebellion in the Sierra Maestra had taken hold,

Castro did not head a homogeneous movement, and the larger it grew, the less homogeneous it became."[20] It is true that Castro had promised to restore the Constitution of 1940, a document by no means free of ambiguity and contradiction. The fact is that Castro's middle-class supporters went along with the postponement of elections and other substantial modifications of constitutional procedure in early 1959. It was only after Castro turned decisively against their material interests that they branded this unconstitutional behavior a betrayal.

Furthermore, even if it were agreed that Castro indeed betrayed the middle class (or the revolution), there would remain the crucial problem of explaining what conditions permitted this betrayal of an entire people or, at least, of a major social class. This is a sociological and political question, and attempting to answer it can be far more fruitful than asserting the useful but limited knowledge that an individual leader is not to be trusted. In short, whether or not the Cuban middle classes were "betrayed," it is essential to explain how Castro was able first to obtain their support and then to turn against them.

A Bonapartist Revolution

Although an understanding of Cuban social classes and their political behavior is of crucial importance for an analysis of the Cuban Revolution, existing interpretations which view the revolution as primarily the expression of any one class are unsatisfactory and even misleading. This has been understood by several writers on Cuba. For example, in his second book on Cuba, Theodore Draper abandoned (without an explicit acknowledgment) his previous thesis of the middle-class revolution betrayed and adopted the more realistic thesis that this was a "*declassé* revolution" where "the *declassé* revolutionaries who have determined Cuba's fate have used one class or another or a combination of classes, for different purposes at different times. Their leader functions above classes, cuts across classes, or maneuvers between them."[21] If Draper's newer thesis is valid, it then becomes necessary to identify the conditions that enabled Fidel Castro and his close associates to be free from restraints or controls of any class institutions. Such an inquiry presents an analytical task even more difficult than the analysis of revolutions whose leadership was in some way responsive to powerful class movements; in the analysis, Karl Marx's concept of "Bonapartism" will, I think, be very helpful.

The Theory of Bonapartism

In trying to explain the rise of Louis Napoleon Bonaparte in France, Marx had to face the difficult problem of the relations between social classes and political leaders. While the bourgeoisie was clearly the predominant economic class in France in 1851, it was equally clear that the bourgeoisie was not ruling the country politically, for Louis Napoleon was not a direct agent of the bourgeoisie. Neither was he a free agent, suspended in midair; but although he supported bourgeois interests it was he who politically dictated to the bourgeoisie rather than the other way around. The bourgeoisie had exchanged the troubles and dangers of its own political rule for the social and economic security provided by a strong government. This exchange was the end result of trends visible for many years in French society. The bourgeois classes had become more conservative in the face of a growing and increasingly militant working class. Universal suffrage itself had become a serious threat to bourgeois interests and privileges. The bourgeoisie and petty bourgeoisie became politically more fearful and less confident and consequently less able to provide their own political leadership.[22] At the same time, while the bourgeoisie and petty bourgeoisie were decaying politically, neither the peasantry nor the working class was yet in a position to take state power away from the bourgeoisie. Thus a kind of political vacuum was created, and Louis Napoleon stepped in.

Marx emphasized the importance of this social and political deadlock in his explanation of Bonapartism. Once a deadlock exists, he suggested, it is not necessary that the rising leader have great popularity or personal magnetism; sometimes it is sufficient that the main social classes be on the defensive and that they accept or put up with a political leader for largely negative reasons.[23] Marx also suggested that we consider the specific traits of the major classes themselves. Bonapartism is possible not only when no single class can exercise hegemony over the others but also as a result of the very composition of certain classes. Thus, although Marx stated that Louis Napoleon Bonaparte "represented" the peasantry, this representation was quite different from the way a leader represents the bourgeoisie in a bourgeois democracy. Marx unambiguously stated that the peasantry could not be a ruling class. The peasantry was too atomized and lacked the cohesion and organization necessary to exercise power on its own behalf. An objectively defined class may be large or economically important but will not constitute a class in the full sense of the term if

> the identity of their interests begets no community, no national bond and no political organization among them. . . . They are consequently incapable of enforcing their class interest in their own name, whether through a parliament or through a convention. They cannot represent themselves, they must be represented. Their representative must at the same time appear as their master, as an authority over them, as an unlimited governmental power that protects them against the other classes and sends them rain and sunshine from above.[24]

Here Marx was beginning to spell out a sociology of authoritarianism: classes or groups with a low degree of cohesion, of economic and political organization, and of political consciousness are susceptible to authoritarian leaders. The *lumpenproletariat* is a good example. It was a demoralized and disorganized stratum that could be bought and manipulated, as in fact it was by Louis Napoleon.[25] Louis Napoleon was able to stay in power for a long period of time by keeping the opposition divided and by obtaining support from several sources. One of his bases of support was the growing governmental bureaucracy, which permitted "uniform action from a supreme center" and annihilated "the aristocratic intermediary grades between the mass of the people and the state power," thus creating an important source of jobs for the unemployed and making them pliable tools in the hands of Louis Napoleon.[26]

Marx's use of the concept of Bonapartism was not restricted to his analysis of Louis Napoleon. As Hal Draper has pointed out, Marx also applied the concept to Simón Bolívar and his authoritarian leadership and control of the Spanish American independence movement, and to Soulouque, the dictator of Haiti.[27] This broader use of the term, though somewhat less precise, still helped to clarify the complicated relations between political leaders and social classes. Frederick Engels applied the same concept to his analysis of Boulanger and Bismarck, going so far as to suggest that Bonapartism was a permanent trait of bourgeois rule and adding that, "when there is no oligarchy, as there is in England, to take over in exchange for good pay, the management of state and society in the interests of the bourgeoisie, a Bonapartist semidictatorship is the normal form."[28]

The concept of Bonapartism thus became part of the Marxist tradition. The formation of mass political parties in the second half of the nineteenth century introduced a new and significant mediating element in the relationship between political leaders and social classes, and the concept of Bonapartism was appropriately used in this context. Edward Bernstein, for example, analyzed the role of Ferdinand Lassalle in terms which suggested that Lassalle was a Bonapartist leader who was able to lead a working-class party in its early stages of development, before maturity.[29] Leon Trotsky explained a good deal of the process of consolidation of Russian Stalinism in terms of the transformation of the Bolshevik party from a strongly disciplined group of autonomous and conscious individuals into an atomized mass of submissive, conforming members. Trotsky attributed this development to what he described as Stalinist Bonapartism, the success of which was facilitated by the wholesale destruction wrought by the civil war. A key event in the transformation of the Bolshevik party was Stalin's "Leninist levy" by which a large number of new members were brought into the party ranks. According to Trotsky, the purpose of this levy was "to dissolve the revolutionary vanguard in raw human material, without experience, without independence, and yet with the old habit of submitting to the authorities. . . . The chief merit of a Bolshevik was declared to be obedience."[30]

The Marxist concept of Bonapartism, in its broadest rather than in its historically narrowest sense, can be usefully applied to contemporary Cuban history as well, despite the obvious differences between mid-nineteenth-century France and Cuba after 1933, and those between Louis Napoleon, Batista, and Castro. Batista often ruled above and beyond Cuba's social classes in order to preserve the social and economic status quo, and Castro did the same in order to destroy the power of the old social classes and thereby make possible the transition toward a social system and ruling class like those in the "socialist" countries.

Fulgencio Batista as a Bonapartist Conservative

After the frustrated Revolution of 1933, neither the Cuban bourgeoisie and its North American allies nor their more or less revolutionary opponents were in a position to consolidate power on their own best terms. This contributed to the success of the Sergeants' Revolt of September 1933 and of its leader Fulgencio Batista. Batista was a young and unknown army sergeant of humble origins who had become politically articulate while serving as military court stenographer. At the beginning, there was a good deal of uncertainty concerning the political road Batista would eventually choose; for a while Batista was quite possibly unsure himself. This uncertainty was aggravated by the critical and highly fluid political situation existing in Cuba after the overthrow of Machado in 1933. Batista soon threw in his lot with the counterrevolutionary side and obtained the support of the United States government and Cuban and American businessmen.

Batista, however, was not the usual reactionary. During most of his first period in power (1933–44), he supported a variety of reforms in the labor and social fields. His "revolutionary" opponents in the Auténtico party were not in fact much more reform-minded than Batista; the main difference was that Auténtico reformism was civilian and democratic while Batista's reformism was militaristic and authoritarian. While Batista's main base of support was the armed forces, he repeatedly tried to broaden his support during his first period in power by maneuvering and forming alliances with practically every politician and political party, conservative as well as reformist. While he was rebuffed by a majority of the Auténtico party, he successfully formed an alliance with the Communist party which lasted for several years. Many conservative Cubans criticized this alliance, but they were unable to develop an effective opposition to it. Given the favorable international situation, Batista was able to maintain his Communist support without alienating his North American protectors. The Communist-led labor movement was thus effectively neutralized as a potential revolutionary force, and the Cuban bourgeoisie also got its returns in the form of domestic law and order.

During most of this first Batista regime, which was significantly different from his second period in power (1952–59), Batista successfully manipulated the main social classes in Cuba and maintained an essentially unaltered status quo, while employing liberal and even left-wing rhetoric on appropriate occasions. He once told a *New York Times* interviewer that Cuba should have a "renovated democracy, under which there should be discipline of the masses" so they might be taught "a new idea of democracy and learn to discipline themselves." Batista added that he could be described as a "progressive Socialist" since there are two kinds of socialism: "one means anarchy, and the other functions under the discipline of the government."[31]

In spite of the significant political support Batista obtained from the Communists and from various traditional political parties and politicians, the army remained his most reliable source of power. The successful Sergeants' Coup had eliminated the old officer corps which was closely tied to the old Cuban upper classes. In its place, Batista created a new officer corps of middle- and lower-class extraction. As the Cuban scholars Emeterio S. Santovenia (a well-known

Cuban historian who had been a leader of the ABC party and was for many years a collaborator of Batista) and Raúl M. Shelton have pointed out, this new officialdom became a privileged caste which eventually broke its allegiance to the laws of the country and its ties with the interests of the lower and middle classes. According to Santovenia and Shelton, "In a state of open disintegration, the officialdom paid attention only to the enjoyment of prebends, privileges, perquisites, and commissions."[32] I might add that this officialdom became increasingly alienated from most of the upper classes as well. In short, Batista's army became an essentially mercenary institution. The lower ranks of the army also benefited from the fruits of corruption, which built a great deal of solidarity within the army while it was becoming increasingly isolated from the rest of society. At the same time, American support for Batista's army rendered it even less dependent on internal Cuban support. A high number of Cuban army officers received training in United States military installations, and the United States supplied the Cuban armed forces with a great number of weapons and plenty of ammunition.

This corrupt Cuban army fell apart when put to the test of fighting a guerrilla army with very high morale. Castro did not defeat this army in a strictly military test of strength; rebel political warfare was a more powerful weapon than Batista's tanks. Batista's army had not been of a Prussian or totalitarian bent; the extreme brutality that characterized it was motivated by crass utilitarianism rather than by ideology or solidarity with upper-class interests. The army ranks were voluntarily recruited from the most demoralized sections of unemployed Cuban youth. The mercenary character of the army made it more difficult for political rebellion to succeed within the army itself or for significant numbers of soldiers to join the revolutionaries out of political conviction. In such a situation, it was difficult for the army, or large parts of it, to change sides while retaining power, as is often true in Latin American "revolutions." The alternatives were victory for Batista's army or complete disintegration and defeat.

Fidel Castro as a Bonapartist Revolutionary

A parallel can be drawn between the conservative Bonapartism of Fulgencio Batista and Castro's revolutionary Bonapartism. Fidel Castro was able to achieve and maintain power while remaining independent from the control of any major social class because he obtained political support from first one class or group and then another without linking himself irrevocably to any one of them. Although there were some significant but isolated working-class struggles during the Batista dictatorship, the Fidelista revolutionary leadership did not make a serious effort to tie these class actions to the ongoing political struggle. While there were some attempts to organize general strikes, these strikes were conceived as purely anti-Batista political acts with little or no social and class content. Furthermore, the lack of strong class consciousness in the Cuban working class allowed Castro to avoid choosing sides among the rival classes.

Thus the revolutionary leadership opted for a policy of militant opposition to the Batista regime combined with a moderate stance on social questions. Castro became the enormously popular leader of a very broad and heterogeneous anti-Batista coalition which had the sympathy and support of the overwhelming majority of the Cuban population, regardless of class membership. This coalition was similar to many other movements against traditional dictator-ships in Latin American countries except in one major way: the Cuban coalition was led not by older, traditional, liberal or populist politicians but by a young leadership with little or no background in traditional Cuban politics. Castro and most of his close associates had emerged from the militant student and youth movements rather than from the top leadership of the traditional political par-ties. Yet this youthful leadership felt that it badly needed the sup-port of the middle classes and of some traditional politicians and that it could not afford to alienate them with a strong pro-peasant or pro-working-class stance.

Castro's coalition would not have come into being if any of the traditional political organizations had retained any strength. Shortly after Batista's coup, all of the old opposition parties and groups collapsed, and the way was thus left open for Castro. At the same time the upper and middle classes were becoming increasingly alienated from the Batista regime, and in the light of Castro's reassuring stand on social questions they felt safe in becoming enthusiastic supporters of the growing militant movement against the dictatorship. Although some prominent middle-class political personalities publicly joined Castro in the Sierra Maestra headquarters, they never became a part of Castro's inner circle. However, this middle-class presence in the Sierra Maestra was extremely important in helping to provide greater legitimacy and respectability to a movement run by unknowns who happened to be close associates of Castro. Many of these unknowns had been with Castro at least since the days of the attack on the Moncada barracks in 1953. Historian Hugh Thomas has compiled a list of the occupations of the participants in the original Moncada attack; the list includes accountants, agricultural workers, bus workers, businessmen, shop assistants, plumbers, students, and the like. Although the majority seem to have been workers by origin or current occupation, very few of them had been active in trade-union or working-class politics. It can be safely concluded that these individuals were not representative of any one class or group in Cuban society. Nineteen of these men were with Castro on the yacht *Granma,* and the social composition of this later group was also diverse although more of them had a higher education than at Moncada. According to Thomas, both of these groups were composed of men who loyally followed Castro as their chieftain. Eventually, peasants in the Sierra joined the rebel ranks and deepened the knowledge of the largely urban rebels, but, as Hugh Thomas points out, "it is doubtful if they had much effect on the programmes of the revolutionaries."[33] The only social and demographic trait common to Castro and his loyal followers was their youth. The rapid degeneration of a number of revolutionary generations, such as those of 1895 and 1933, had produced a significant discontinuity in the revolutionary populist tradition, and new cohorts of young people had arisen to fill the positions of leadership.

Fidel Castro abandoned the social "honeymoon" of class conciliation soon after the overthrow of the Batista dictatorship. He turned against his former supporters in the upper and middle classes and encouraged popular hostility toward them. While the revolutionary government shifted its orientation from one social class to another, it always retained complete initiative and control of the process of drastic social transformation. James O'Connor, a student of Cuba who supports the Castro regime, has aptly summarized the unique traits of Cuba's transformation, throwing a good deal of light on the character of Castro's leadership and control. O'Connor points out that the liquidation of Cuba's private property system was initiated everywhere by the ruling group. The revolutionary government had outlawed spontaneous seizures of land, but there was no need to enforce the law, for there were no peasant attempts to seize land. Neither did the urban or sugar mill workers attempt to take over the factories and mills. It was the rebel army and militia units that took over factories and farms under the direction of the central government. O'Connor explains that the social revolution was more or less orderly because the political revolution transferred power from one relatively small group of men to another, and because the masses of Cubans at least passively supported the social revolution. Comparing the Cuban Revolution to the Russian, Mexican, Chinese, and Bolivian revolutions, O'Connor shows that the Cuban case was unique: in all these other revolutions, spontaneous mass action made it more difficult for the revolutionary leaders to keep control of land and industry; the absence of such spontaneity in the Cuban Revolution simplified and facilitated the process of state collectivization of the economy. O'Connor correctly indicates that this central trait of the post-1959 social revolution was closely connected to the character of the pre-1959 political revolution which was fought by a small group of young people without any significant involvement of the working class or peasantry.[34]

It is worth noting that the Cuban Revolution passed very

rapidly through a series of stages while the same top leadership remained in power. Usually, the successive stages of a revolutionary process are associated with the shift of power from one social stratum to another. These power shifts in turn produce changes in the revolutionary leadership: a given leadership is associated with and depends on a certain social class or stratum, and when that social stratum is defeated so is the leadership. But Castro was above and beyond social ties which might have doomed his leadership. We should also note that the closely related phenomenon of "dual power" did not appear in Cuba. That is, there was no time when conflicting social strata or classes formed rival centers of power in the course of the revolutionary process. Dual power often precedes a radical leadership change in which one of the contending social classes or strata defeats the previously dominant and usually moderate revolutionary leadership. Thus, the Bolshevik-led Soviets were a center of "dual power" vis-à-vis the central government dominated by Kerensky and the Social Revolutionary-Menshevik alliance.[35] In Cuba, the brief interlude at the beginning of 1959 when there was a moderate cabinet in office was not a situation of dual power because it was perfectly clear at the time that ultimate power resided in Castro, who, for tactical reasons, did not yet want to assume formal control of the government. Fidel Castro was able to carry out his own kind of "permanent revolution" and consolidate his power without the political situation ever threatening to get out of his hands.

While Marx analyzed the social bases of Louis Napoleon's regime in terms of the nature of the peasantry and the stalemate among the rival social classes, I would go further in accounting for Castro's revolutionary Bonapartism, spelling out the factors in Cuban historical and social development that produced a political paralysis of the peasantry and working class while at the same time weakening the hegemony of the upper and middle classes. It is possible to conceive of a class deadlock in which powerful class giants cannot easily defeat each other, as in pre-Hitler Germany. In Cuba, the class deadlock took place at a far lower level; the main social classes, while numerically large, were fairly weak in terms of organization and political consciousness.

It would be a mistake to assume that Castro's revolutionary Bonapartism was unexpected in Cuban politics. The predominance of amorphous populist politics, as opposed to clearly articulated class politics, was another political symptom closely related to the existence of Bonapartism in the 1933–59 period. Populism and Bonapartism were two sides of the same political coin: large numbers of Cubans were attracted to inarticulate and vague populist moods and movements; and this was a reflection of the absence of more defined social classes, parties, and programs. This situation encouraged both conservative rulers and emerging revolutionary leaders to assume Bonapartist roles which, in their turn, further hindered the development of independent class organizations that could have challenged their individual power.

The 1933 Revolution: A Major Turning Point

The structural conditions that permitted and encouraged the existence of Bonapartism, both conservative and revolutionary, have been sketched briefly. These structural conditions were both cause and effect of certain historical processes and events in contemporary Cuba, and the specific developments of the 1933–59 period were of crucial significance in setting the stage for the major upheavals brought about by the Cuban Revolution. Let us now turn to a study of the 1933 Revolution and the ensuing period so we can analyze the interplay of these structural conditions and historical processes and events.

2 | The Revolution of 1933

Independence from Spain

CUBA was a latecomer to political independence from Spain. The liberation movements of the first half of the nineteenth century in Spanish America bypassed the "Pearl of the Antilles." For a variety of reasons, Simón Bolívar had not extended his military efforts to the relatively distant island of Cuba. For a period of time, black African slaves outnumbered the white Creoles in Cuba, which made the latter very timid in their anti-Spanish exertions: the fear of another Haiti was too strong to be easily put aside. In 1868 major hostilities began between the increasingly nationally conscious Cubans led by a Creole aristocracy and the Spanish colonialists. Spain was able to defeat this struggle for independence, which lasted ten years. Despite the fact that the Creoles in arms had liberated many slaves and actually incorporated them into the rebel armies, this stage of revolt was marked, by and large, by its aristocratic character: the aristocratic Céspedes and Agramonte families symbolized the leadership of this Ten Years' War, as it came to be known.

It was not until 1895 that another *major* effort to obtain independence from Spain was initiated. This time, however, the social composition and politics of the rebels were significantly different. Many Cuban patricians participated in the war effort, but its most salient stamp was given to it not by the leadership of the Céspedes and the Agramontes but by the plebeians: Antonio Maceo, a black rebel general, and José Martí, the son of a Spanish noncommissioned officer, who was to become Cuba's foremost historical hero, a writer, poet, and revolutionary.

José Martí

The thought and actions of José Martí were highly revealing of the character of this War of Independence in Cuba and its major differences from the emancipation movements of Spanish America much earlier in the nineteenth century. More than fifty years of social and political struggles on the European continent had intervened, and the United States itself was moving farther away from an agrarian society. Martí had certainly been influenced by the French and American revolutions, as his liberator predecessors in South America had been; but he also had been influenced by Giuseppe Mazzini, Victor Hugo, and Walt Whitman, and by important figures of the progressive movements of the second half of the nineteenth century. Martí's thoughts and actions were populist rather than aristocratic, democratic rather than pervaded by the authoritarianism of a Bolívar; and although he was not a socialist his politics were certainly socially conscious.

Two Martí scholars, Manuel Pedro González and Iván E. Schulman, have described his thought as "the most exemplary and diaphanous that the democratic ideology has produced in the Hispanic countries up to now. It has as a firm basis the dignity of the citizen and has as a goal individual liberty and collective welfare within the legal order."[1] They go on to explain that Martí repudiated the concept of oligarchy and classes and proposed a society without privileged people and without dominating castes, that he advocated economic democracy in order to make political democracy effective. For him the two were inseparable. But, they added, "Martí did not go beyond the borders of democratic individualism, whether in the economic or political order. If he condemned excessive or ill-gotten riches or the exploitation of the helpless, he also defended [the] possession [of wealth] when it was the product of honest effort without detriment to the proletariat." What was of interest to Martí was man, particularly if that man was needy.[2]

José Martí is important in Cuban history not only because of the way he influenced the character of the War of Independence but also because a habit of quoting Martí on every ideological question developed in Cuba, particularly among idealistic young people. This was not an unmixed blessing, considering that the many admirable traits of Martí's thinking were accompanied by a strong element of voluntarism and romanticism which came to pervade the Cuban populist tradition.[3] As a result strong dedication, sacrifice, and heroism were sometimes perceived as sufficient weapons in the harsh sphere of political action, and particularly of revolutionary action. It is not that Martí did not analyze the society of his time; he did. But his primary focus lay elsewhere, and his romantic imitators were at least partially justified in their perception of him. C. A. M. Hennessy has observed that, for Martí, "the basic conflict was not between classes or races but between good and evil in which personal redemption could be found through self-sacrifice for the *patria* [fatherland]."[4] Far from being the spontaneous mass uprising and quick overthrow of the Spanish government Martí had envisioned, says Hennessy, the War of Independence became a protracted struggle which dragged on for three years and ended with the foreign intervention Martí had hoped its quickness would forestall.

The Consequences of United States Intervention: The Platt Amendment

The United States government eventually intervened in the warfare between the Cuban rebels and Spain and soon defeated the latter.[5] Characteristically, North American troops proceeded to snub the rebel troops and then to occupy the country for four years, during which North American interests acquired and consolidated substantial holdings on the island. Finally, a Cuban Constituent Assembly was called in 1901, and the delegates were clearly told that if they wanted a United States withdrawal and political independence they would have to accept the Platt Amendment to the Cuban Constitution, which would give to the United States legal rights to intervene in Cuba. By a narrow margin, the assembly accepted this proviso, and the Platt Amendment became an integral part of the Republic of Cuba, which was inaugurated on May 20, 1902. This amendment gave a series of rights to the United States, such as the right to maintain military bases (eventually reduced to one in Guantánamo) and kept open the question of possession of the Isle of Pines, finally settled in 1925 when the United States Senate ratified a 1903 treaty granting Cuba sovereignty over the island.

The most important American prerogatives were spelled out in title III, which gave the United States "the right to intervene for the preservation of Cuban independence, the maintenance of a government adequate for the protection of life, property and individual liberty, and for discharging the obligations with respect to Cuba imposed by the Treaty of Paris," and in title IV, which ratified and validated "all acts of the United States in Cuba during its military occupancy."[6] Title III is practically self-explanatory, although it should be pointed out that no representatives of the Cuban revolutionaries were invited to attend, or allowed to participate in, the negotiations that led to the signing of the Treaty of Paris.

During the next thirty-two years of Cuban history, the United States intervened repeatedly in internal Cuban affairs, whether by landing troops or by threatening to do so. This interventionism reached such a level that it elicited protests even from the otherwise accommodating Cuban authorities. Foreign domination, in combination with a conservative native social system, produced a political situation where the almost indistinguishable Conservatives and Liberals alternated in office through the leadership of their usually corrupt chieftains. All of these politicians accommodated themselves to the internal and external status quo of the country; some of them had had direct business ties with American business corporations (e.g., Presidents Menocal and Machado).[7]

The importance of title IV of the Platt Amendment was far greater than may appear on the surface. During their occupation of Cuba, United States military authorities had given concessions to United States enterprises in various fields, particularly public utilities, and the purpose of this provision of the amendment was to ensure that none of those concessions would be declared invalid by any native Cuban government. But even more important than these concessions were the changes that had taken place in the sugar industry. As Sidney W. Mintz has pointed out, a profound technological revolution had begun in the sugar industry even before the United States intervention in Cuba.[8] During the North American occupation, those tendencies toward technological advance were greatly accelerated, under the impact of protected American capital which invaded the island at the turn of the century. As more and more modern mills were constructed, more and more land had to be devoted to growing sugarcane to keep pace with plant capacity. "Thus," writes Robert B. Batchelder, "the old system of communal lands underwent change because clear title of ownership was necessary if new mills were to obtain control of greater acreages."[9] During the period of United States occupation, the communal estates were divided by special court process and the foundation was laid for the corporate development of vast private estates or *latifundios*.[10] Because Spanish suppression of Cuban resistance through such policies as *reconcentración* (i.e., making Cuban cities virtual concentration camps for the rural population) had ruined many Cuban landholders and practically wiped out Cuban agriculture, it was relatively easy for American investors to buy up extensive amounts of land. Title IV gave legal blessing and some degree of permanence to these land grabs.

The Social Structure and the "Sugar Mentality" (1898–1933)

Compared with the situation that existed in many Spanish-American countries immediately after independence, the Cuban oligarchy in early Republican Cuba was weak. Divisions between upper-class Spanish parents and their nationally conscious Cuban children resulted in a lack of cohesion within the Cuban upper class, a lack that was often reinforced by the continuing immigration of

Spaniards even after the loss of one of their last remaining colonies. This lack of upper-class cohesion made itself felt in a weakened Cuban oligarchy. The destruction caused by the events of the Spanish-Cuban-American War further contributed to the weakness of Cuban society as a whole and of its upper strata in particular. The newly acquired political power, in spite of all the limitations resulting from North American interference, offered tempting career alternatives to many displaced upper- and middle-class Cubans. The situation was shrewdly described by Lino Novás Calvo, a well-known Cuban literary figure now in exile:

> Cuba won its independence, but the winners lost, by the same process, their economic power. A good part of their landholdings were destroyed by the war of 1898. . . . Another part of what remained was abandoned or transferred to a new class of buyers: Americans and . . . once again to Spaniards, but of quite a new and different type and kind. The sons of the old owning class were too occupied with political power, with the new liberty and its privileges, to pay any attention to the new estate, plantation or workshop.
>
> The old Spanish political aristocracy disappeared as well as the old Cuban landed aristocracy. Social expectations then came to consist of administrative posts and the liberal professions.[11]

While this process was taking place, some members of the Cuban upper and middle classes participated in important economic enterprises but often as managers and supervisory personnel for United States concerns. There were some children of Spaniards who followed in the footsteps of their enterprising business fathers, but many more entered the professions, white-collar work, or politics.[12]

The sugar industry had not completely eliminated the rural middle class in Cuba. A small but significant number of sugar farmers (*colonos*) managed an arrangement with the sugar mills by which they would contract with them for the sale of cane; but, given the capitalist dynamics of the sugar market, this was a highly unstable arrangement (at least until the mid-thirties, when the industry became highly regulated by the state). A prominent Cuban expert on the sugar industry and its history, Ramiro Guerra, explained that enough cane for each *zafra* (sugar crop or season) at a cost low enough to meet competition within the industry could be ensured only by reducing the colono's independence and "making him a vassal of the mill, bound by contract and prevented from freely selling his product, or by purchasing lands and administering them as cane farms or having them sharecropped or rented by *colonos* dependent on the mill."[13]

All of the above-mentioned features of the Cuban economy contributed to the creation of capitalist latifundia and to the consequent displacement of independent farmers, weakening of the rural middle classes, elimination of subsistence cultivation, creation of total dependence of landless employees on cash, and stimulation of political consciousness on a class basis.[14]

The development of the Cuban economy under the specific impact of sugar had very marked effects on the demographic patterns of Cuba, as well as on the peculiar development of its social classes: the upper and middle classes, the peasantry, and the working class (rural and urban). Sidney W. Mintz, on the basis of Guerra's classic work, points out that the plantation (or latifundium) urbanizes while it proletarianizes, creating company towns and a factory situation, albeit a rural one. He goes on to say:

> A rural proletariat working on modern plantations inevitably becomes culturally and behaviorally distinct from the peasantry. Its members neither have nor (eventually) want land. Their special economic and social circumstances lead them . . . [to] prefer standardized wage minimums, maximum work weeks, adequate medical and educational services, increased buying power, and similar benefits and protections. In these ways, they differ both from the peasantry — who are often conservative, suspicious, frugal, traditionalistic — and from the farmers, who are the agricultural businessman, the forward-looking, cash oriented, rural middle class.[15]

Up until the fifties the rural proletariat in Cuba has outnumbered the more traditional peasantry (i.e., sharecroppers, renters, and the like) by about two to one; thus the latter have remained an important minority in the rural population.

Seymour Martin Lipset, in his *Agrarian Socialism*, has observed that the helpless dependence of Saskatchewan farmers on the vagaries of the prices of wheat in the world markets created there, as a similar dependence on sugar did in Cuba, a situation where farmers were strongly inclined to engage in independent and collective political activity. Yet Lipset was speaking not about agricultural workers but about what are essentially "middle-class farmers," in Mintz's terminology. Thus, in the Canadian case dependence on arbitrary price oscillation beyond the control of the Saskatchewan farmers was a strategic factor. However, from Lipset's own comparison of Saskatchewan with the Dakotas in the United States, it appears that such a factor must be accompanied by other favorable circumstances if attempts at collective political action are to be as successful as they were in Saskatchewan. In Cuba, the agricultural proletariat later developed strong ties to the trade-union movement in the cities (in the first half of the thirties); but these political ties were weakened by various political and historic circumstances. Meanwhile, Cuba's "traditional peasants" (such as the ones in the Sierra Maestra) were usually far more distant from any kind of organization, whether trade union or otherwise, except for some sporadic Ligas Campesinas (Peasant Leagues) which were often founded for a limited and specific purpose, such as stopping evictions, and would then disappear.

Sugar also affected what we might term the Cuban "national character." From time to time the price of sugar skyrocketed, producing a period of speculation and "high living"; the post-World War I period of sugar prosperity was nicknamed the period of the Dance of the Millions, or of the Fat Cows (*Vacas Gordas*). This prosperity was not, to be sure, equally beneficial to all social strata. After all, this was a period in Cuba of almost complete laissez faire, with hardly any unionization of the working class, when sugar capital, domestic and foreign, was indeed absolute king. This prosperity turned into a serious depression when the world sugar market took a sudden and unexpected turn for the worse. These kinds of changes, combined with the frequent political disappointments of Cubans, helped to produce cynicism and what one author has described as "the sugar mentality . . . a kind of economic opportunism or shiftlessness, arising from the awareness that Cuba's economic welfare was at the mercy of persons and forces outside the Cuban setting."[16]

The Revolutionary Period of 1933–1935

Following the well-established tradition of the political seesaw of Liberals and Conservatives alternating in power, with occasional violent interruptions to be sure, Gerardo Machado was elected president in 1924; at the end of his mandate, a rubber-stamp constitutional assembly extended his tenure of office for another term. This outraged large sections of the Cuban people, particularly the gradually growing student and labor movements. In addition, the Great Depression broke out during Machado's second term in office, seriously aggravating the already building resistance to his regime. Machado responded with increasing brutality toward his opponents, mostly student and labor leaders and a large part of the traditional political forces in the country. By 1933, the situation in Cuba had become extremely serious: Machado would not consider resignation as a way out of the political crisis. Government-initiated assassinations of oppositionists became a frequent occurrence, and the opposition retaliated with its own acts of terrorism.

In the meantime, President Franklin D. Roosevelt had just taken office in the United States and announced a new "Good Neighbor" policy toward the countries of Latin America. Without a doubt Cuba would be the acid test of this policy; in fact, the Cuban situation was one of the most critical foreign policy problems facing Roosevelt. Accordingly, Assistant Secretary of State Sumner Welles was dispatched to Cuba where he arrived as the new United States ambassador in May 1933. Immediately Welles set himself up as a mediator of the crisis in Cuba and called on most political groups, both government and the opposition, to meet with him. Opposition groups like the Cuban Communist party were not invited to the talks, and others, such as the important Student Directorate, the largest and most important university student group, refused to participate in the negotiations, although by and large they engaged only in relatively moderate criticism of the negotiations. At the cost of a split in its ranks the ABC, an important terrorist organization, accepted negotiations and, in so doing, gave additional legitimacy to the political maneuvers of Ambassador Welles.

The negotiations did not make much progress, but by the end of July things were brought to a head by a nationwide general strike movement. Charles A. Thomson, a historian of this short but crucial period of Cuban history, described the movement as follows:

> On July 25, Havana omnibus drivers ceased work in protest against heavy taxes imposed by José Izquierdo, Machado appointee as Mayor of the capital. A bloody clash between the strikers and the police on August 1 brought truck and taxi drivers to the support of the movement, and its ranks were soon swelled by street-car workers, stevedores and newspaper employees. Transportation was tied up both in the capital and throughout the country; Havana newspapers suspended publication. President Machado, absent on a fishing trip, hurried back to the capital. By August 5 the strike, under the direction of the National Confederation of Labor and the Havana Labor Federation, had been transformed from a limited economic movement into a political crusade openly anti-governmental in character. Commerce and industry joined forces with labor. . . . The capital, with its streets almost empty, took on the aspect of a deserted city.[17]

At this juncture, Welles moved quickly and, in alliance with the army's top brass, obtained Machado's resignation. Machado left the island on August 12.

Céspedes' Conservative Regime

Machado's departure was received with widespread enthusiasm and followed by a massive upheaval. The army officers, with the support of Welles and the conservative opponents of Machado, established a conservative provisional government headed by the patrician Carlos Manuel de Céspedes, a son of the famous Cuban patriot of the same name. The ABC organization (discussed further in Chapter 3), taking one step further in its decline as a revolutionary organization, agreed to participate in this provisional government. The situation was very unstable. Welles and the Cuban conservatives acted as if there had been a mere palace revolt, while in fact a mass upheaval was taking place in the country, encouraged, ironically enough, by Welles's actions, which had undermined the apparent solidity of Machado's regime.

The Céspedes administration ended only the most blatant brutality and suppression of elementary democratic rights but instituted no social reforms. Even in the strictly political field, the Céspedes regime moved with great caution and legalistic timidity, particularly when it came to dissolving Machado's undemocratically elected, rubber-stamp Congress. There is no question that, to a large extent, this caution was the result of Welles's personal influence. He planned to maintain all the legal trappings of the previous regime, have Machado formally resign or take a leave of absence, and then have the Cuban Congress sponsor free elections at the expiration of its term of office in 1935. This was too much for even the otherwise accommodating ABC, which threatened to withdraw its two cabinet representatives unless immediate action was taken to effect constitutional reform.[18] Finally, Congress was dissolved by the Céspedes cabinet and the 1928 Machado Constitution was abolished, but nothing else was done in the way of reform. Popular impatience was further increased by the inability of the new government to proceed to a swift punishment of the most brutal police functionaries of the Machado regime. Thus the door was opened to exasperation which expressed itself in the violence — individual and collective — that became a political tradition in Cuba.

The students and workers wanted a new constitution which would include widespread social and political reforms. It is little wonder that the Céspedes regime was soon in deep trouble; even the army was reported to be undisciplined and rebellious.[19] If there was unrest in the army, the situation in the erupting labor movement can only be described as revolutionary. The Communist party, now in its Third Period of ultraleftist policies, made a significant contribution to this virtual state of insurrection, vividly depicted by the Foreign Policy Association in its report *Problems of the New Cuba:*

> Students, Communists and some members of the ABC were reported active in the task of labor organization. Strikes were spreading on the sugar plantations, the workers demanding higher wages, recognition of their unions and better living conditions. On August 21, the workers seized the first sugar mill — at Punta Alegre, in Camaguey Province. Within less than a month the number of mills under labor control was estimated at thirty-six. Soviets were reported to have been organized at Mabay, Jaronú, Senado, Santa Lucía, and other *centrales* [sugar mills]. At various points mill managers were held prisoners by the workers. Labor guards were formed, armed with clubs, sticks and a few revolvers, a red armband serving as uniform. Workers fraternized with the soldiers and police. During the first stage of the movement, demonstrations in Camaguey and Oriente were often headed by a worker, a peasant and a soldier. At some of the *centrales* in Santa Clara, Camaguey and Oriente provinces, the workers occupied not only the mills, but also the company railroad systems, and extended their control to the sub-ports and the neighboring small towns and agricultural areas. Relief committees supplied food to the strikers and their families, and in some cases became subsistence commissions for the whole population of the strike area. At various points these committees allocated parcels of land to be cultivated by the field workers. [20]

Nothing like this took place when Batista was overthrown in 1959, nor was there on or before January 1, 1959, the open anti-imperialism expressed during the struggle against the Machado regime. The stark visibility of Welles's interference and the Platt Amendment further encouraged an open anti-imperialism which, unlike that expressed in the fifties, extended far beyond the ranks of the Communist party and its supporters. It is also true, however, that, although there were soviets in Cuba in 1933, there was no socialist or communist movement of *decisive* importance, and many militant revolutionaries did not in fact go beyond social reform in their program and ideology. In the Cuban revolution as in many others, actual or potential revolutionary actions were not necessarily accompanied by a clear distinction between the desire for reforms from a more revolutionary ideology. Thus Rufo López Fresquet, first treasury minister under Castro and now an exile, is not far off the mark when he points out that the similarities between the 1933 and the original 1959 revolution lay in the desire for an economic revolution that would permit the industrialization of the country and eliminate the single-crop economy; "a social revolution to erase the privileges enjoyed by a few — such as not paying taxes — in order to extend to the many the benefit of better education, proper medical attention, and the other basic obligations of a modern democratic government"; and "a political revolution to punish corrupt politicians and to establish human freedoms and civil rights."[21] This was essentially the ideology of the very influential Student Directorate and nominally that of the ABC. As we have noted, the ABC was only too willing to forget its demands, but the student organization was more persistent.

The Emergence of Grau and Batista

The support of Welles and of conservative Cubans was not sufficient to maintain the Céspedes regime in power. Before a month had passed, this government was overthrown by what was perhaps one of the most bizarre events in Cuban history. Accounts of what actually happened are not in complete agreement, but it is clear that on September 4 a group of army sergeants, led by an unknown Sergeant Fulgencio Batista, among others, rebelled against their officers. More successful than they apparently had expected to be, they ended up with full state power in their hands. Then, realizing that they desperately needed civilian support to hold and administer this newly acquired power, the sergeants called on the Student Directorate and other revolutionary elements, who agreed to constitute themselves as a revolutionary government with the support of the successful army rebels.[22]

The rebel sergeants, who had apparently set out with far more modest goals for their rebellion, signed a joint proclamation with their revolutionary allies. This proclamation included the following points: economic reconstruction, a constitutional convention, immediate removal and full punishment of all those responsible for the previous situation, strict recognition of the debts and obligations contracted by the republic, and the execution of all measures not foreseen in the proclamation that might prove necessary to begin the march toward the creation of a new Cuba founded upon an immovable foundation of justice and on the most modern concept of democracy.[23] This was without doubt a weak compromise document; there were no promises of any specific measures concerning such things as national sovereignty, rights for labor, or agrarian reform. The students and other revolutionaries (which did not include the Communists and their allies in the Student Left Wing) were achieving power on the basis of precarious support lent to them by forces with at best doubtful revolutionary dedication. Initially, a five-man government was formed with Batista as head of the armed forces; but this arrangement soon proved unworkable, and Ramón Grau San Martín, a university professor closely allied with the students, was named president, while Batista continued in his military post, now having been promoted to colonel.

Before long, ideological differences became apparent within the Grau government: Interior Minister Antonio Guiteras y Holmes was on the Left, Batista was on the Right, and Grau himself held the center. Opposing the government from the Right were the ABC organization and almost all Cuban conservatives. Opposing the government from the Left, on the grounds that Grau and Guiteras were essentially "social fascists," was the Communist party. Sumner Welles and Jefferson Caffery, who replaced him as United States ambassador to Cuba, refused to recognize the Grau government and threatened intervention, following instructions from Washington. After Welles's short-lived defense of the officer class's resistance to the Sergeants' Coup, he and Caffery found a close affinity with Batista in what became a tacit alliance against Grau and particularly against Guiteras. Nothing is more revealing of the developing United States alliance with Batista than the following dispatch to the secretary of state filed by Sumner Welles on October 4, 1933:

Batista came to the Embassy this morning to see me and I had a conversation with him alone for about one hour and a half. . . . He then told me, in response to an inquiry from me as to whether he intended to permit a continuance of the intolerable conditions which had now existed for the last 5 weeks on the sugar plantations, that the Army would seize all foreign agitators and arrange for their immediate expulsion from Cuba and at the same time imprison Cuban Communistic leaders and would also guarantee the rights of the legitimate managers of such properties. . . . He asked me for my advice as well as my opinion and I gave it to him. I told him that in my judgment he himself was the only individual in Cuba today who represented authority. . . . In some manner it must be evident to him, I said, that the present government of Cuba did not fill any of the conditions which the United States Government had announced as making possible recognition by us. . . . I urged him in the interest of the Republic of Cuba itself to act as intermediary between the groups now at variance and through the force of authority which he represented in his person to insist that an immediate, fair and reasonable solution be found.[24]

Thus there came into being at least three conflicting forces or groups: the Grau–student government coalition; the alliance of Batista, the United States, and conservative Cubans; and the Communist party and its trade unions, which opposed all the others. The Grau government, at the prodding of its own left wing led by Guiteras, initiated a fairly wide program of social legislation, but this did not consolidate sufficient support among the masses of Cubans to prevent its eventual overthrow. Grau's inability to purge Batista from the government eventually compromised him in the eyes of many of his own supporters, despite his several confrontations with the open United States opposition to his government. This made it easier for the United States, in alliance with Cuban, Spanish, and American conservative elements on the island and, by late 1933, with Batista himself, to get rid of Grau. Grau's vacillating reformism lost him the support of his main political base, the university students. On January 6, 1934, there was an unambiguous vote of opposition to his government by an assembly of university students, who were angered by the apparent predominance of military influence in the government.[25] As Luis E. Aguilar explained

rejected many of the workers' demands. The men struck and a crisis ensued:

> For three hours Havana was paralyzed — without light, power, or street-car service. As the city's water supply is pumped by electricity there was an immediate menace to health. The Grau government, by Decree No. 172, therefore intervened provisionally in the administration of the company — a move which brought back the strikers.
>
> Rafael Giraud, an auditor of the company, one of the leading spirits in the strike movement, was named provisional general manager. His first act was to order the suspension from work and pay of 35 officials consisting of all the company executives and department heads, with their assistants and secretaries — a total of 67. . . .
>
> During the period of three weeks in which the property was under government management, the operation was actually in the hands of the workers.[30]

There is little doubt that this incident greatly intensified United States hostility to the Grau regime, which was brought down shortly afterward.

The Repressive Batista-Mendieta Regime

Grau's exit in January 1934 left Batista and his conservative Cuban and foreign allies as the undisputed bosses of Cuba. To replace Grau, Batista installed in the presidency a traditional politician who had been an opponent of the Machado regime and who was safely conservative, Carlos Mendieta. The latter was supported, initially at least, by the ABC organization, by most of the traditional politicians and parties, and by Spanish, Cuban, and North American business interests. This regime was promptly recognized by the United States government and, thus encouraged, began systematically suppressing its opponents, sometimes in a manner even more thorough than that of the Machado regime.

The negative and restrictive elements in Grau's labor legislation, which had been tempered by that regime's benevolent attitude toward labor, were now sharply increased without any accompanying benevolence to sweeten the pill. Strikes could be called only after a compulsory waiting period, and then only after at least eight days' notice had been given to the Ministry of Labor. Disputes had to be submitted to "commissions of social cooperation."[31] Then came a prolonged period of negotiation and appeal, following which, if workers were still dissatisfied, they could theoretically proceed to strike, "except in cases where the demands had been satisfied, or had been declared illegitimate by the Commission (Article 3)."[32] This legislation was ineffective in counteracting labor militancy; and, in fact, the government was soon faced with another strike wave. This government, however, was determined to stop labor no matter what the cost, and it began to implement even more repressive legislation, much of it inspired by the fascistic elements in the ABC organization who were still participating in the government.

During March 1934, Mendieta's regime promulgated and enacted a series of extremely repressive measures. As described in *Problems of the New Cuba,*

> On March 6 President Mendieta promulgated a Law of National Defense, designating as common criminals (*reos de delito*) all those who advocated governmental change by illegal means or issued other subversive propaganda, and those who violated the laws regulating strikes, engaged in progressive sympathetic strike (*huelga escalonada y progresiva*), or presented new demands to an employer within the six months immediately following a strike.[33]

In spite of this law and subsequent decrees aimed at suppressing labor, however, strikes continued to take place. Strike leaders and militants were arrested, and the number of political prisoners in Cuba grew once more. Sometimes the Mendieta administration and Batista were willing to give concessions if it seemed more costly to deny them. Thus the crisis in the electricity company eventually was settled with the strikers obtaining some substantial concessions.

The United States, eager to bolster the Mendieta-Batista regime's prestige, proceeded to prompt negotiations and abolition of the Platt Amendment, although this was to be followed by a new commercial treaty disadvantageous to Cuba and by United States retention of the Guantánamo Naval Base as well. By and large, however, this was a period of such harsh reaction that the government eventually started losing some of its own previous supporters. Thus, even the ABC organization was finally forced to withdraw from the cabinet in protest against that body's failure to establish any of the moderate reforms the ABC had hoped for.[34]

The General Strike of March 1935

Although Cuba experienced some economic improvement, partly as the result of United States economic concessions that bolstered the Cuban economy after the overthrow of Grau, the state of revolutionary ferment which expressed itself in all forms of political and labor agitation remained unaltered. The abolition of the Platt Amendment, although welcomed by all Cubans, was not sufficient to mollify the resentment felt by many Cubans against Ambassador Caffery's thinly veiled support for the Batista-Mendieta regime. No substantial reforms had been enacted by the new government, and the aspirations of 1933 were still unsatisfied. The culmination of these frustrations has been described by Charles Thomson:

> In March 1935 this discontent came to a head in a general strike movement more widely supported than that which had contributed to the overthrow of General Machado in August, 1933. Estimates placed the total number of strikers at 400,000 to 500,000. The movement, which throughout was substantially one of passive resistance, began on February 12 with a walk-out of teachers and students. This promptly led to the closing of every school on the island from kindergarten to the University. The demands were listed under five heads: abolition of Army rule, restoration of democratic principles in government, release of political prisoners, suppression of summary courts (Tribunales de Urgencia) and increased expenditures for education. . . . Organized labor was the last important group to give its backing, and only after some hesitation agreed to call a general strike for Monday, March 11. Dissension in its ranks prevented unity in the labor offensive. But on the date set, a state of virtual anarchy reigned in Cuba.[35]

The strike was ruthlessly suppressed by a show of force of the army and police, led by Colonel Batista operating under martial law. Some strikers were killed and hundreds were injured and arrested; in the repression that followed the strike, most Cuban labor unions were dissolved and their headquarters raided. Military rule was established throughout the country, opposition newspapers were closed, the death penalty was established for certain crimes such as sabotage, and school and government offices were purged of strike sympathizers.[36]

The failure of the strike and the intense and effective repression that followed brought to a close the revolutionary period of 1933–35. The defeat of this strike had a traumatic effect on the Cuban Left and labor movement and would remain in the memory of future generations of political activists. There is no question that disunity on the Left, political as well as organizational, was a crucial factor. At the time, there existed close to twenty left-wing political groups of various kinds.[37] Furthermore, the Communist party was at that time going through a stage of transition from its Third Period to the Popular Front period. The Communists had not yet completely abandoned ultrasectarianism and were uncertain as to what attitude to adopt toward other groups and what tactics to employ. That this strike, like others that would take place in Cuba, failed not because of basic weaknesses of the working class as a class (such as its degree of militancy and level of consciousness, both of which were relatively high), but rather because of organizational weaknesses in the superstructure, which the students at least partly avoided on this occasion, is suggested in an intelligent analysis of the strike made by Aureliano Sánchez Arango, at that time a left-wing student leader in exile:

> It is curious and highly interesting that the only call for a general strike after the downfall of Machado which received unanimous echo was sent out by the students of the University, who have an amorphous social composition. . . . The students . . . knew how to interpret exactly the objective and subjective circumstances of the moment. From this point of view the call to strike was a resounding success. The United Front, however, could not be achieved. The internal differences between the organizations of the proletariat were carried into the very meeting in which the beginning and duration of the strike were planned. . . . Four fronts arose, in each one of which the University Committee was represented. They were united only by

this chain, and by the memorandum of demands prepared by the Student Assembly.

The disorganization of the strike began then. Without central control it was impossible to avoid premature actions.[38]

The Failure of the Revolution of 1933

In the years from 1933 to 1935, Cubans witnessed a veritable classical revolutionary situation in their country. Various issues and grievances, each of which had revolutionary potential, were telescoped into each other. In the context of the kind of social structure described earlier, Machado's ruthless political dictatorship emerged. Against it arose a vigorous opposition composed of students, workers, and some traditional politicians. Their struggle took place during the Great Depression, which had disastrous effects on the price of sugar and, consequently, on the very center of the Cuban economy. This rapidly intensified the desperate labor protest of a working class which was deprived of the most elementary trade-union rights, and which, in many places under Communist leadership, would rebel against both the dictatorship and the employers. If all this was not enough, the situation was further aggravated and complicated by the presence of imperialist intervention in the form of the Platt Amendment and by the presence in Cuba of Ambassadors Welles and Caffery who, under instructions from Washington, openly interfered in Cuban internal political affairs. As in the successful Revolution of 1959, there had been a struggle against dictatorship, with the active involvement of vigorous groups of students and intellectuals; but in contrast to the fifties there was also vigorous working-class participation, at least partially produced by an economic crisis which had no counterpart in the fifties. Finally, the character of imperialist pressures and intervention was different in the two situations: direct and effective in the thirties, indirect and less effective in the fifties.

Yet a successful social revolution did not take place in 1933–35. While it was relatively easy to shake Cuban society and politics to its very roots, it proved to be quite difficult to go beyond this, smashing it completely in order to rebuild it along new lines. For the weakness in Cuban society which had allowed it to be shaken with relative ease, by the same token prevented the formation of alternative political structures which could bring about that society's wholesale replacement and renewal. These social peculiarities were reflected particularly in the fact that the forces and parties of revolution were fragmented. Unlike the situation in the late fifties, in the 1933–35 period no single movement was clearly predominant in the struggle against Machado and its aftermath. For a while it seemed as if the ABC organization could achieve such predominance, but it soon suffered a loss of prestige as well as splits and defections due to its accommodation to the United States embassy and the conservative forces in the island.

The various opposition groups were divided along several axes. In the first place, there was a crucial organizational and political separation between the labor movement and the rest of the opposition. This was almost entirely the result of the separation of the Communist party from the rest of the opposition. The Communists were highly influential in the nascent labor movement but had less strength among the students and other popular opposition elements, while the reverse was true of other opposition groups, with some exceptions, like the labor support Grau obtained from the Federación Obrera de la Habana.

The non-Communist opposition was also divided into various groups which differed in their degree of radicalism, their tactics, and the like. These groups included the Student Directorate, the ABC organization, and the old politicians. Until the arrival of Sumner Welles, the non-Communist opposition had been relatively united, but Welles's mediation drove in the first wedge of disunity.[39] The conflict between the ABC and the students regarding mediation was later reinforced by the sharply conflicting attitudes of the two groups toward the Céspedes and Grau regimes. The two most important reform groups were now opposed to each other, and this proved to be an important factor in subsequent developments.

Thus, fragmentation of political groups was perhaps the crucial weakness of the 1933 Revolution, but this was a cause as well as a consequence of other powerful factors analyzed in more detail in Chapter 3.[40]

3 | The Social Context of Revolutionary Failure

DURING THE STRUGGLE against the Machado dictatorship, there were two main forces that clearly embodied the Cuban populist tradition: the ABC organization and especially the student movement as represented by the Student Directorate (Directorio Estudiantil). Both of them advocated structural reforms of traditional Republican Cuba and both shared the sharp generational consciousness that was such a crucial characteristic of Cuban political and revolutionary thought in 1959 as well as in 1933.[1] Young people have very often been in the vanguard of political change in Cuba but, as we shall see, they were a more decisive factor in the struggle against the Batista dictatorship.

The ABC: A Curious Ideological Mixture

The ABC was a political organization of striking peculiarity and heterogeneity. At various points in its history, and sometimes simultaneously, the ABC stood for a variety of trends and tendencies: generational revolt against the national humiliation of Cuba under the first Republican generations, intellectual and political elitism, democratic demands, opposition to laissez-faire capitalism, veiled racism, concern for economic development, fascist tendencies, and middle-class fears in the face of working-class militancy — all of these found a place, at one time or another, within the confines of the ABC. Its name, structure, and ritual were peculiar, if not altogether obscure and bizarre, and showed an unusually strong hierarchical and secretive bent, even if we grant that the latter attribute developed in the midst of repression.

Ruby Hart Phillips, an observer definitely sympathetic to this group, has explained that the structure of the ABC was copied from a secret society formed in France before the French Revolution. The basic unit was the "cell." There were "seven A men, the executive or directing body," each of whom had under his control ten B men, who in turn each controlled ten C men, a plan of organization that prevented traitors from betraying any members outside their own immediate group.[2] Lower cell members often acted as spies, penetrating every branch of government, including the police and secret service divisions. The actual terrorist squads "were composed of not more than one hundred fifty youths, the majority of them university students who were willing to sacrifice their lives."[3] This organizational structure and activity were closely related to the essentially middle-class, elitist nature of the organization.[4] Its major and almost only strategy in the fight against Machado was a campaign of terrorism against government figures, in the course of which ABC militants demonstrated great heroism and courage and for a time made theirs the most respected and admired organization combatting the regime.

A certain popular political mystique began to develop around the ABC, but this was soon to fade away, for, as indicated in Chapter 2, the ABC revealed that it was able to combine heroism with compromise, particularly if the alternative was a radical confrontation with either the United States government or the native upper classes. Mrs. Phillips has described how she and her husband (then the *New York Times* correspondent in Cuba) went to see Ambassador Welles and in fact acted as go-betweens for the ABC and the North American government:

> Phil and I went to see the Ambassador. The Ambassador sat behind his big desk in the Embassy with the window at his back and listened gravely as I explained that I thought an assassination might be avoided. The Ambassador appeared surprised but almost immediately agreed to see the youths, although he did ask me what type they were.

I told him they were well educated, one spoke perfect English, both were quite charming boys, outside of their tendency to throw bombs. I have wondered what he had previously thought of the terroristic groups. Possibly he visualized them as being long-haired, bearded, typical anarchists.

The Ambassador talked with the boys that afternoon and later told Phil he was extremely glad to have had contact established and was much interested in getting the point of view of this group. They agreed to curtail terroristic activities, although in their meeting held after the interview the boys told me they had a most difficult time persuading the others. On Wednesday of the following week the ABC Revolutionary Organization publicly accepted mediation and pledged themselves to refrain from terroristic activities.[5]

The tendency to compromise had even been written into the ABC Manifesto, an outline of the political program of the organization written shortly after its founding in 1932.[6] This manifesto deserves a closer look because of the great influence it has had on politically aware Cubans, ABC members and nonmembers alike. The manifesto brilliantly analyzed the failure of the "generation of 1895" (that is, the generation that survived the War of Independence). It pointed out that Cubans had been displaced from control of their economy and that it was necessary to eliminate the colonial characteristics of the Cuban economy and the negative role of the United States in it. However, the manifesto's hostility toward imperialism and its commitment to domestic social reform were immediately tempered by a statement to the effect that "realism" should be the guiding policy.[7] And if any ambiguity remained in that formulation, the compromising intent of the manifesto was made crystal clear on the same page when, in order to temper the anti-imperialism of the manifesto, its authors wrote:

> What is NOW [manifesto's emphasis] inescapable is that we are a young American republic, without any economy of our own, located, whether we like it or not, within the political and economic orbit of the United States.
>
> This situation limits and conditions our possibilities much less than is commonly assumed: but it certainly does so to the degree that it will not be possible to experiment with the basic constitution of our

nation. As long as the United States remains within the social and economic system under which it is ruled today, Cuba will not be able to escape from that system; when the United States abandons it, Cuba will have no recourse but to abandon it.

This passage is almost classic in the way it typifies the historical fatalism and submissiveness that had plagued Cuba for so long.

The net effect of the manifesto was not negative for the ABC, particularly because the ABC's audacious activities had won respect among the masses and thus an extremely large audience. Clearly the ABC could not ignore the great influence of Communists and, to a lesser extent, that of Trotskyists and anarchists. There is little doubt that these cautious passages in the manifesto were encouraged at least in part by its authors' fear of leftist activities, which were especially threatening because the ABC had very little organized strength in, or orientation toward, the nascent labor movement and was no match for the Communists there.[8]

The ABC's concern about left-wing influence is made clear in a passage where the manifesto explicitly opposes inciting one class against another.[9] Cuba is a country where all classes are indigent, it argues, and where strong national cohesion must be built. The task is to conquer the economy for the country and not to socialize it. The manifesto then spells out its alternative to a socialist policy, namely: protection of small rural property; measures to encourage the gradual disappearance of *latifundia,* such as a progressive tax on land and limits on the right of corporations to buy land; encouragement of cooperatives; nationalization of public services that tend toward monopoly; protection of small traders and industrialists; adoption of labor legislation to protect the worker, such as the eight-hour work day, social insurance, and the "right to strike, conciliation and arbitration"; and finally the adoption of antitrust measures and the cancellation of unused mining concessions.[10] Yet the manifesto also proposes some "reforms" that are indeed shocking and alarming. Section C of the manifesto proposes the "replacement of the Senate by a Corporate Chamber," and section E recommends the "suppression of the illiterates' right to vote."[11] This, of course, did not prevent the manifesto from explicitly condemning the undemocratic systems of fascism and Communism.[12]

In many ways, this curious ideological mixture was highly representative of the past experience of the ABC's leadership and of a Cuban middle class which was humiliated and resentful but also fearful of major social upheavals. The ABC leadership seems to have come from the intellectual elite of the Cuban middle class. These men and women were part of a new generation which had succeeded in removing itself from the direct influence of both the traditional Spanish groups and older Cuban political circles (veteran generals and officers of the War of Independence). Many of their followers were bureaucrats, professionals, teachers, and students who were repelled by the corruption of the older Republican generation and its inability to attain full political independence, let alone economic independence. The personal enrichment of the older politicians had only served to discredit them further. But these ABC leaders and many of their followers were also afraid of the "ignorant masses," which explains their proposal to deny suffrage to illiterates and their racist inclinations. At the same time, the ABC hoped that clean government and social reforms from above would improve the Cuban masses and make them "safe" participants in politics in the future.

A well-known Cuban journalist and a founder of the ABC, Francisco Ichaso, explained that the ABC "was the outburst of a slow and growing process of nonconformism which . . . expressed itself for many years in the form of philosophical, artistic, and literary rebellions, maintaining itself at the margin of Cuban politics because of its lack of trust in it and its loathing for it . . . [and for] the way in which, with very few exceptions, politics were conducted in Cuba."[13] This mistrust and loathing had led significant sectors of the middle class away from politics into other endeavors; but the Machado dictatorship, with its excessive brutality and its disregard for elementary civility, forced many of these people back into politics. In an almost classic response, a good number chose terrorism, with all of its well-known shortcomings, as the sufficient means of change. Of course, other intellectuals had joined the not yet discredited Communist party. Intellectuals from both ABC and the Communist party as well as others, had been members of the Grupo de Avance. This, as its very name suggests, was an avant-garde group which concentrated mainly on the creative arts and other intellectual pursuits. But it had also shown political awareness and sensitivity and would in fact be highly influential in the formative period of a whole generation of Cuba's top creative, academic, and political intelligentsia.[14]

The Decline of the ABC

Up to and even shortly after Welles's mediation, the ABC organization was, without doubt, the single most important political force in Cuba, although by no means as clearly predominant as the 26th of July Movement would be many years later. Its slogan, "ABC is the hope of Cuba," had a ring of credibility if for no other reason than the near mystique it had created in the country. As the revolution developed, however, its "realism" soon proved to be a policy of "crackpot realism," as C. Wright Mills would have put it, and of utter reaction as well. The acceptance of Welles's mediation produced the first split: the ABC radicals under the leadership of Oscar de la Torre created a rival group. Participation in the Céspedes conservative administration, opposition to the Grau regime, and participation in the repressive Mendieta regime led to further defections and great loss in popularity and prestige for the organization. Its leadership had been caught in a dilemma: on one hand, its elitism and compromising attitudes led it to participate in governmental maneuvering in the hope of obtaining a few concessions; on the other hand, its natural constituency, no matter what conservative tendencies it might have had, was basically reformist. To the extent that the ABC was willing to be a junior partner in conservative governments, it lost its appeal to its natural supporters. This tension produced a zigzag policy which tended to discredit the movement even more. Still, the traditional forces of conservatism-as-usual could not come to terms with and live at ease with the ABC.

At the same time, the authoritarian and corporatist tendencies in the ABC leadership were asserting themselves. Its hierarchical leanings were underscored when it made Joaquín Martínez Sáenz "dictator" of the organization. During the Mendieta regime, the ABC became noted for its substantial contribution to repressive antilabor legislation. Even after going to such reactionary lengths, however, the ABC continued to pursue its zigzag policies. Eventually it withdrew from the Mendieta regime in protest against the absence of reforms and participated in the 1935 strike. After 1935 the ABC went into a rapid decline, and it became just another sect of notables until a rump formally dissolved it in 1947 and then joined, significantly, the newly formed Ortodoxo party. At the end its leaders were dispersed over a wide political spectrum, and some of them, notably Martínez Sáenz, Ramón Hermida, and Carlos Saladrigas, were to be important figures in the first and second Batista dictatorships.

There is little question but that the policies and actions of the ABC were an important factor in assuring the defeat of the revolutionary aspirations of 1933 and in helping to shape the events of that time. In many ways, what the ABC did could have been predicted. Although the organization went through a definitely "populist" period during the struggle against Machado, eventually it expressed itself as a faithful representative of the politics of substantial middle-class sectors. Not only had the ABC expressed compromising attitudes and even submissiveness toward the United States in its own early manifesto; but, more importantly, its caution, vacillation, and fear of a rebellious working class had led it to prefer an alliance with conservatism and even reaction in order to stop revolution in its tracks. Most of these conservative forces had little use for organizations such as the ABC and contributed to its eventual ruin.

To be sure, the ABC was not merely a "representative" of important sectors of the Cuban middle class. It also had its own relatively autonomous political and ideological development which led it to achieve a peculiar ideological synthesis, no doubt influenced by many national as well as international factors, including the growth of fascism. To a significant extent, the ABC was outside the Cuban populist traditions; and, by and large, it remained an almost unclassifiable political mixture.

The Students

As the ABC became increasingly conservative and lost most of its populistic traits in the course of the revolution, the students, together with their close ally Grau, came to symbolize the populist tradition; in fact, many former ABC supporters and members became supporters of the student-Grau government. The overwhelming majority of the university students were of either middle- or upper-class background; but, even though their background might have been no different from that of the ABC leadership, the students were much more militant, a fact that can be partly explained by their peculiar social status. Outside the regular hierarchies of society, at least for several years, and therefore partly sheltered from their impact, students are also in direct touch with an educational experience that brings them closer to high ideals.

At a crucial point, the drawbacks of student populism became evident. Thus, their voluntarism made it possible for them to accept political office from Sergeant Fulgencio Batista after the coup of September 4, 1933, without seeing or understanding the limitations inherent in such a political transaction. As long as this power was based not on organized popular mobilization but on the endurance of the armed forces, it could only prove to be extremely precarious and could only compromise both the student leadership and Grau in the eyes of their supporters.

Lacking a strategy that dealt seriously with the rising and militant working-class movement,[15] the students never succeeded in creating a revolutionary program. The student leaders failed in this regard because, largely as a result of social background and other factors, they were not determined social revolutionaries, nor were they certain what they actually wanted, aside from some social and nationalist reforms. This programmatic uncertainty was accompanied by a failure of will at crucial moments when decisive action against the enemy was necessary. This student hesitancy is revealed in Ambassador Sumner Welles's report on negotiations the students conducted with him to obtain United States recognition and is somewhat reminiscent of tendencies in the ABC leadership. In Welles's own words:

> In my conversation with the members of the student group last night I gained the very distinct impression that the three or four real leaders of the Directorio were weakening materially in the uncompromising attitude they had heretofore taken. They are gravely worried by the fact that the soldiers are no longer inclined to obey any orders issued and that the labor agitation seems to have passed beyond the control which they had deluded themselves they possessed. . . . The [State] Department will understand that Grau San Martín is entirely under their orders and whatever decision they reach he will be forced to abide by. . . . The general impression I gained was one of complete immaturity, of a failure to grasp even in a rudimentary sense the grave dangers which the Republic confronts and a feeling of almost impermeable self-satisfaction. I am having [A. A.] Berle explain to three or four of them today who have some slight grasp of economics just what the Cuban financial and economic picture really is. . . . Once they realize these very obvious and simple facts, I am inclined to think that the already shattered morale of the student leaders will be further weakened and a more patriotic and conciliatory attitude will be adopted.[16]

Even if we allow for Welles's bias and possible exaggeration, given the fact that he was building a case for nonrecognition of the Grau-student government, he is nonetheless pointing to some real traits of the student movement and its leadership: the separation and lack of serious relations between the students and the labor movement and, of course, their alienation from the army. In fact, the students and Grau had no organic ties to any major group in society and were, to a large extent, operating in a vacuum and wasting the fund of popular *sympathy* which was, aside from the initial support of the army, their only basis of power. Although social reforms, legislation, and chauvinistic appeals allowed them to retain sympathetic support, without organized popular mobilization this support was not sufficient to maintain them in power in the face of the subsequent onslaught of the army–native conservatives–United States government alliance.

The Partido Revolucionario Cubano (Auténticos)

In February 1934, while in exile, Grau founded a new political party with most of the leaders of the Student Directorate, who had by now ceased being students. Significantly, they named it Partido Revolucionario Cubano (Auténtico), after the political party Martí had founded in his fight for Cuban independence. Thus Grau and the former student and revolutionary leaders wanted to establish the populist nationalist credentials of their party, which were confirmed by the early nature, social composition, and program of the organization. Basing its appeal on the reformist and nationalist stance of the short-lived Grau government, the party was eventually successful in appealing to many lower-middle and working-class elements, as well as to the peasants. At this time, and for a considerable period afterward, the party tended to appeal to workers and to the poor in their individual roles as underdogs, rather than to the *organized* working-class movement.

In spite of the fact that Grau was personally more moderate than many of his populist followers, he went along with the latter; and the early program and appeal of the party were closely modeled on the Aprista party of Peru, founded and led by Victor Raúl Haya de la Torre. The main planks of the Auténtico program — "constructive nationalism"; a "new socialism" to take political and economic action to benefit the popular majorities; "scientific anti-imperialism," which viewed imperialism as an economic phenomenon resulting from the development of the internal forces of capitalism; a united front of classes instead of class struggle; and double political tactics through the stategy of a "maximum program" and a "minimum program" — clearly showed the Aprista influence.[17] It is ironic that it was only *after* they lost power that Grau and his followers went about forming a party. The Auténticos did not take their programs very seriously, and they did not last as a true mass party. Yet they were open to a reexamination of the failure of the Grau government, and for some time at least they had the potential of becoming a real force for political and social progress in Cuba.

The period of repression following the overthrow of the Grau government seriously affected the Auténtico militants, who were one of the main targets of the persecution organized by Batista's army and police. By the time of the March 1935 general strike, many Auténticos had been killed, arrested, and imprisoned. As previously pointed out, lack of unity in the Left was a crucial factor in the defeat of that strike. Perhaps it was in response to this that Grau subsequently developed his own strategy for unity. It was based on the idea of the Auténticos becoming a broad party, including all the forces that were independently organized, such as the Joven Cuba ("Young Cuba") organization founded and led by Antonio Guiteras.[18]

Joven Cuba

Not all members of the deposed Grau regime joined with him in forming the Auténtico party. Antonio Guiteras y Holmes, a militant Cuban nationalist born in Philadelphia who had been minister of interior in the Grau regime, founded the Joven Cuba [Young Cuba] organization. This group was more militant than the Auténticos, ready to engage in illegal and armed activity.[19] Even before the coup that brought Grau and Guiteras to office, Guiteras had helped to prepare a program for a group of revolutionaries in Oriente Province, which included: (1) punishment for all who directly or indirectly participated in the recently overthrown regime; (2) confiscation of all assets legally acquired "under the protection of that situation of force and illegality"; (3) reform of the Constitution; (4) initiation of a socialist policy; (5) general elections.[20] Guiteras appealed to the most radical elements outside the Communist party who had given support to the Grau regime. Although he was definitely more interested in working-class affairs than Grau, like other populists he lacked a systematic strategy for working-class organization. Yet there are indications that Guiteras's vision was broader than that of most Auténticos. As a Cuban Trotskyist, R. S. de la Torre, observed of Joven Cuba, "The basis of its program is the 'anti-imperialist' struggle and it advocates a broad reformist program in favor of the working masses. Guiteras had a broader view than his successors. He had an international perspective for the Cuban revolution."[21]

Joven Cuba confirms again the heterogeneity of the middle classes and their politics. There is little doubt that essentially different groups are classified as "middle class" and that in Cuba many members of the lower middle class, for example, were supporters of the militant policy of Guiteras while others had gone along with the Auténticos or even with the ABC. In this context it is important to point out that, to a great extent, the Cuban lower middle class was anchored in the state bureaucracy. As de la Torre observed,

> the Cuban petty bourgeoisie is distinguished from that of other countries by the fact that it does not have an economic base of its own. It is not rooted in small business, in small industry and in small-scale property, but consists exclusively of state employees. . . . [The] relative consolidation of Mendieta, the reactionary, and the lack of faith in electoral methods, caused this social layer, in black despair, to turn to its only way out . . . insurrection.[22]

This despair encouraged a terrorist and voluntarist approach to politics and revolution in Joven Cuba, as well as in many smaller revolutionary groups in this period of Cuban history. The "Revolutionary Deed" was often seen as a goal in itself, rather than in close connection with the revolutionary mobilization of broader social groups or with a clear social and political program. Even though Guiteras's program was more radical and working-class oriented than that of Grau, it was still rather vague, and Joven Cuba was unable to grow and become an organizational alternative to Grau or to the Communists.[23]

Guiteras was killed by Batista's troops on May 8, 1935, after which Joven Cuba declined in importance. Eventually most of its members joined the Auténtico party when the latter successfully persuaded various revolutionary groups to dissolve and merge into it. Yet Guiteras's influence as an ideological precursor of non-Communist revolutionary nationalists would remain.

The Cuban Working Class

A crucial factor in the development of revolutionary events in the 1933–35 period was the role played by the working-class movement and by the Communist party, which was closely related to it. The fairly large Cuban working class included many workers, both rural and urban, in the sugar industry, as well as the usual city proletariat in services and manufacturing.[24] With the exception of railroad workers and a few other trades, it was hardly organized at all in the period preceding the revolution. This was a period in which employer domination was almost absolute, given the lack of strong working-class organization and governmental support for employers. The post-World War I period had been a time of prosperity, and this no doubt stimulated the appetite of many workers; but the prosperity did not last too many years. Furthermore, in the late twenties the Great Depression took its toll on the Cuban sugar economy, and workers' living standards dropped sharply. The crisis was so severe that by 1933 even the more secure public employees had not received their pay for several months and there was actual starvation in some sectors of the population.

These factors, in combination with the Third Period policy of the Communist International and the ongoing struggle against the Machado dictatorship, produced a highly explosive situation and stimulated revolutionary sentiment among many Cuban workers. Of course, some of these factors, under other circumstances, might have produced less rather than more militancy. For instance, mass unemployment can have a debilitating effect on working-class protest. In this instance, however, the vacillations of the Machado regime, when faced with pressure from Ambassador Sumner Welles and the opposition of most Cubans, only encouraged and gave confidence to the growing spirit of revolt among workers. The great economic distress which affected all Cubans also served to partially erase some of the divisions within the working class, such as those between skilled and unskilled, blue- and white-collar. When the first general strike erupted in August of 1933, it was supported not only by all workers but even by store owners who were also sharing in the general political and economic despair, thus making it a national, as well as a working-class, struggle.

Working-Class Organizations

Anarchist influence was strong in working-class circles in Cuba in the first twenty-five or thirty years of this century; the American Federation of Labor, which at various times sent organizers to Cuba, also made its influence felt. In 1925 the very small and just recently established Communist party played a major role in organizing the CNOC (Confederación Nacional de Obreros de Cuba), which years later was to become the most important national labor organization. By the early thirties a number of Trotskyists, under the leadership of Sandalio Junco, a Black trade-union leader, had split from the Communists and had become an influential force in the Havana Federation of Labor, where there also existed strong anarchist influence.

Until the early thirties none of these radical groups were successful in organizing a large number of workers. Their failure was due in part to the fact that a socialist tradition was practically nonexistent among Cuban workers. There was no significant number of immigrants from countries like Germany and Italy to import this tradition, as they did in Argentina. Some Spanish workers brought anarchist ideas and practices with them, but that was all.[25] Although most workers were individually sympathetic to the populist groups, the influence of such groups remained marginal in the organized working class during the thirties.

The Appeal of the Communist Party

One important piece of evidence of the virtual absence of a socialist tradition in Cuba was the fact that, despite the crucial world events of 1914–18, there was no significant socialist party and the Cuban Communist party was not founded until 1925. Even in 1928 the Communist party had no more than a hundred or so members,[26] making it more a sect than a party. At that time, the party included a few intellectuals, some students, and a number of workers, some of them Jewish immigrants from Russia and Poland. Subsequently various intellectuals from the original 1927 Grupo de Avance also joined the party.

A key figure in the early history of the Cuban Communist party was Julio Antonio Mella, who could be considered the founder of the Cuban student movement. Mella is perhaps exceptional in his having remained an historic hero to both the Communist and the populist sections of the Cuban Left. Mella, a handsome athlete and revolutionary, had become the leading Cuban representative of the Latin American movement for university reform, often referred to as the Córdoba Movement. Mella had also developed a strong orientation toward the working-class movement. At a relatively early date, however, Mella was forced into exile in Mexico, where he was assassinated in 1929 under obscure circumstances. Whether because of Mella's absence or for other reasons, the Communists never were able to exercise as much influence among the students as they later did among the Cuban working class. The Student Left Wing (Ala Izquierda Estudiantil), which had links with the Communists, had some influence among university students, but it was never a serious match for the more "moderate" leadership of the Student Directorate.

The early death of Julio Antonio Mella and that of the poet Rubén Martínez Villena a few years later left the Communist party with a more purely bureaucratic leadership. In addition, the date of the party's founding meant that it was born practically Stalinized, thus largely bypassing the heroic period of the Communist International, when internal controversy and fresh thinking were still appreciated. A Trotskyist group did split off, but, as Robert Alexander points out, "it soon joined the newly formed Auténtico Party and became the core of that party's labor support, losing all connection with the international Trotskyite movement."[27] Otherwise, the Cuban Communists were an unusually monolithic organization, even by Communist standards, and the party's leadership remained essentially intact from the late twenties until the sixties, relatively few splits taking place. Even in the midst of serious crises, such as the denunciation of Earl Browder in the forties, the leadership managed to reverse itself and stay at the helm, following the new Moscow line as faithfully as it had followed the previous line. Yet this rigid bureaucratic organization to an extent benefited the Communists in their organizing tasks in the trade-union movement when the populist revolutionary forces were fragmented and rather uninterested in the working class. It is quite easy to see why the Communists proved to be so successful among workers at a time when the latter were eager and overripe for organization and only the Communists were around to do the job.

The massive popular upheavals of the revolution against Machado and its aftermath greatly increased the membership and power of the Communist party, particularly in the working-class movement. Yet the sectarianism of the Communist party hurt the revolution's chances of success. In addition, a separation existed between most populist groups and organized labor, and the Communists adopted a viciously hostile policy toward *all* populist groups. A resolution of the Second Congress of the Cuban Communist party in 1934 stated that, "of all the groups and parties in Cuba, the most dangerous for the revolution are the parties of the 'Left,' chiefly the Cuban Revolutionary Party of Grau."[28] This resolution expressed the belief that the principal threat to the revolution was from groups who would "canalize the mass discontent and use it for their own purposes" or "divert the masses from the road of revolution in order to safeguard the bourgeois-landlord-imperialist domination."[29]

Comintern policies influenced Cuba's internal events to such an extent because sectarian policies in world Communism coincided with a major revolutionary upsurge in Cuba. Not only did the Communists fail to make any distinctions among non-Communist groups, thus lumping Grau, Guiteras, and the ABC together as if they were all the same,[30] but at some points they made concrete policy decisions that, if widely adopted, would have seriously endangered the triumph of the revolutionaries. Such an instance was the last-minute Communist pullout from the August 1933 general strike against Machado. There is an historical controversy as to what were the actual motives of the Communists in doing so. Their opponents have argued that the Communists had worked out a private deal with the Machado dictatorship for their own sectarian benefit,[31] while an important Communist leader many years later explained that the Communist leadership had failed to see that the strike had changed from an economic and solidarity strike to "a unified political act on the part of all the nation, under the slogan 'Down with Machado!' " He added that the Communist leaders at the time erroneously concluded that, "since it was impossible to replace Machado immediately by a revolutionary workers' government, the struggle of the working class would only have the objective effect of aiding the bourgeois opposition to gain power."[32] Regardless of the validity of any of these explanations, there is no question that, even if we accept the interpretation most favorable to the Communist party, the unilateral withdrawal of the Communists from a national strike of a variety of forces and groups showed a marked sectarian character; the political priorities of the Communist party clearly were put before those of a widespread popular movement. Fortunately, in this particular instance, the Communist call went largely ignored and thus had a smaller effect than it might have had otherwise.

By early 1935 a shift had begun taking place in the political line of the Comintern as it searched desperately for allies, sometimes, as in Cuba, going far to the right. This new policy did not arrive early enough to prevent the Cuban Communist party from contributing to the disunity of the revolutionary forces. At the time of the March 1935 strike (the second general strike and the last major revolutionary event of this period), the Communists were still in the initial stages of their new policy, and the Left remained disunited at this crucial juncture.

It did not take long for the party to confess to many of its previous errors. Thus, in October 1935, when the new policy was being consolidated, Comrade Marín, Cuban delegate to the Seventh World Congress of the Communist International, acknowledged that "this 'neutral' position taken by the party with regard to the struggle between the Grau government and the reactionary ABC party . . . objectively facilitated the coming to power of the present reactionary government." He went on to add that the party had incorrectly characterized as "fascist" even Joven Cuba, headed by Guiteras. This mistake was accompanied, Marín added, by another basic error: "mechanically setting off the class interests of the proletariat against the interests of the national-liberation struggle, the aims of the bourgeois-democratic, agrarian and anti-imperialist revolution in Cuba."[33]

These confessions of guilt were accompanied by overtures to Joven Cuba and to the Auténticos to form a Popular Front.[34] The overtures to Joven Cuba led to no agreement, and that organization lost strength after the death of Guiteras in May 1935. As we have seen, Grau rejected the Communist overtures. This did not deter the Communists in their search for alliances, including one with Batista a few years later.

In the meantime, the policies of the Communist party had seriously affected the course of the revolutionary movement. In terms of its impact on the development of working-class consciousness, the sectarianism and ultrarevolutionism of the Communist party in its Third Period had prevented it from laying the basis for a solid socialist and revolutionary tradition. The sudden shift to a policy of conciliation of political forces of a conservative nature only served to create a justified distrust and cynicism among many militant Cubans. It was at this time that the undemocratic and elitist nature of the Communist party became increasingly apparent.

The Role of United States Imperialism

We have already discussed the decisive role played by United States interests, both private and governmental, in the internal affairs of Cuba throughout the Republican period. This could not fail to have a great impact on the political attitudes of the Cuban people; yet, as is so often true, these attitudes were in some respects inconsistent, depending in part on whether the prevailing political mood of Cubans was one of self-confidence and militancy or one of pessimism regarding the success of their own political efforts. Thus, Ruby Hart Phillips was not exaggerating unduly when she described how many long-suffering Cubans heralded American Ambassador Sumner Welles on May 7, 1933, as their savior. She added, "The majority of Cubans still looked to the United States to free them from oppression."[35] This dependency and submissiveness changed to defiance and struggle in a matter of months. Before the end of 1933, the revolutionary upheaval had created strong anti-imperialist sentiment even though it was often accompanied by a recognition of the objective powerlessness of Cubans. Nothing reveals this powerless anger more clearly than the popular anecdote of the militant Cuban who, during the time the United States was threatening Grau, started firing at an American warship anchored across from Havana Bay — with a revolver. These contradictory attitudes of defiance and submissive fatalism — the idea that "nothing can be done in this country without the approval of the United States" — would continue to alternate in the Cuban mind during the historical epoch to come.

Of course, United States intervention was decisive in a much more concrete way than in its effect on the political ideology of the Cuban people. Through the use of economic and military threats, the United States became a powerful factor in defeating and emasculating the Revolution of 1933 in two fundamental ways. First, the backing of Welles and Caffery was essential to bolster the confidence of an inexperienced Batista who had not yet consolidated the power of the army — which he proceeded to do at the expense of the revolution and its program, always counting on the support of an American government which wanted the reestablishment of law and order. Second, the United States ambassadors allowed the traditional politicians to play a role in Cuban politics that would otherwise have been beyond them. The Revolution of 1933 had dealt a serious blow not only to Machado but also to his traditional opponents such as Mendieta. Yet support from the army and the United States allowed such elements to come back and play their old political games.[36] In fact, these political games were essential to the interests of Batista and of North American ruling groups because it was very important to give the impression that everything had returned to "normal" in Cuba, and to avoid any appearance of naked army rule. Thus, Cuba missed an opportunity to clear away outmoded and corrupt political figures completely. The influence of these old politicians and the oligarchic social groups they represented was changed by the events of 1933–35. In the meantime, however, the United States had succeeded in bringing the revolutionary process to a halt without having to use its troops. It did this through the agency of the Cuban army and traditional politicians in a manner not dissimilar to what would take place in Guatemala in 1954 but very much unlike the Cuban Revolution of 1959, where the United States would have *liked* to do the same but was in no position to implement such a policy.

The United States could not continue its relations with Cuba in the old openly imperialist fashion. The outburst of 1933 had produced too many changes in Cuba, and these changes combined with the new Good Neighbor policy to produce a new and subtler policy under which political intervention was less visible.[37] The Platt Amendment was abolished soon after Mendieta took office, and in exchange Cuba allowed the United States to keep one naval base at Guantánamo. What is more important, the United States and Cuba signed the 1934 Trade Reciprocity Treaty. Though it underwent some modification over the years, this treaty remained the model for the neo-imperialist relations between the United States and Cuba. Under it the island was forced to remain an undiversified and economically dependent country. Robert F. Smith, an American historian of United States–Cuban relations, has explained that

> the new treaty gave Cuba certain tariffs benefits for sugar, rum, tabacco, and vegetables. In return, Cuba made six general concessions to the United States: (1) Import duties on many American goods were lowered, usually by increasing the preferential reduction. Small electric light bulbs, for example, were given a 60 percent preferential reduction; the old rate had been 25 percent. Tires received a 40 percent preferential reduction, and inner tubes a reduction of 30 percent. Both had received 20 percent reductions under the old treaty. (2) Cuba agreed not to increase the existing rates of duties on a large number of American products during the life of the treaty. (3) Cuba agreed to abolish or to reduce internal taxes on many American products. (5) No quantitative restriction would be placed on any article receiving the benefit of tariff reduction in the treaty. (6) No new restrictions would be placed on the transfer and means of payment for goods.[38]

For the next twenty-five years, Cuba would maintain an overall pattern of economic stagnation, primarily caused by distorted and anarchic capitalist economic development, itself the result of a self-perpetuating one-crop economy which was largely an appendage of the dominant United States imperial economy. The United States sold all kinds of manufactured products and even foodstuffs to Cuba while the island virtually depended on sugar alone to pay back its purchases from the monopolistic imperial salesman. Thus Cuba often found itself in an unfavorable position concerning price levels and foreign exchange balances, as well as in the generally degrading position of economic and political dependence on its northern neighbor.

The Role of the Armed Forces

The relative weakness of the Cuban oligarchy during the Republican period almost inevitably had a weakening effect on two usually traditional and conservative institutions of Latin American society:

the army and the church. In the case of the army, this relative weakness was further encouraged by the fact that, at the end of hostilities against Spain, the United States interventionist government and the Cuban governments that followed disarmed the Cuban rebels and literally pensioned them off. Only a rather small army (as well as an even smaller navy and police force) remained in existence, with a few Cuban generals in command. As a result, the most pronounced characteristics of early Republican Cuba were not those familiar elsewhere in Latin America — military *caudillos* with their large armed followings of former independence fighters battling each other for the spoils of office. To be sure, there was an element of this in Cuba during that time, but a more typical figure was the provincial or regional civilian *cacique* ("political boss") fighting other caciques and their followers for the spoils of office. Some of these caciques had served as generals in the War of Independence, but by and large their struggle was based on patronage of the usual political sort rather than on military force. There was more of Tammany Hall than of the military spirit in them.

Yet there did exist a small group of officers, mostly members of the upper class, who had been professionally trained in United States military academies and who shared the authoritarian and somewhat aristocratic values of typical officer corps. Under the stresses and tensions of the Machado dictatorship and the revolutionary period, their authority was greatly weakened, and it finally gave way altogether in the Sergeants' Coup. At the time, a former officer in the army told Ruby Hart Phillips about the kind of institutional crisis that eventually led to the events of September 1933. Although some parts of this report may be biased or inaccurate, it is worth quoting because it gives an interesting overall picture of the nature of the conflict involving Machado, his army officers, and the troops: "Machado himself feared . . . the group of younger officers who were completely divorced from politics and were career men. One hundred forty-six of this group had been trained in American military schools and were imbued with the high ideals of the American armed forces."[39] By extending various favors, Machado tried to gain the active support of this group but failed.

His next step was to have the higher and most trusted of his officers weaken the disciplinary hold of the subaltern officers on the troops. . . . On every occasion the authority of the subaltern officer was disregarded and belittled by his supporters. Therefore, the troops came to look on their immediate officers as mere figureheads without any real power.

When Machado fell and the highest officers of the army fled, the troops, composed of the uneducated classes of the island, were completely disorganized. They had no desire to submit to the authority of the officers then in command. They had been taught to disregard them and to look to the higher category of officials as their commanding officers. Thus the next logical step was for the enlisted men to assume control. . . .

The fourth of September rebellion started as . . . a movement within the ranks destined to force compliance with certain conditions or demands made by the troops with regard to their own status, and was never intended to become an insurrection with removal of officers and a change of administration. . . . The leaders . . . removed the officers. . . . Then they found themselves forced to establish a government which would continue their action. In something like panic they called in the student element.[40]

Throughout the revolution against Machado and afterward, the United States ambassador kept in close touch with military circles, relying on them as a guarantee that whatever changes took place would not endanger the status quo. Thus, Welles, through his assurances of backing and support, was instrumental in persuading the officers finally to get rid of Machado;[41] and the ties between Welles and the officers continued even after the latter had been fired by Batista. In fact, the officers actively resisted Batista's control of the armed forces until they were at last defeated in the "battle" of the Hotel Nacional, an armed confrontation that took place after the officer corps barricaded itself inside what was then the largest hotel in Cuba. Immediately, Welles got in close touch with Batista as well, making sure that the latter would maintain the army and Cuba on a safe conservative course; this policy was continued under the auspices of Ambassador Caffery. Welles's strategy can be better understood in light of his explanation to the state Department of the significance of the clash at the Hotel Nacional and its outcome:

I wish, however, to make it very plain that the capture of the officers does not indicate consolidation of the position of the government but solely a decidedly increased prestige for the Army as distinguished from the government. I appreciate fully the difficulty of realizing that such a distinction can exist in view of the apparent identification of the Army with the Grau San Martín government. It might be remarked, however, that the army mutiny did not take place in order to place Grau San Martín in power. It occurred for the sole purpose of displacing the officers, and when Batista and the other ringleaders found at the last moment that the students and a few others would join with them they then agreed to support a so-called revolutionary government in which Grau San Martín participated. The divergence between the Army and the civilian elements in the government is fast becoming daily more marked. As Batista becomes more influential the power of the students and Grau San Martín diminishes. [42]

Perhaps Welles underestimated the at least temporary increase in Grau's power as well as Batista's; but, by and large, his analysis was sound, particularly in regard to the distinction he made between the army and the government, a distinction that allowed him to pursue more effectively the conservative interests of his own government.

It is necessary to correct any impression that the army ranks were solidly inclined toward an antirevolutionary position. Batista himself found it convenient to use reformist rhetoric, and the populist revolutionaries and even the Communists had influence within the military establishment. The Communists published a paper especially aimed at soldiers (*El Sentinela*), and Guiteras had also been assiduously cultivating sections of the armed forces. Thus, as late as November 6, 1933, Welles himself left open the possibility of the "displacement of Batista through violence by elements in the Army, upon whom Guiteras, the present Secretary of Gobernación is working."[43] Yet, Batista's greater strength, and his own roots in the army, proved to be decisive, and he soon became the undisputed leader and chief of the Cuban armed forces. This leadership he consolidated through a systematic policy of military sectarianism, where the size and importance of the armed forces was constantly increased and the living standards of the troops were improved. Few of the civilians who served as tools of Batista dared to challenge such military supremacy; those who did (e.g., President Miguel Mariano Gómez) were quickly eliminated from the political scene. The supremacy of the military was further reinforced after the defeat of the March 1935 general strike. As early as February 1934, Batista's control of the military, as against the pretensions of the former officer corps, had been legalized by governmental decree.

The power and privileges enjoyed by the military could not but influence the financial and social scale of priorities of the Cuban state. Charles A. Thomson has reported that, "of a total budget of $55,395,000 for 1934–35, the army and navy were allotted $12,201,000 or 22 per cent. Subsequent credits approved by the cabinet increased this total by $5,000,000. . . . During the Machado regime, however, the revenue absorbed by the army and navy had ranged as low as 14 per cent for some years and for the final period of depression and terrorism had not exceeded 19 per cent."[44]

With augmented financial support, the total force was increased by 8,000 men, growing to almost twice its strength under Machado: there were a total of 22,100 men in the armed forces (army, navy and national police) under the control of Colonel Batista. They were better paid and more adequately fed and housed than ever before. Certain distinctions between officers and enlisted men were abolished. Large quantities of arms, ammunition, and airplanes were purchased, and American instructors were hired to train a new air corps.[45]

Even more important was the new and very special role the armed forces, through their chieftain Batista, would come to play in the social and political system that came into existence in Cuba after the close of the 1933–35 revolutionary period. This sytem, while antirevolutionary, was also significantly different from the prerevolutionary situation.

As we have seen, the peculiarities and weaknesses of various social and political forces contributed to the political fragmentation that led to the defeat of the Revolution of 1933. Thus a situation with almost all the elements of "classical" revolution did not lead to a victory of the revolutionary forces. Instead, it led to an impasse: the new revolutionary forces lacked the necessary strength and unity to take over, while the older conservative forces, considerably weakened, were effectively prevented from reasserting their power in the old terms. Although there was a period of sharp repression, particularly from 1934 to 1936, this was not to be the permanent basis of the new postrevolutionary status quo; the fall of the Céspedes government had brought down the remnants of a traditional caste of military officers and greatly discredited the old conservative and liberal political parties. All of this produced a further weakening of the traditional Cuban oligarchies. From this time on, the traditional politicians would continue to play a role but only to the extent that they were strongly bolstered by new middle-class and *arriviste* elements (e.g., the Auténticos) or by Batista's plebeian leadership of a new military caste. This caste was to play a unique and crucial role in the postrevolutionary situation.

The failure of the Revolution of 1933 left a feeling of frustration and malaise among most Cubans. The aspirations of 1933 had not been fulfilled, nor had the prerevolutionary state of affairs been restored. Unfulfilled expectations accompanied this frustration and malaise, often resulting in a kind of cynical disillusionment; this was not, however, the same as a state of somnolent and ignorant indifference. Future political generations would have a basically ambivalent attitude toward the events of 1933–35: on one hand, they would take pride in the rebellious past and in some of the gains of the period; on the other hand, they would feel shame and frustration over the corruption of the revolutionary generation and its failure to achieve basic social transformations. This ambivalence could, under appropriate circumstances, be transformed into a fervent desire for a new revolutionary attempt.

4 | The Counterrevolution of 1935

Batista and Conservative Bonapartism

Few situations could be more propitious for the development of Bonapartism than the state of Cuban society in the wake of the overthrow of Machado's regime in August 1933; in fact, some of the traits of this period are similar to those discussed by Marx in connection with the rise of Louis Napoleon Bonaparte. While the weakened Cuban oligarchy was trying unsuccessfully to maintain order and to bolster a badly shaken power structure through the efforts of the Céspedes regime, which had the strong backing of the United States, the fragmented opposition was unable to rally the united power necessary to continue the revolution and lead it to any sort of successful conclusion. Neither the conservative bourgeoisie nor its populist opponents were in a position to gain and consolidate power on their own terms, as was proven by the weaknesses and failure of the Grau government. Eventually, the successful sergeants of September 1933, after getting rid of Grau and his supporters, found themselves filling a power vacuum. The leadership of these sergeants and soldiers was assumed by Fulgencio Batista y Zaldívar.

Of humble origins, Batista was at that time an obscure sergeant in his early thirties. He had held a variety of jobs before becoming a stenographer in the army with the rank of sergeant, attached to General Headquarters as a court reporter. This literate milieu probably contributed to making him a quick and fluent speaker.

It would be a mistake to conceive of Batista as an ordinary reactionary. While there is no question that his ideas and actions were profoundly counterrevolutionary and repressive, he did not think and act like a typical conservative politician. Thus, even at the height of his repressive activities, he was still speaking in almost reformist terms about the rights of labor and the evils of working-class exploitation. He added, however, "Cuba is a geographical accident. . . . Whether Cubans like the idea or not, Cuba is compelled through her own necessities to be close friends with the United States and I believe that the majority of the islanders feel as I do on this subject."[1] Indeed, Batista's formulations about class impartiality and geographical fatalism vis-à-vis the United States are highly reminiscent of the ABC organization of which he reportedly was a rank-and-file member while a sergeant in the army. Of course, this "reformism" was accompanied by a strong authoritarian and militaristic bent which was not quite the same as that of the ABC.

When Batista and his sergeants came to power, the situation was so fluid and unclear that it provided Batista with a certain freedom of choice as to the political direction he would take. There was, of course, the threat of direct United States intervention in the country, but this was not the only factor that influenced Batista's decisions. He was not long in making up his mind and coming to an understanding with the cause of conservatism and counter-revolution. His participation on this side of the Cuban conflict proved to be indispensable; in the two or three years following his emergence from obscurity, Batista made himself the leader of a strengthened and flattered army, which then attempted to stamp out the revolutionary forces on the island, an effort that culminated in the complete suppression of the general strike of March 1935.

From Repression to "Normalization"

The period of intense repression and political reaction that followed the defeat of the March 1935 general strike did not last long. After the defeat and demoralization of the students, the working class, and other revolutionary forces in 1935, a new stage of Batista's rule began. Intense repression had initially made him highly unpopular with the overwhelming majority of Cubans, and his popularity was restricted to the still-narrow base of the increasingly strong armed forces, plus a few conservative Cubans. Not a few members of the Cuban upper classes often disapproved of Batista's methods, but their timidity and fear of revolution made them unable to oppose him effectively, a situation very similar to that discussed by Marx in *The Eighteenth Brumaire.*

As a Bonapartist figure, Batista had been able to rule during the intense revolutionary crisis of 1933–35 only because his narrow base of popularity was not much of an obstacle when the task at hand was one of pure repression. After the revolution had been suppressed, Batista and his allies came to realize that the business of society could not be permanently conducted on the basis of force alone. In fact, the Cuban intellectual Jorge Mañach saw as the central characteristic of what he called "Septembrismo" (after the coup of September 1933) not merely the predominance of military men over civilians but "a militarism . . . which prefers to act not through pure and simple orders but with a civilian screen. . . . It is moved by desires for public welfare in education and health, provided that they be under military jurisdiction. . . . It provides, finally, a tolerance which is not quite liberty; a discipline which is not quite order; a quietude which is not yet peace."[2]

Batista had to broaden his political base; and in fact, the history of the second half of the thirties in Cuba is a record of accommodations and political soundings aimed at normalizing the political order disrupted in the 1933–35 period. During this time Batista held no political office, preferring to rule indirectly through civilian presidents while he maintained his position as head of the army. At various times and on various occasions, Batista replaced these civilian presidents and/or looked for a convenient action or ally to enhance his own strength and broaden his political support. Much of the milder conservatism that followed was the result of pressure from Washington.[3] Roosevelt did not want naked army rule in Cuba, especially in view of the storm of protest registered in the

United States, particularly in the liberal and radical press, against Batista's activities.

This pressure was not lost on Batista. Aided by a slackening in the economic crisis of the early thirties, he attempted to "normalize" Cuban society on as conservative a basis as circumstances allowed, employing a kind of authoritarian socialism from above "under which there should be discipline of the masses and of institutions so we can establish a progressive state under which the masses may be taught a new idea of democracy and learn to discipline themselves."[4] Batista explained that he believed in a philosophy of authority, not of force. He described himself as a "progressive socialist" and said that the army, imbued with a "spirit of realism," wanted "to teach the masses that capital and labor both are necessary and should cooperate. We want to drive out utopian ideas which will not work, but which so many of our people hold."[5]

This new stage in Batista's rule did allow him to gain more support than had the previous stage of pure repression and force. Combined with some new and unexpected political alliances, this modicum of popularity allowed him to stabilize his rule and to exercise power, whether openly or not, for quite a few years. In this manner, the crisis of the revolutionary period of 1933–35 was temporarily contained, at the price of leaving untouched the fundamental social and political structure of the country and ignoring the continuing frustration arising from the fact that crucial problems, such as the need for agrarian reforms, were being left essentially unresolved. In the meantime some rather minor reforms and concessions were granted for the sake of reducing the tensions inherited from 1933 and before, and the state and its bureaucratic apparatus grew in importance and even in relative autonomy vis-à-vis the economically powerful business classes. For this reason, Batista's Bonapartism played a crucial role during all those years when a new "stability" was being sought and an "outside" arbiter — Batista — took charge to adjudicate whatever disputes occurred in the process of establishing new social rules.

Thus, by 1936, a less extreme policy on the part of Cuba's conservative forces had become predominant. When President

Miguel Mariano Gómez took office in May 1936, after an election that was boycotted by practically all revolutionary parties and groups, he called for amnesty for political exiles, autonomy for the University of Havana, and some social reforms.[6]

As candidates for his puppet electoral posts, Batista revived traditional Cuban politicians who were always willing to play the electoral game. Some of these politicians were younger than their most corrupt predecessors, but they adhered nonetheless to the spirit of the previous political generation. One such politician was Gómez, who was eventually overthrown by Batista when he started taking his presidency a little too seriously. As Russell Fitzgibbon and H. Max Healey remarked concerning the period of Gómez and his contemporary Cruz:

> Gómez and Cruz . . . are of a younger generation — both were boys at the time of the War of Independence — but their political habits and thought patterns are molded after those of the "men of '95." That, to the forward-looking Cuban, means a conventionalized reaction to politics which thinks in terms of the *"chivo"* ("graft") and *"botellas"* ("soft jobs") and rejects any notion of a social and economic revolution. Old-school politics, the young reformers say, has captured the stage and nothing is to be expected of it. . . . The flame of enthusiasm has given way to ashes of bitterness and disillusion.[7]

This bitterness and disillusion could not help but have a very damaging effect on the political self-confidence and combativeness of oppositionists and revolutionaries. Most had abstained from participating in the fraudulent elections held by Batista, and there were some hopes of armed resistance which did not materialize. Some revolutionaries, in their hopelessness over the Cuban political situation, turned their attention elsewhere. A few, mostly intellectuals, returned to purely esthetic pursuits. Others, equally hopeless about the Cuban situation but willing to fight, turned their attention — and sometimes their efforts — to the Spanish Civil War. Pablo de la Torriente Brau, a kind of Cuban John Reed who died fighting for the Spanish Republican cause, was one of the latter. A friend of Brau's has said that, "if in Cuba there had been a glimmer of any possibility of renewing the struggle initiated years before, without a doubt

[Brau] would have flown to Cuba. But in 1936, Cuba was a cemetery of illusions and revolutionary plans."[8]

Of course, most oppositionists and revolutionaries neither went to Spain nor took refuge in purely esthetic pursuits. Instead, many of them joined either the Auténtico or, to a lesser extent, the Communist party when, a few years later, the situation improved enough to make possible their participation in "normal" political activity. They returned, however, not to the revolutionary politics of 1933–35 but to a far more subdued and reformist politics. Their frustrations with the failures of the 1933 Revolution continued and, consequently, so did their search for the fulfillment of those aspirations in a new political context.

By the end of the thirties, the situation in Cuba was in many ways opposite to that of 1933–35. While in the early thirties a number of potentially revolutionary issues reinforced each other, in the late thirties there was a telescoping of conditions leading to reformism, if not to outright conservatism. On the foreign front, the nature of United States imperialism vis-à-vis Cuba had changed. The granting of some concessions and the implementation of the Good Neighbor policy substituted a more refined politico-economic domination, accompanied by liberal and even left-wing rhetoric, for the old Big Stick policy of landing marines. The Communist policy of Popular Front and "unity" against fascism strongly contributed to reformist sentiment and to an even greater decline of explicit anti-imperialist politics than had already occurred as a result of the new United States policy. All these factors had their effect on the Left, both Communist and non-Communist, and they also affected the Cuban Right, particularly the regime and policies of Fulgencio Batista and his puppet presidents.

Batista's Bonapartism and the Political Parties

The shifting, opportunistic policies of Batista's regime in the thirties led him to look for alliances with *all* major political parties, including the Communists and the Auténticos, both of which had strongly opposed him. In his search for a base of support broader than the armed forces, Batista could not be satisfied with the support that he had previously obtained from the completely discredited traditional parties and politicians, who had lost so much strength and prestige since the overthrow of Machado; he had to look for more substantial alliances. As we shall see, he was turned down by the majority of the Auténticos, but he was successful in forging a close alliance with the Communist party, a rather amazing turn of events.

The Communist Party

After the defeat of the general strike of March 1935, the Communist party and its clandestine press continued their sharp attacks on the Batista dictatorship; and, under the auspices of the international Popular Front line, they tried to make an alliance with the other major opposition groups. By this time, however, the Communist party had become more moderate in its tactics than the groups it had previously denounced as "social fascists" and the like, and no agreement was reached on how to go about combatting Batista. As one Cuban Communist put it at the time:

> The delay in the formation of the People's Front was mainly due to the fact that the Revolutionary Cuban Party and "Young Cuba" regarded immediate revolt as the sole way out, whilst the prerequisites for this were by no means ready. . . . The Communist Party had repeatedly proposed joint participation with the Left parties instead of the policy of abstention from elections pursued by these Left parties. Had the proposals of the Communist Party been accepted, then without a doubt several important positions would to-day be in the hands of the revolutionary elements, which would form an important basis for the fight within the administration, against the imperialist dictatorship.[9]

The Communists were probably right in their assessment of the inadequacy of a strategy of "immediate revolt," given the widespread demoralization existing at the time; but the alternative they offered was even worse, since it consisted mainly of participation in and acceptance of the obviously phony electoral game that Batista and Gómez had brought into being.

The more moderate opposition of the Cuban Communist party and its failure to establish a Popular Front with Grau's Auténticos and the other populist groups coincided with Batista's search for political allies after a new phase in his political orientation began around 1936. It is not known when the first contacts took place between Batista and the Communists, but in 1937 the Partido Unión Revolucionaria, a Communist front group, was founded and allowed legal existence by the government. On May 1, 1938, the Communist daily newspaper *HOY* started publishing legally, and on September 25, 1938, the Communist party, which had been declared illegal in 1935, was finally allowed to become a legal party. By this time the Communists had started holding rallies and resumed open and legal work in the trade unions. The position of the Communist party had changed in the meantime from moderate opposition to one of friendly support for Batista and his controlled regimes, though Batista and the Communists reserved the right to disagree with each other on a variety of issues. The Communist party soon began to make great organizational strides. According to Blas Roca, then general secretary of the Cuban Communist party, the membership of the party grew from only 2,800 members in January 1938 to 5,000 members in September 1938 and 23,300 members in February 1939, the time of his report. Roca also reported that 71 per cent of the members were workers and only 8.2 per cent were peasants.[10]

All of these events are indications of what had taken place: Batista, in exchange for political support from the Communists, had allowed them a free hand in their trade-union work. They managed to obtain a following and to recruit workers into the party on the basis of a policy qualitatively different from their Third Period ultra-leftism. This Communist trade-union work was accompanied by the unmistakable paternalism of the Ministry of Labor, which now grew beyond anything the first Grau government might have imagined. The ministry, among other things, favored Communist trade-union officials as against those of other political persuasions, which was not an unimportant factor in producing an easy Communist hegemony when the CTC (Confederación de Trabajadores de Cuba, or Confederation of Cuban Workers) was legally founded. It is symptomatic of the relations of the unions with the government that the Workers' Palace, headquarters of the CTC, was to be built with the proceeds from two state lotteries which the Batista-controlled government had granted to the Communist-controlled trade-union movement.

There is no doubt that this Batista-Communist alliance was possible only because of favorable international circumstances in the years 1936–38. The Popular Front policy and their liberal approach to fascism made the Communists sufficiently respectable for the United States to tolerate such an alliance on its own doorstep. Batista had made a visit to Lázaro Cárdenas in Mexico and to the United States. After giving all proper assurances of his support for United States policy, he returned home to a triumphant welcome, organized with the active participation of the Communist party.[11] Yet, once the alliance had been established and consolidated, even new and less favorable international circumstances would not break it. Thus, the brief interlude of the Nazi-Soviet Pact did not serve to sever the ties between Batista and the Communists, which was rather unusual, considering the many other Popular Front alliances ruined after the Ribbentrop-Molotov agreement.

Both Batista and the Communist party had a lot to lose from a break in their alliance. The Communist party would have endangered its increasingly important control of the newly reorganized labor movement; and Batista, on the eve of the opening of the Constitutional Convention and of the general elections which were to crown his long efforts to "normalize" Cuban politics, would have been left again in the sole company of the army and a variety of weak and discredited traditional politicians.

A variety of national and international factors had thus allowed Batista to utilize an opportunistic alliance with the Communists to ensure his own power. This alliance met a fair amount of disapproval on the part of many conservative supporters of Batista; but Batista was able to straddle and manipulate these various forces without any undue strain. In many ways he had a better knowledge of the long-range interests of the Cuban capitalist classes than did they themselves. Thus, he was able to obtain more profit for conservatism from the Popular Front policy than the Communists did for their own cause. For a variety of reasons the Cuban bourgeoisie would have been in no position to obtain the same results, acting on its own behalf without the "outside help" of Batista. Batista was not "representing" the latter; he was dictating policies which the bourgeoisie accepted because of their compatibility with its basic interests even though it disapproved of some of their aspects.

In the meantime, Batista's successful alliance with the Communists had ensured the continuation of a profound split in the Cuban Left, which in fact was by now becoming almost permanently divided into two quite distinct political traditions: the "populist" one of the Auténticos and that of the Communists. Batista, in pursuing his Bonapartist policies, had tried to manipulate the Auténticos as well, but most of them refused to go along and remained the main opposition force.

The Cuban Revolutionary Party (Auténticos)

After the defeat of the 1935 general strike, many of the Auténtico leaders went into exile, some of them joining Grau, who had left Cuba in early 1934. The Auténticos, as well as other opposition and revolutionary groups, continued to call for the violent overthrow of the Batista dictatorship; but in fact, nothing significant happened in this direction. In many ways, the Auténtico policy was abstentionist rather than either revolutionary or collaborationist (like the Communists). This abstentionism did not last very long, however, particularly after Batista adopted more conciliatory policies toward the opposition. By early 1937, Grau was announcing his willingness to return to Cuba "if there is a free and sovereign Constituent Assembly."[12] Grau's plans to return to Cuba were joined with various efforts to regroup the non-Communist opposition and revolutionary factions within the Auténtico party. Thus, on August 15, 1937, at a meeting in the city of Havana, representatives of the Auténticos,

Joven Cuba, and other groups, and various independents took steps to reconstitute a unified Auténtico party,[13] a process successfully completed by 1938.

The return to legality due to the new moderation of Batista and the regrouping of the various populist groups under the Auténtico banner was accompanied by a visible moderation of the Auténticos and their more radical allies. Not only did the international climate of liberal anti-fascism and Popular Frontism have its own somewhat smaller yet definite effect on the Auténticos as it had on the Communists, but also the defeatism of 1935 and shortly afterward had made many despair about revolutionary possibilities. In this context of demoralization, the conciliatory moves on the part of Batista were successful in decreasing populist militancy and radicalism. Thus, while Grau had been talking, as late as 1936, about the trinity of "socialism, nationalism, and anti-imperialism," and about the need for a revolution that would effect profound transformations in the economic, political, and social spheres,[14] by the time he was announcing in early 1937 that he would return to Cuba if there was a free Constituent Assembly, he was also explaining that his "criterion for a revolution is fundamentally different from any extremist idea."[15]

A situation was now developing where *all* major political groups were moving in a more moderate and conservative direction. The Auténticos had somewhat different reasons from the Communists for doing so, and they did not at this time go as far as the latter toward collaboration. But the fact remains that Batista's new and more moderate policy was successfully dissipating a good deal, though by no means all, of the surviving revolutionary tensions and currents from the 1933–35 period. This process continued throughout the late thirties, particularly when the various parties were preparing to engage in the electoral politics of the period of liberal democracy inaugurated with the Constitution of 1940 and the general elections of that year. By 1939, the Auténticos, who were now the largest single party in the country, had adopted a political program that was significantly more moderate than anything they had previously offered. In April 1939, the intellectual Guillermo de Zéndegui wrote, on behalf of and with the explicit approval of the National Political Bureau of the Auténtico party, the latter's ideological program for the coming period of the Constituent Assembly and general elections.[16] This document praises nationalism but does not mention the term imperialism in either the Aprista or the Leninist sense, nor is the United States mentioned in any context that might suggest its imperialist character. The document criticizes both laissez faire capitalism and Communism and advocates a "coexistence of classes" as a goal for Cuban society. The program is still critical of the traditional and unprincipled Cuban electoral parties, and it continues to demand agrarian reform that would safeguard small family property and redistribute land, though it does not say a word about the scope of such a reform or its methods of compensation, distribution, and the like. The document is in many ways a good example of Cuban populist politics and attitudes from 1938 to 1959.

In fact, by this time the distinguishing characteristic of the Auténticos was not so much that they were the broad party of the Left as that they had become the party that advocated a civilian and democratic version of reform rather than a militarist and authoritarian one. As far as reforms went, the Auténtico programs and actions were at the most only slightly more radical (and sometimes less radical) than those of the other major parties, including the Batista-Communist-conservative alliance of the late thirties and early forties. The Auténticos were able to appeal to the very powerful anti-Batista and antimilitarist tradition in the country, a tradition that had retained its strength.

The contrast between the civilian-democratic and the militarist-authoritarian traditions remained for a long time one of the key lines of political cleavage despite the efforts of groups like the Communist party to blur the distinction. In fact, as a result of their associations with the tradition of militarism, the Communists discredited themselves among a great number of Cubans who rightly perceived them as a completely opportunistic and undemocratic group which in addition violated cardinal rules of Cuban nationalism by their subservience to Moscow. These Cubans, and especially many workers who belonged to Communist-led unions, would usually acknowledge the personal honesty and dedication of most Communists, unusual traits in an increasingly corrupt country. Yet the Communists remained separated from the rest of the Left, and Cuba, unlike other countries, did not have a single "movement of the Left" within which the Communists were one element. This came about not only because the Communists refused to support the 1933 Grau government and then supported Batista but also because Grau and the Auténticos were on most occasions adamant in their refusal to make a pact with the Communists, even when the latter definitely wanted to do so in the mid-thirties. The Auténticos' refusal could be attributed, at least in part, to their different social base; also Grau's plan to create a single non-Communist reform party turned out to be reasonably successful for a while in spite of crucial structural weaknesses of the Auténtico party, as well as its increasing conservatism and corruption.

The Auténticos were by no means immune to the persistent efforts of Batista to manipulate as many political groups and parties as he could for the benefit of consolidating his own independent power above groups, parties, and classes. In late 1938, Batista, after having arrived at an understanding with the Communists, actually approached the Auténticos and tried to obtain the support of the latter for the formation of some kind of reformist coalition; however, he was turned down by Grau and most of the leadership of the party. In spite of this, Batista's power and attraction were sufficient to cause a split in the Auténtico party in 1937–38; the "Realists," under the leadership of such well-known figures as Sergio Carbó and Rubén de León, two leaders of the 1933 Revolution, supported Batista and broke with the "Orthodox" majority, led by Grau, who refused to go along with them.[17]

These maneuvers, as well as the increasing moderation of the major parties, were signs of their accommodation to the period of electoral politics which started in the late thirties, a period when the opportunities offered by a climate of relatively great civil liberties were wasted in politicking and corruption of the worst sort. The Auténticos, who had so often opposed traditional politicking, were in 1940 signing an electoral pact with the Republican party, a small group of old conservative machine politicians, and the Communists took similar steps when they found it convenient. This was to be the state of Cuban politics during the coming years of popular disappointment, cynicism, and frustration of the not-yet-forgotten aspirations of 1933.

Capitalist Development Pays a Price

Capitalist development also paid a share of the price for the new state of affairs in Cuba. Partly because of unstable conditions in the world sugar market and partly because of the labor situation in the country, the state intervened in the conduct of business, particularly that of the sugar industry. Thus, in 1937, the Ley de Coordinación Azucarera legalized state control of the total sugar acreage, state allocation of quotas to producers, and regulation of prices and wages, and established measures protecting the rights of the small and medium-sized sugar farmers (colonos), thus containing the process of their elimination by bigger holdings.[18] Under the terms of this law, representatives of sugar mill owners, sugar farmers (colonos), workers, and the government would jointly determine the rules that were to govern the state's regulation of the industry. Wages and regulations for each mill would become the objects of yearly bargaining; and in this manner, various political and national and international economic considerations would influence the relative gains of each of the "factors of production" in the sugar industry. Under these conditions of state control, politics became much more important to the masses of Cubans; the role of the state bureaucracy and its usefulness to Batista and his successors continued to gain in importance; and one more link was forged between the unions and the state.

There is little doubt that this regulation of a highly unstable industry contributed to the creation of an even greater unwillingness on the part of many capitalists, particularly foreign, to invest in Cuba. Thus, the typical predicament of most less-developed countries was created: distorted development due to the economics of imperialism, insufficient and disharmonious investments, and lack of diversification eventually lead to state-capitalist regulation even on the part of native conservative governments, which then often discourages the capitalists from even their usual limited investments in the country.

Let us now return, in Chapter 5, to our analysis of political developments in the period 1933–1959 by taking a close look at the constitutional period that began in 1940.

5 | The Constitutional Period of the Forties

BATISTA'S POLICY of "normalizing" Cuban politics and society after the revolutionary agitation of the first half of the thirties was fairly successful. The end of the sharp economic crisis brought about by the depression, the relative calm in the labor front after some concessions had been granted to the working class and an agreement had been reached between Batista and the Communist party, and the increasing integration of the Auténticos into the politics of legality and electoralism had brought about some changes in what was still status quo politics. At the same time, revolutionary undercurrents had not disappeared. Cuba had not yet achieved full legal and political normality given the continuing constitutional vacuum and rule by decree, and the absence of succession procedures for the rotation of officeholders. By the late thirties, Batista's rule was sufficiently secure to allow him to look forward to a more permanent political stabilization of Cuban politics and society on the basis of a legitimation of the changes that had taken place in the country's economy and politics since the overthrow of Machado. For this purpose, the puppet government of President Federico Laredo Bru called a Constitutional Convention.

The Cuban Constitution of 1940

On November 15, 1939, Cubans went to the polls to elect delegates to the Constitutional Convention which was to take place the following year. In spite of the fact that these were the first reasonably honest elections Cuba had seen in many years, opportunism and lack of political principles still strongly colored the delegate election process. Two blocks of delegates faced each other during and after the elections: one supporting the government and one opposing it. Both blocks contained reformists as well as reactionaries, new as well as old politicians. The opposition was led by the Auténticos, who elected the single largest number of delegates, but it also contained the conservative forces, led by the traditional politicians Mario G. Menocal and Miguel Mariano Gómez, as well as the zigzagging ABC party, which by now had greatly decreased in importance. The government side included the Communists as well as the conservative and discredited Liberal and Unión Nacionalista parties. After the opposition had won 44 out of the 81 seats and had just installed Grau as president of the convention, Menocal's group, in a move typical of the increasing corruption of Cuban politics, went over to the government side, which thus obtained a majority and replaced Grau with Carlos Marquez Sterling.[1]

In spite of the predominance of government delegates, the mood of the Constitutional Convention was one of liberalism and of a desire to establish a fairly democratic constitution. For one thing, the lines separating the government and opposition coalitions were by no means rigid ones; and often Auténticos, Communists, and other Left-leaning delegates would vote on the same side of an issue against the conservatives, regardless of their affiliations with the government or the opposition.[2] The final result was a constitution that was, without a doubt, one of the most liberal and progressive ever written in the American hemisphere. Besides establishing universal suffrage, free elections, freedom to organize political parties, and a large variety of protected civil and political rights, it also spelled out maximum hours and minimum wages; included provisions for old age, accident, and other forms of insurance; established annual one-month paid vacations for every worker; guaranteed the right to strike; and included measures for the "protection" of women and children.[3] Yet many of its articles, especially the most advanced and progressive ones, were couched in vague terms and ended with a proviso leaving to future congressional action the passage of laws that would put these social innovations into effect. In many instances, as in the establishment of the National Bank of Cuba, it took years for Congress to enact such legislation; in other instances the legislation was never passed because the constitutional provision, although unspecific, was nonetheless too radical and too "hot" for Cuban politicians to handle. This was true of the famous Article 90 of the Constitution, which established agrarian reform:

> Large landholdings are proscribed, and to do away with them the maximum amount of land that each person or entity can have, for each kind of exploitation to which land is devoted, and bearing in mind the respective peculiarities, shall be specified by law.
>
> The acquisition and possession of land by foreign persons and companies shall be restrictively limited by law, which shall provide measures tending to restore the land to Cubans.[4]

The vagueness of its most progressive articles was not by any means the only peculiarity of the Constitution of 1940. Properly speaking, it was not really a constitution in the usual sense of the term, but rather a long document setting forth a large number of provisions, often without corresponding enforcement procedures. It was full of inconsistencies and contradictions, which is understandable for a document written after a lengthy process of compromise and bargaining among delegates chosen across a wide political spectrum. Another result of this diversity of delegates was the inclusion of constitutional provisions designed to safeguard sectional interests of varying legitimacy.

These weaknesses and peculiarities have been pointed out in many critiques of the Constitution. Rufo López Fresquet, an economist who was Castro's first treasury minister, wrote just such a critique. He claimed that the Constitution "became an absurdity" and pointed out that it included many precepts based on arithmetic puzzles. For instance, both public teachers' minimum monthly salaries and the University of Havana's budget were defined as a percentage of the total national budget; thus any government investments made to enlarge the capital assets of the country necessarily forced an increase in teachers' salaries and the university budget. The Communists included the provision that a person remaining more than six months in a given job would acquire the right to hold it permanently; according to Fresquet's procapitalist analysis, this provision handicapped the economic development of Cuba because it made any labor hired for more than six months become a permanent mortgage on the assets of the entrepreneur, a mortgage many investors were loath to assume. Interested in public finance, conservative elements included in the Constitution a clause prohibiting any public disbursements without establishing corresponding sources of revenue *through taxes;* thus it was impossible to follow the now common practice of anticyclical or compensatory government expenditures.[5]

Cuban governments, however, found many ways of circumventing whatever constitutional provisions became too troublesome. For example, two kinds of budgets came into existence: the "ordinary" and the "extraordinary," the latter not being considered in dealing with the various group claims and other measures that the Constitution had tied to the annual budgets.

On a more fundamental level, the Constitution was an attempt to establish in theory and on paper what the Revolution of 1933 had failed to bring about in practice. It represented the result of conflict and power relations among the various social classes and forces, which the delegates tried to sublimate into abstract formulas meaning various things to various kinds of people; sometimes this was impossible or unnecessary, and more concrete measures were established (e.g., in the realm of individual liberties).

In such areas as social legislation, the Constitution often came to act as a promissory note rather than as an actual body of legal commands. For example, constitutional and legal provisions dealing with labor were enforced in those plants where unions were strong enough to insist that they be; otherwise employers, through such means as the bribery and corruption of public officials, very often managed to ignore these provisions. This was true, for example, in the large number of small businesses and plants where labor could not exercise decisive influence and power. To a significant extent, this lack of enforcement resulted from the fact that many provisions of the Constitution actually hampered economic development under capitalist auspices. Thus, various Cuban governments and functionaries were encouraged to engage in selective enforcement and even sabotage of provisions that made it more difficult for capitalism to function. Some shrewd observers realized from the very beginning the real meaning and importance of this Constitution. Thus, in October 1940 *Business Week* analyzed it in the following terms:

> Whether it is ever enforced or not, Cuba's spectacular new charter has created a powerful implement for social and economic reforms demanded by the country. . . . Sudden and drastic enforcement of the new regulations is not anticipated. Cuba is too closely tied to the United States, both economically and politically, to be able to afford measures against foreign holdings comparable to Mexico's expropriation of foreign oil properties. . . . Insiders expect the enforcement of clauses restricting foreign ownership of land and providing for the eventual reversion of present holdings to Cuban hands to be accomplished gradually, if at all. More probably, the constitutional provisions will be held in reserve to be used to force concessions for Cuban workers and to insure more Cuban participation in management.[6]

The Constitution came to play a unique role in the political and ideological development of Cuba in the period following 1940. On one hand, the advanced, progressive character of most of the Constitution made it a banner for the Left, and particularly its populist elements. In the face of repeated violations of the rights and benefits established by the Constitution, it provided a strong and very important source of legitimacy for protest movements against various forms of injustice and abuse. On the other hand, the Constitution's liberal and progressive character helped to obscure the social and economic realities of Cuban society because it encouraged the belief that all that was needed to usher in a utopian era was simple enforcement of the laws and the Constitution. This faith was not accompanied by an appropriate understanding of the socioeconomic realities underlying those very violations of the Constitution and the law. Very often, an admirable revulsion against venality and corruption did not go beyond the symptoms and did not try to determine the more fundamental causes of those social ills, as is apparent in the militant reformism that characterized so much of Cuban politics in the forties and fifties.

While the Constitution became an ideological and political weapon for movements and struggles against the status quo (at least among the more politically aware elements in the population), it also encouraged, in its own way, a spirit of cynicism and disillusionment which could sometimes be converted into militant activity. The fact that all sorts of good things legislated on paper were ignored and had no immediate effect on the actual conditions of daily life led many to adopt a cynical attitude toward the law in general, especially when it was realized that, by and large, the law was enforced to the extent that one could obtain power to back up demands for fair treatment.[7]

A Weak Oligarchy and a Fragmented Middle Class

It is only within the context of the growth of the Cuban middle classes and a relative improvement in the Cuban economic situation throughout the forties that we can understand the pressures building on Batista and his successors to allow and maintain a more liberal regime which included wider civil liberties and some form of free elections for local and national offices. However, it would be very misleading to look only at the numerical size of the Cuban middle classes in order to assess their influence. It is far more important to know who made up these middle classes, what they thought, and how they came to think as they did.

A crucial element in the formulation of middle-class ideology was the relationship between the middle and upper classes in Cuba. Twentieth-century Cuba was never "feudal": its economic and social relations were essentially capitalist, even though it was a dependent form of capitalism. After the older landlord class was almost completely ruined by the drawn-out guerrilla struggle against Spain, the capitalist sugar industry consolidated its predominance. As a result, a strong and old-fashioned landed oligarchy like that in some other Latin American countries never fully developed.

The weakness of the oligarchy seriously affected the behavior of the middle classes, particularly in respect to the formation of class consciousness. The Cuban middle classes were, on the whole, dependent and parasitic. Middle-class Cubans sought bureaucratic employment as a way of avoiding poverty. For their part, the upper classes were more ostentatious than bigoted (aside from the race question), more opportunistic than ideologically committed to a firm set of conservative values. Thus, the Cuban middle classes had no ideological mentors to provide a legitimation and ideological defense of the status quo, with the possible exception of the United States, whose influence was not sufficiently acculturated to be decisive. Imitation of the North American way of life was no substitute for the creation of an ideologically and culturally hegemonic ruling class which took itself seriously enough that other classes could believe in and/or fear its rule.

Mid-twentieth-century Cuba was controlled by ostentatious and rather vulgar *nouveaux riches* who had little sense of social and political tradition. Edmundo Desnoes, perhaps the most sophisticated pro-Castro novelist, has one of his characters describe the prerevolutionary bourgeoisie:

> That's the only thing I have to thank the revolution for: they really fucked up all the damned half-wits who hoarded everything here. I can't say "governed" because they didn't have the foggiest idea of what a ruling class is all about. They never even took the trouble to find out. . . . Cuban society women dressed like whores. At least among the people that has a certain charm: women with loud dresses tightly accentuating all their curves and protuberances; but among the bourgeoisie it was pitiful to see those women dressed up like that and topping it off with jewelry. . . . I can't think of the Cuban bourgeoisie without foaming at the mouth. I hate them with tenderness. Feel sorry for them: for what they could have been and what they wasted out of plain stupidity. For a time I tried to convince them to go into politics, throw out all those professional politicos and tin soldiers, find out what was happening in the rest of the world. I insisted that they had to modernize the country: put an end to all those thatched huts

and all that Cuban rhythm and primitive gaiety and force everybody to study mathematics. Nothing. All wasted.[8]

Thus, class struggle in prerevolutionary Cuba, although often very sharp, was less culturally and socially pervasive than in most countries. The working class and the poor were more likely to be contemptuous of the myriads of Cuban-style Babbits than to nurture the type of crystallized hatred which is transmitted from generation to generation among workers in other countries. This lack of crystallized consciousness is one of the reasons the frequent militancy of Cuban workers failed to develop into socialist consciousness and organization; there was no compelling need to form counterinstitutions and a counterculture, for there was no strongly classconscious upper or middle class approximating the ideological and cultural models of an oligarchy. A relatively small sector of the upper class, for which the reactionary newspaper *Diario de la Marina* was the main representative, did have an oligarchic tradition. However, the *Diario de la Marina* catered to an audience that was heavily Spanish in composition and orientation; the Cuban offspring of its Spanish readers were less likely to read or be influenced by the newspaper. The most important sectors of Cuban capitalism were not, in any case, the Spanish diehards of the import business but the Cuban-born capitalists, often the descendants of Spanish businessmen, who had close ties with United States capital.

Many authors have noted the lack of leadership and fighting spirit in the Cuban middle class as a class.[9] Others have pointed out that this class was fragmented and not united in defense of its common interests. Juan F. Carvajal suggested in 1950 that a class war would fragment the middle class "in accordance with its small partial interests" and that each of the resulting fragments would then align itself with the sector offering it the greatest guarantees.[10] The fragmentation and the lack of developed class consciousness of the middle classes were largely the result of their social and economic dependence and of the absence of oligarchic ideology and leadership. It is not surprising that Castro would later be able to defeat the middle classes precisely by playing on their fragmentation. Instead of alienating all of them at once, Castro successfully dealt with various sectors of the middle classes one at a time.

There is little question that the Cuban middle classes as a whole, given their economic and political weaknesses and even bankruptcy, could not and did not play the progressive role that so many theorists of Latin American society have attributed to them. Of course, part of the problem with some of these theories is that they try to explain so much with the use of broad and ambiguous terms like "middle sectors" that they become meaningless and of very little use for purposes of analyses.[11] Also, a good deal of the confusion surrounding discussion of the middle classes results from the fact that many theorists have failed to make a clear distinction between the bourgeoisie of the early capitalist countries in Western Europe and the *middle classes* of late-developing capitalist countries, two groups that probably have more differences than similarities. As G. D. H. Cole wisely put it:

> In truth "middle class" and *bourgeois* are not only different words, but stand for essentially different ideas. *Bourgeois,* to any historically-minded person, calls up at once the image of a body of citizens asserting their collective as well as their individual independence of a social system dominated by feudal power based on landholding and on the services attached to it; whereas the words "middle class" call up the quite different image of a body of persons who are placed between two other bodies — or perhaps more than two — in some sort of stratified social order. The *bourgeois* is by his very name a claimant, not for himself alone but for a group with which he identifies his claim, to social power and recognition.[12]

War-Created Prosperity

World War II and particularly the postwar economic upswing had a decisive effect on the Cuban economy. If Cuba had been seriously affected by the Great Depression in the thirties, by the same token she also enjoyed the benefits of the international sugar boom that began in the mid-forties, when an increase in consumption occurred before the wartorn sugar-growing countries in the Far East and elsewhere had time to reconstruct and begin competing in the world market. As a result, Cuba experienced a period of prosperity during which, according to the International Bank's *Report on Cuba*, it achieved an income level among the highest in Latin America, as per capita income rose by 30 per cent in a single decade. Sugar sales reached values not attained since 1920, domestic industrial and commercial activity was high, and there were large imports of agricultural and industrial machinery and of various types of consumer goods.[13] Even the slowdown at the end of the forties was reversed by the Korean War and the consequent increase in sugar consumption by the United States. In June of 1950, the United States purchased the 600,000-ton Cuban sugar surplus.[14]

It is very important to point out, however, that there were many negative economic factors that seriously limited Cuban economic advancement, even in this period of prosperity. Given the fact that no fundamental structural improvements had been made to combat such perennial Cuban problems as chronic unemployment and lack of agrarian reform, large sections of the population were still not fully incorporated within the Cuban economy as effective consumers. This fact helped to produce fairly serious inflation, particularly when large exports produced a surplus of United States dollars,[15] many of which were spent on luxury imports. In addition, an appreciable share of the savings generated in the Cuban economy, far from being used to raise internal productive capacity, were hoarded or invested abroad.[16]

Thus, the lack of structural reforms and the essentially parasitic and consumptionist nature of the upper and much of the middle classes led to a situation where the prosperity of the period was greatly misused. The opportunity to use favorable economic circumstances to develop the productive potential of the country was wasted. This failure is dramatically revealed by the figures of the Economic Commission for Latin America which point out that, during the 1946–52 period, gross fixed investment as a percentage of gross income was only 9.3 per cent for Cuba while it was 18.7 per cent for Argentina, 15.7 per cent for Brazil, 13.1 per cent for Chile,

18.6 per cent for Colombia, and 13.4 per cent for Mexico.[17] The controllers of the Cuban economy simply used up the existing capacity of the economy during the boom and paid little attention to technological modernization or to expansion into new fields which might have brought about a more balanced and diversified economy.

In spite of this, and despite obvious social and economic inequalities, the prosperity was felt in the country and these years — the late forties to the late fifties — were crucial in that they made Cuba somewhat better off than most "underdeveloped" countries. In fact, many economists place Cuba in an "intermediate" group of nations which fall between the "highly developed" and the "underdeveloped" groups. This was the classification used for Cuba by Eugene Staley, the chief economist of the International Bank mission that investigated the Cuban economy in 1950. Staley grouped Cuba together with such countries as Argentina, Chile, Poland, Hungary, and Spain.[18]

The relative prosperity of the forties, combined with the increasing dislike of United States capitalists for Cuban restrictions on labor and other aspects of the economy, led to an increasing role in the economy for Cuban capitalists. Thus, while in 1939 only 28 per cent of sugar mills were Cuban owned, by 1946 the proportion had increased to 45 per cent. (It reached 59 per cent in 1955.) The proportion of bank deposits in Cuban banks (as opposed to deposits in foreign banks in Cuba) rose throughout this period and grew from 16.8 per cent in 1939 to 60.2 per cent in 1955.[19] It should not be inferred from this, however, that there was any kind of clear separation between American and Cuban capital; Cuban and United States capitalists had close relations which included sharing of investments. It is clear that the Cuban bourgeoisie was becoming a junior partner rather than remaining a mere appendage to North American capital.

Yet socioeconomic traits harmful to Cuban economic development persisted. Thus, while there was an increase in the role of Cuban banks, they continued a policy of high liquidity which was harmful to economic growth and contributed to Cuban stagnation.[20] Many Cuban capitalists continued to spend large amounts of money to enhance their prestige, often purchasing land for recreational purposes or for status alone. Robin Blackburn, examining the land records of an area near Santa Ana, Matanzas, found evidence pointing to the relative weakness of Cuba's landed oligarchic past and to the parasitism of the new rich of the forties:

> Apart from the land owned directly by the sugar *central* there were forty medium-sized estates: none had possessed the same owner since the beginning of the Republic (1902), indeed, few of them had existed at that date. Most appeared to have been acquired as investment properties since the period of prosperity created by the Second World War. For from the 1940's onwards, the countryside was increasingly repossessed by the urban *noveaux riches* of Cuba. For the successful businessmen and politicians of the towns, country estates became prized insignia of prestige. These parvenu owners rarely improved productivity. The land was either left untouched (for cane-growing or rent extortion from small subsistence peasants) or else converted into grandiose "ranches" imitated from Texas, with absurdly low cattle densities.[21]

This period of prosperity also led to the development of new groups within the Cuban middle classes, diverse groups like professionals, small businessmen, middle bureaucrats, and people in new occupations. Theodore Draper termed one of these "a rising group of modern technicians, many of them wholly or partially trained in the United States." Calling these groups "innovating and invigorating," he added that "this vital force in Cuban life was increasingly visible after World War II in business, the technical professions, and the governmental bureaucracy."[22]

Using figures from the 1953 Cuban census and other sources, observers have made a variety of estimates concerning the size of the Cuban middle classes. The Argentinian sociologist Gino Germani estimated that the middle and upper classes made up 22 per cent of the total population of Cuba, as compared with 36 per cent in Argentina, 15 per cent in Brazil, 8 per cent in Bolivia, 22 per cent in Chile and Colombia, and 18 per cent in Peru.[23] Carlos Raggi Ageo estimated that the middle classes in Cuba represented as much as

33 per cent of the population, although his figure seems somewhat exaggerated.[24]

A numerically large class or group of people may not be very important if its characteristics tend to diminish rather than to increase its social weight. The Cuban middle classes were disproportionately urban in composition. In fact, the small size of the rural middle classes in Cuba led some students of the Cuban countryside to question whether there was a middle class in the country.[25] In Cuba, as in other Latin American countries, middle-class urban employment does not often provide the economic and social independence historically associated with the development of the middle class in the Western European world. The *Economic Bulletin for Latin America* has pointed out that, alongside industrialization in the form of large and efficient plants, there sprang up in the urban centers "a vast mushroom growth of small inefficient workshops," which could operate at a profit because of an ample supply of cheap labor provided "by the steady immigration of rural population to towns and by the already-existing local stock of marginal population."[26]

In Cuba, an even more important factor in the existence of a dependent middle class was the inflated size of bureaucratic employment, both private and public. At the end of 1949, there were no fewer than 186,450 active and 29,524 retired employees on the state payroll.[27] Many of these were not members of the middle class, but a large number of them doubtless were. Bureaucratic employment and the liberal professions came to be highly prized among most members of the Cuban middle classes. As a result supply far exceeded demand for the available bureaucratic positions. Commented Lino Novás Calvo, "The white Cuban from the city . . . dedicated himself with all his effort to the hunting of one prize: the bureaucratic position. . . . Ministries . . . law offices, offices of all kinds: these were the object of his aspirations. But there was no room for all at the desks."[28]

During the years from 1944 to 1952, when the Auténticos assumed power and tried to run Cuban political life along relatively non-Bonapartist parliamentary lines, their failure resulted in no small measure from the social and political shortcomings of the Cuban middle classes, even in the midst of a period of prosperity.

Constitutional Governments

In 1940, as the tasks of the Constitutional Convention neared completion, general elections were held throughout the country with Ramón Grau San Martín opposing Fulgencio Batista for the presidency. Batista won, though the circumstances surrounding his victory are somewhat questionable, and for the first time he became the official head of the Cuban state. During his period of constitutional rule, he essentially continued his previous policies except that individual and political rights were somewhat better protected by the provisions of the new Constitution. Cuba officially declared war on the Axis powers, and World War II further encouraged the growing pro-Allied and pro-American sentiment in the country, particularly among the middle classes. The Communists continued to control the trade-union movement, which they built and streamlined, but without abandoning their wartime no-strike policy. This only further contributed to the social stagnation and growing frustration of the country during these years when no significant social changes were made. In fact, the Cuban working class and the masses of the population probably lost some ground economically because of a variety of wartime controls their unions supported. A critic of the Communist leaders of the Cuban Confederation of Labor (Confederación de Trabajadores de Cuba) "credited" them with both the increase in nominal wages during the early war years, "long since . . . outraced by living costs," and the later freezing of wages.[29]

Grau and the Auténticos capitalized on this growing social and political frustration by building up their forces and propaganda, looking forward to the general elections of 1944. In the process of local and provincial electoral preparations, the Auténtico party had been gradually changing its nature and becoming further removed from its revolutionary origins of the early thirties. This process had actually started at the end of the thirties, when the Auténticos increasingly became a vehicle for the political and electoral advancement of a variety of ambitious people. Rubén de León, a former top Auténtico leader, has explained that between 1938 and 1944 the Cuban Revolutionary Party (Auténtico) was converted into a traditionalist party under the influence of the "new Auténticos"; these new leaders, most of whom lacked a revolutionary background, "introduced the politics of electoral frauds, especially in the provinces of Las Villas and Matanzas." He added that, as a result, the men who were elected represented the extreme right, the very ideas the Revolution of 1933 had fought; and the true Auténticos, who represented the principles that underlay the revolution, "would obtain a candidacy . . . only by pure miracle. . . . The Auténtico Party wasn't the same anymore. It was much older now."[30]

This process of corruption and weakening of the Auténticos as a party of reform was accompanied by a dilution of the party's proposed program and by unprincipled appeals based on a wealth of contradictory promises of all things to all people. During the campaigning that preceded the 1944 general elections, both government and Auténtico candidates tried to make themselves attractive to employers and workers alike, and, as in previous years, both sides contained conservative as well as reformist elements within their electoral coalitions. In this situation, the personalities of the candidates became key factors.[31]

In spite of all that had happened, Grau and the Auténticos still represented, with a little justification, the "Cuban Revolution" and the civilian-democratic tradition to the majority of Cubans, who expected them not only to eliminate militarist influence from the government but also to establish wider social reforms and administrative honesty. The Cuban people as a whole became aware of the weaknesses and increasing corruption of the Auténtico party only after its 1944 victory. Before that time Auténtico corruption was still largely confined to the local level and had not affected the top national leadership. Besides, Grau's undeniable charisma helped to obscure the weaknesses of the Auténticos and their program of government. As Carlos González Palacios explained in his discussion of what he called the "Cuban Pseudo-Revolution" of Grau and the Auténticos, "Grau . . . had appropriated a slogan for himself which was elementary and effective with the great popular mass: 'Grau, Cuban President.' It wasn't saying much. Even the higher echelons of his own party did not see their leader as a man of extraordinary brilliance; but [his] personality . . . had an unusual attraction for the crowds.[32]

On June 1, 1944, free general elections were held, and Ramón Grau San Martín, in his famous "glorious journey" of that day, decisively defeated Carlos Saladrigas, the candidate of the "Democratic Socialist Coalition," which included Batista and his supporters among the traditional politicians, as well as the Communist party. Batista left office in October 1944 and went into exile in Florida; and Grau, in order to ensure his tenure in office, replaced and retired many army officers,[33] although the institution itself remained essentially unaltered.

Batista's willingness to observe the constitutional mandate against reelection and his acceptance of the defeat of his protégé Saladrigas have been the subject of wide speculation. Pressures from the United States government may have been a factor in his decision. In any event, an attempt by Batista to stay in power, whether by reelection or by imposing Saladrigas, would have been extremely costly in terms of the turmoil and resistance it would have provoked. Despite the many years of Batistiano rule, great political expectations had been built up before and during the war period. Many of these expectations were built on hopes aroused by the growing Auténticos under the leadership of Grau, who were now seen as the harbingers of a new political era. Despite overall stagnation, a few important social and economic changes had been taking place in Cuban society in the decade preceding 1944; and, as a result of some of these (e.g., relative prosperity), many people had recovered some of the confidence and self-reliance they had lost in the aftermath of 1935, a confidence that was strengthened by the political concessions of the early forties. Given this situation, Batista may have simply decided to take a vacation and enjoy his wealth in Daytona Beach, Florida.

At any rate, Grau became president on October 10, 1944, and one of his first acts was to send a presidential message to Congress (in which Auténticos and their allies were a minority) advocating a program of welfare-state legislation which also envisioned "private initiative and enterprising spirit" as a means of mobilizing new sources of wealth. It almost goes without saying that this message made no mention of anti-imperialism or of any of the radical-sounding pronouncements Grau had made in previous years.[34]

The principal achievement of Grau's administration and of Carlos Prío Socarrás, who succeeded Grau as the second Auténtico president in 1948, was that, with some important exceptions, they were able to maintain a climate of civil liberties after eleven years of Batista's authoritarian Bonapartism, which had restricted political freedom even during its "normal" constitutional period. However, this achievement was more than outweighed by the great failures of these regimes.

Although neither Grau nor Prío played a Bonapartist role of the magnitude of that played by Batista, they still operated in a society that possessed, albeit to a lesser extent, many of the same social and political characteristics that served as the bases of Batista's rule. So long as these basic conditions existed, any head of state would have had to play a role different from that played by the head of an older, more economically developed, bourgeois democracy. As we shall see, the liberal and corrupt Auténtico governments proved to be an inadequate substitute for Batista's authoritarian Bonapartist rule. In spite of the democratic changes that were instituted following Batista's exile, Grau's strong use of presidential authority allowed an element of political continuity with the previous regime. William Stokes has described how, during President Grau's administration, "progress toward a parliamentary system slowed to a walk as a result of . . . recalcitrant personalities, defective mechanics, and pressing public issues," adding that Grau "asserted his leadership in an uncompromising and imperious fashion" and perpetuated through his hard-headed one-man rule many of the administrative abuses he had promised to eradicate.[35]

A more important and decisive trait of the Auténtico regimes was the widespread corruption that engulfed public life and created much cynicism and disillusionment among millions of Cubans who had looked with hope toward the coming to power of those who were ostensibly the political heirs of the Revolution of 1933. Not only was there embezzlement of public funds, but, more than ever before, the holding of important public office became the basis for building political machines through the arbitrary use of patronage. Stokes commented that "Grau's supporters seemed to think of public office as plunder to which they were entitled." It was claimed that in the Ministry of Education alone there were 10,000 changes in personnel by June 1946, and there were 4,000 employees on the payroll with no duties to perform.[36]

The high functionaries in Grau's government were making free use of a traditional and crucial sociopolitical weapon in Cuba: control of the inflated and inefficient state bureaucracy on which so many middle- as well as working-class people depended for their livelihood. With few exceptions, these public employees had no job security and were subject to the whims of new administrators and whatever personnel changes they wanted to make, usually for the purpose of providing jobs for their own followers. The resulting insecurity compounded that which *all* Cubans experienced, whether publicly or privately employed, because of chronic unemployment on the island.

It is not surprising that, in this context of corruption, running for office became an occasion for spending large sums of money to buy votes and to obtain publicity. In another article Stokes has said that the evidence suggests the expenditure of very large sums of money by all sides in elections during the Grau and Prío regimes. He quotes Dr. José Manuel Cortina as having said of congressional elections in the late forties, "I believe the cost for candidates in

Cuba is the highest in the world," with such elections costing the candidate between $50,000 and $100,000.[37]

In sum, the atmosphere of the Auténtico governments was one in which a chaotic and corrupt free-for-all political regime, operating in the midst of the relative prosperity of the post-World War II period, had replaced the more authoritarian rule of Batista. The aspirations for basic reforms, which dated back to 1933, continued to go unsatisfied, and a great cynicism and disappointment with politics spread among the Cuban people. However, the rise of the Auténtico governments represented more than this. The Cuban middle classes had arrived at what was probably the pinnacle of their power and prosperity: their political strength had been sufficient to help drive Batista out of power; but it was not strong enough to implement the changes they desired, or to imitate successfully Western bourgeois democracies such as the United States and Switzerland. What replaced Batista was an expression of the middle classes which did not succeed in establishing a political party capable of maintaining social and political stability and a modicum of governmental honesty and efficiency. The weakness of the Grau government and the even greater weakness of the Prío administration were in many ways similar or parallel to those that doomed the 1933 Revolution to failure. In both situations, organizational weakness, indecision, and the Cuban social structure led to the collapse of attempts to establish a liberal reformist regime in the country.

Middle-Class Politics and Auténtico Failings

The negative traits of the Cuban middle classes tended to augment rather than offset one another, with the result that they proved even less capable of effective political organization than many of their Latin American counterparts. Robin Blackburn has said that debility and disarticulation made the Cuban bourgeoisie "utterly unable to create a lasting or coherent party system. The failure of parliamentarism in Cuba was a common enough phenomenon. But the complete failure to crystallize durable, substantial political parties was exceptional in Latin America."[38]

Thus, the failure of the Auténticos cannot be seen simply as the work of corrupt people. What is more important is that, although Auténtico politicians had emerged from the middle classes, middle-class opinion had no way of controlling or containing those people while they were reaching for and occupying the seats of power. Although the Auténtico regimes could not be meaningfully described as Bonapartist, they did play a somewhat comparable role as a relatively autonomous ruling political machine, unresponsive to long-run social needs.

The changes in the Auténtico party and its consequent failure were no surprise, considering the trends evident within the party *before* it attained the presidency. It was invaded by ambitious professional politicians who saw it as a potential vehicle for the distribution of political spoils in the form of all-important bureaucratic employment. Thus, in the midst of a period of relative prosperity, when state coffers were full, the party became an avenue of social mobility for many ambitious individuals in pursuit of economic success. This was by no means a peculiarly Cuban phenomenon. Merle Kling has point out that,

> while the conventional economic bases of power, landownership and control of mineral resources, represent essentially economic constants in the contemporary equation of power in Latin America, government and the army — often indistinguishable in Latin American society — represent notable variables. For in Latin America, government does not merely constitute the stakes of a struggle among rival economic interests; in Latin America, government itself is a unique base of economic power which, unlike the conventional economic bases of power, is subject to fluctuations in possession. . . . In the distinctive power structure of Latin America, government serves as a special transformer through which pass the currents of economic ambition.[39]

The flexibility of the Cuban political Establishment after 1938 definitely encouraged the trend toward political careerism by opening the doors of office holding and patronage to all the major political forces that had hitherto been in opposition to the Batista regime (i.e., the Auténticos and the Communists).

A more fundamental effect of this flexibility was that it hindered the consolidation of the Auténticos into a mass party of opposition and reform. Those social scientists who have analyzed the rise of mass parties, such as M. Ostrogorski and Max Weber, have correctly traced this growth to the rise of mass suffrage in nineteenth-century Europe. Theirs is a necessary but by no means sufficient explanation of the rise of mass parties, particularly oppositionist ones. For the latter at least, another condition seems necessary: an inflexibility on the part of the ruling classes which forces the subordinate classes to develop a kind of countersociety with its own institutions. This activity is accompanied by the formation of mass political parties of opposition (e.g., the German Social Democratic party at the end of the nineteenth century). Thus, in a dialectical fashion, lack of flexibility on the part of the Establishment may, in the long run, strengthen the organization of the opposition, provided, of course, that there is no complete and successful repression. Thus, Robert Michels explained that German workers were forced to develop leaders from their own ranks precisely because they were isolated from an inflexible German society:

> In Italy, the course of political evolution and a widespread psychological predisposition have caused an afflux into the labor party of a great number of barristers, doctors, and university professors. . . . In other countries, however, such as Germany whilst we find a few intellectuals among the leaders, by far the greater number of these are ex-manual workers. In these lands the bourgeois classes present so firm a front against the revolutionary workers that the deserters from the bourgeoisie who pass over to the socialist camp are exposed to a thoroughgoing social and political boycott.[40]

After the late thirties, the Auténticos began to have varying degrees of access to the sources of political power; this helped to corrupt their oppositionist and reform character, as well as to hinder the effectiveness of their organization for other than purely electoral purposes. To a great extent, the Communists escaped many of the possible consequences of their access to power because of their institutional base among workers and because they were a very special kind of party, a party that, to a large extent, found its raison d'être in factors and situations external to Cuba. No matter how many temptations existed inside Cuba, there was always the discipline and mystique forthcoming from a tightly knit international movement, something that the populist political groups completely lacked.

It may be instructive to contrast the Auténticos with roughly equivalent parties in Peru and Venezuela. There is no doubt that both APRA and Acción Democrática (AD) were much better organized political bodies than the Auténticos ever were. Many factors must be taken into account in explaining this difference, but it is quite reasonable to argue that the much longer alienation of both APRA and AD from their respective national ruling classes played an important part in their development as stronger and more cohesive opposition parties.

The Growing Conservatism of the Middle Classes

World War II and its aftermath were accompanied by a definite move toward conservatism on the part of the middle classes not only in Cuba but in Latin America as a whole. The Chilean social scientist Claudio Véliz has brilliantly described this change:

> This unexpectedly conservative attitude on the part of the Latin American urban middle sectors is relatively new. Until the Second World War their political leadership had maintained a reformist position and had even become associated with a number of national Communist and Socialist parties. In fact, during the years between the wars, several reformist political movements, broadly based on urban middle-class support, managed to get near the sources of political power in their respective countries. By so doing, they reversed the traditional order in which social classes or groups perform their climbing feats. The well-known sequence of social ascent usually begins with the acquisition of wealth, continues with the achievement of political power, and ends in the long and tedious quest for social prestige. The urban middle sectors of Latin America, however, reached the sources of political power with the support of the popular

vote, while they were still economically unimportant. . . . They were recruited from the distributive trades, the bureaucracy, the white-collar workers, the professions, and the intelligentsia. . . . In less than a decade, the leadership of the urban middle sectors became extremely wealthy. Using their access to the sources of power and their influence with the bureaucracy, they allocated tenders, granted licenses, exercised the traditional rights of patronage, and, even, without outright corruption, accumulated considerable fortunes. These economic changes were too swift, unexpected, and accidental to result in significant social changes. No apparent contradictions developed between the aristocratic landowner and the wealthy radical leader; on the contrary, they became fast friends and political colleagues once the rising bureaucrat had bought land and racehorses, joined the local country club, and taken his first golf lessons. Thus in a relatively brief period of time, the violent outspoken reformist leaders of 1938 became the sedate, technically minded, and moderate statesmen of the 1950's.[41]

To be sure, Véliz is generalizing for a whole area, and modifications are needed for individual nations;[42] but the thesis is essentially sound when it points to the generally conservative *trend* of the middle classes throughout Latin America in this period. We must also add that World War II had a conservatizing effect not only because of the relative prosperity it brought to most Latin-American countries but also as a result of the pro-American ideological and political currents it encouraged throughout the area, even within the Left itself. This, coming after the period of the anti-fascist Popular Frontism of the second half of the thirties, further reinforced tendencies that had already come to the surface in the immediately preceding period. Harry Kantor, a student of the Peruvian Aprista movement, explains that "the war led the Apristas to soften their criticism of and their opposition to United States imperialism." With the approach of the war, fear of American imperialism became subordinated to fear of nazism as the greatest threat to Latin America.[43]

These currents of sympathy for the United States during the war period could not fail to have an even greater effect on the Auténticos, who had gone much farther than the Apristas in dropping anti-imperialist politics. The Good Neighbor policy elicited a positive response from Auténtico spokesmen, and Grau went as far as to say that there was no more imperialism: "Conditions have changed greatly during the last few years. . . . Yankee imperialism belongs to the past. Certainly, we in Cuba no longer have any fear of such a policy and I believe all Latin American nations are convinced of the sincerity of the United States in striving to establish a continental union of sovereign nations."[44]

His statement was a long way from the old Autentico trinity of "socialism, nationalism, and anti-imperialism," and the new ideological posture it embodied was yet another factor contributing to the dilution of the reformist identity and of the raison d'être of the Auténtico party and to the conservatization of middle-class politics in Cuba. In fact, open anti-imperialism practically disappeared from the Cuban political scene in the forties and fifties, although there remained a latent undercurrent of resentment against United States power in Cuba. In the absence of appropriate channels of political expression, this resentment very often expressed itself in the form of cultural nationalism which sometimes took ludicrous xenophobic turns. A popular congressman in the early fifties, for example, introduced a bill that would have forbidden businesses from having any foreign words in their names.

This increasing conservatism of the Auténticos and the Cuban middle classes was accompanied by their failure to achieve even the rather modest goals that they had set for themselves. We shall analyze this failure and its consequences in Chapter 6.

6 | The Failure of Constitutional Politics and Its Consequences

THE FAILURE and moral bankruptcy of the Auténtico administrations seriously affected the revolutionary and populist groups. These groups found themselves without a political party or vehicle through which they could express their aspirations for a better Cuba. This was particularly true of the more radically inclined, who had joined or supported the Auténticos in the hope that Grau would eventually follow in the traditions of revolutionaries such as Antonio Guiteras. The Auténtico debacle provoked a crisis in the nationalist and populist Left, and the political revolutionary consciousness of these people had to face the perennial question, What is to be done? Eventually the formation of the new Ortodoxo party in 1947 provided one political and organizational answer; but by the time this party appeared the demoralization and hopelessness produced by the decay of the Auténticos had already contributed greatly to the growth of a peculiar Cuban political phenomenon of the 1940s: political gangsterism.

The Political Gangster

Factors preceding the rise of the Auténticos had contributed earlier to the birth of political gangsterism. The failure of the post-Machado administrations to administer swift punishment to those who had abused and killed citizens under the protection of the Machado dictatorship encouraged the growth of the Cuban political tradition of aggrieved parties taking the law into their own hands and proceeding to punish those who were presumed to be guilty of political abuses and crimes. For example, almost ten years after the over-throw of Machado, a man who had been police lieutenant during that regime was shot and killed near his home. His assailants left a card accusing their victim of having been a participant in the August 1933 massacre by Machado officials. Commented Ruby Hart Phillips, "Cubans, it seems, never forgive or forget."[1] Such events helped to create a political climate of individual and group violence, particularly among the populist revolutionary groups which organized so many of these acts of retribution and vengeance. In addition, a few of these revolutionaries had fought in Spain on the side of the Republic, and some had even joined the Allies in World War II. These foreign experiences only encouraged what had already become a well-established Cuban tradition of political violence.

Most of the violent elements of the populist Left supported Grau and the Auténtico party. Although political gangsterism in fact originated during the latter part of Batista's eleven-year regime (the so-called *bonches* at the University of Havana, for example, began in the early forties), it did not reach its peak until after the arrival of the Auténticos in the presidency and ministries. Once the corruption of the Auténtico administration became evident and the hope of a revolutionary alternative was dimmed by the climate of relative prosperity and political disillusion existing in the country, a situation was created where there were few, if any, restraints on the utter corruption of a large number of "revolutionary" elements. Grau, for his part, was more than willing to help in the process of cooptation whereby all kinds of patronage, including important positions in the armed forces and hundreds of paid positions in the various ministries where there was no work whatsoever involved (*botellas*), were given to members of various groups; but he very shrewdly encouraged petty personal and group rivalries at the same time. This created no small amount of public disorder because gangs fought one another over political spoils; but it was highly effective in defusing a revolutionary challenge to the Grau government. Fidel Castro, who was himself involved with one of these gangs (UIR, Unión Insurreccional Revolucionaria) while a student at the Univer-

sity of Havana and before he became a member of the newly formed
Ortodoxo party, explained that young men who had endured eleven
years of abuse and injustice under the Batista regime wanted to
avenge the murders of their colleagues. Because the Auténtico regime was not capable of doing justice, it allowed such acts of vengeance. Continued Castro, "The blame cannot be placed on the
young men who, moved by natural yearning and the legend of a
heroic era, longed for a revolution that had not taken place and at
the time could not be started. Many of those victims of deceit who
died as gangsters could very well be heroes today."[2] The irony is
that the very activities of these political gangsters contributed to a
growing sense of popular futility in respect to political action. These
"revolutionaries" had become corrupt and were fighting each other
in the streets for private gain, which aroused great public disgust
and cynicism.

According to William S. Stokes, during 1949 and 1950 the
organized use of force in Cuban urban areas was characteristic of
party factions, university terrorist groups, and labor unions, with
the University of Havana being one of the principal sources of political power in Cuban politics. Assassinations and street battles were
common. He writes, "The year 1949 began with the assassination of
two students, supposedly for having participated in the shooting of a
police sergeant, who in turn reputedly took part in the shooting of
Manolo Castro, president of the Havana University Student Federation." Sessions of the social sciences faculty were once interrupted
by a fusillade of revolver shots. In front of the COCO broadcasting
station assassins gunned down the vice-president of the University
Student Federation, riddling his body with bullets. Police officers
invaded the school of agronomy, arresting fourteen persons and
confiscating machine guns, rifles, revolvers, and thousands of bullets. Observed Stokes, "The struggle for control of student offices in
the university and for the spoils of government in the capital continues."[3]

These Cuban gangs support Merle Kling's thesis that politics
and the state are avenues of mobility and enrichment in Latin America. Although gang leaders and members seldom won much pres-

tige, the financial and political stakes were increasingly high, and some of these gangs even branched out into areas other than state patronage. However, the groups still wanted to keep some form of political image, and their names and presumed "ideologies" bear witness to this desire: besides the UIR, which pretended to anarchism, there were Acción Revolucionaria Guiteras (ARG) and the Movimiento Socialista Revolucionario (MSR), whose names clearly indicate their ideological pretensions. Groups such as these were usually very crude and politically unsophisticated. Their leaders believed chaos to be "a wonderful thing for a revolutionary" and found it easier to do away with someone than to write a speech or formulate a political program.[4]

The Auténtico administration encouraged gangster groups for another reason. As a result of the Cold War, a split was developing in the organized labor movement, with the Communists and the Auténticos forming two rival labor federations. Traditionally weak within the organized working class, the Auténticos desperately needed anti-Communist labor cadres. The gangster groups, particularly the ARG, helped to fill this role and eventually controlled various unions such as the Tramway Workers' Union. The ARG members were probably some of the fiercest opponents of the Communists inside the trade-union movement. They contributed to making the labor movement subservient to the interests of the Auténtico governments, which continued the tradition of trade-union–government collusion consolidated during the Batista years. Charles Page, a student of the Cuban labor movement, has described how the ARG, claiming a national membership of 8,000 (the great majority of whom appeared to be labor gangsters originally trained in the anti-Machado terrorist underground), did not attempt to reach the masses but tried to develop leaders, and even established the Georges Sorel School for Leadership. Their tactics were primarily direct action, particularly the slowdown. Yet they made a pact with the government, becoming the Communists' most bitter and violent enemies and the goons of the pro-Auténtico CTC, known as the CTC(a). In this role, the ARG received $100 per month for each of two ARG *activistas* ("agitators") in the six provinces of the island. Commented Page, "The alliance is an unnatural one, but at present is mutually advantageous."[5] The ARG succeeded in placing nine of its members in the secretariat of the CTC(a) and twenty-three on the CTC(a) executive committee. An ARG member was even appointed to the Minimum Wage Commission of the Ministry of Labor as a delegate of the CTC(a).[6]

The political gangs were a real obstacle to the work of serious political reformers and revolutionaries. At the University of Havana, for example, university reformers and political students who were serious about their views were forced to carry on long struggles against gangster domination of university politics. Eventually the gangsters disappeared, not so much because of the opposition of the students and faculty, but because, after the overthrow of the Auténticos by Batista in 1952, the gangster groups suddenly lost their political role: Batista, unlike the Auténticos, had no reason to appeal to or to pacify these particular elements. Some individual gangsters, such as Rolando Masferrer, joined the Batista regime and became well known for the atrocities they later committed on behalf of the government. Gangsterism similarly declined within organized labor, where Batista's suppression of both the Communists and other oppositionists left little need for the use of any such gangs. With the gangsters out of the way, the road was left open for the building of a serious movement of opposition to Batista, particularly among the students at the University of Havana.

This relatively short-lived political gangsterism in Cuba followed a pattern in some ways similar to what E. J. Hobsbawm described as the evolution of the Mafia in Italian towns. In many places the Mafia gradually faded out as modern left-wing movements took root. It did not invariably become a politically conservative force, but nowhere, so far as is known, was it *collectively* converted into a left-wing organization, though in some places it did become a right-wing pressure group. Writes Hobsbawm, "The chief tendency of Mafia's development is away from a social movement and towards at best a political pressure-group and at worst a complex of extortion rackets. . . . In the absence of conscious organization and ideology . . . it inevitably tends to operate through gangsters, because it is incapable of producing professional revolutionaries. But gangsters have a vested interest in private property, as pirates have a vested interest in legitimate commerce, being parasitic upon it."[7]

Political gangsterism was both cause and effect of the political demoralization and disintegration under the Auténtico governments. However, the climate of corruption also provoked a very different political phenomenon: the birth and growth of the Party of the Cuban People under the leadership of Eduardo Chibás.

The Ortodoxo Party

Much of the discontent with the Grau regime was channeled into a new political vehicle when, in 1947, Eduardo Chibás, a former student activist and an important leader of the Auténtico party, split from the latter and founded the Party of the Cuban People (Orthodox) — Partido del Pueblo Cubano (Ortodoxos). The main purpose of this new party was to protest and struggle against the corruption of the Auténtico administration. Chibás was accompanied in this new enterprise by a wide variety of elements, including Auténtico politicians such as "Millo" Ochoa, college professors, students, and many individual workers and peasants. In 1948 the recently founded party ran a ticket against the Auténticos and made a fair showing considering the lack of resources at its disposal at the time. In a very short time the party managed to build an impressive following based on the popularity of its top leader and on the moral message it tried to put across to the Cuban people.

Chibás was one of the leaders of the 1927 Student Directorate; and since the days of the struggle against Machado he had shown great talents for political propaganda. Although regarded by many Cubans as being physically unattractive, Chibás was unquestionably a highly popular leader. In time, he became a master of radio in the same way that years later Castro became a master of television.

Chibás was a passionate individual who had many a duel during his agitated political career and who managed to remain unsullied by the corruption of the Grau regime. This gave him moral authority with many Cubans, and he skillfully channeled this prestige into building a new party.

The politics of Chibás could best be summarized as a kind of democratic populism. Although himself a descendant of a wealthy family, Chibás always inclined toward *los humildes* ("the humble"), a political concept deeply immersed in the populistic tradition going back to José Martí. Chibás had strongly defended the cause of the Spanish Republic[8] and always manifested political hostility toward Communist systems.[9] Yet he did not join in most of the abuses and McCarthyite attacks against the Communists during the Auténtico administrations. For example, he thought that the fight against the Communist leadership of the trade unions should be carried on in such a way as not to endanger the unity of working-class organizations,[10] and he strongly condemned such acts as the government-inspired assassination of Aracelio Iglesias, a Communist trade-union leader.[11]

With the beginning of the Cold War, Chibás took a pro-West position very similar to that of many liberal and social-democratic leaders in Latin America. At the same time he criticized United States support for dictators and the conservative foreign policies of Washington. In crucial conflicts like Korea, however, Chibás supported the United States position.[12] This was to be the policy of the Ortodoxo party during its entire history. Thus, Roberto Agramonte, the top Ortodoxo leader after Chibás's suicide, while opposed to sending Cuban troops to Korea, gave political support to the United States.[13] This pro-West position was rooted in Chibás's strong pro-New Deal and pro-Roosevelt sentiments — sentiments that were rather common within Cuban political circles during the thirties and forties.[14]

In spite of Chibás's reputation for excitability and even recklessness and extremism, the evidence seems to indicate that he was both cautious and prudent. As far back as his student days, Chibás was fond of quoting Lenin's *Left-Wing Communism: An Infantile Disorder* against his Communist opponents, particularly during their Third Period of hostility to other Left groups. Yet Chibás never quoted or followed Lenin on anything else and certainly not on writings like *State and Revolution.* In 1937, Chibás strongly supported Grau's policy of bringing all revolutionary and nationalist groups into a single party, disagreeing with those who wanted to maintain their own groups to the left of the Auténticos. Although he strongly opposed the "Realist" Auténticos in their desire for an alliance with Batista, he went along with Grau's wishes to come to an electoral agreement with the conservative Republican party. In sum, he acted as a reform politican who had a variety of goals and priorities to consider, and not simply as the "crazy agitator" many thought he was. On the other hand, some have perhaps more plausibly accused him of having split from the Auténticos because Grau refused to endorse him as the Auténtico presidential candidate in 1948. However, it is possible to accept this as the major reason for the split and at the same time to interpret it as part of Chibás's strategy as a reform politician. It would have been in character for Chibás to conclude, once he was prevented from achieving any kind of control over the Auténtico party, that there was no more hope for the latter and it was thus necessary to make a new beginning.

The heterogeneous mass that joined and supported the Ortodoxo party under the leadership of Chibás did so with a minimal political program. In essence the program had two main points: administrative honesty and no electoral pacts or coalitions with any other parties. Chibás had repeatedly denounced many scandals of the Auténtico administration, and on this basis he appealed to countless Cubans who wanted to throw the rascals out of office. Yet the Ortodoxo denunciations of corruption were seldom based on any serious analysis of the social roots of corruption in Cuba and of the basic social changes required to end it. In other words, there was no serious attempt to spell out the social conditions under which relative administrative honesty would be possible in Cuba. At best, the Ortodoxos talked about the need to provide security, right of tenure, and a merit system for public employees. There was also talk of enforcing all laws and constitutional provisions but, once again, without properly discussing the kinds of actions that would be necessary to achieve this goal.

It is tempting to compare the Ortodoxo plank of administrative honesty with William Jennings Bryan's Free Silver platform of the 1896 election in the United States. In both instances, a wide coalition was put together on the basis of an all-encompassing single-plank platform which could not be spelled out in more detail because of the risk that doing so would make the coalition fall apart. Both "Free Silver" and "Administrative Honesty" were, to different degrees, fetishistic slogans that obscured the real problems. In the case of the Ortodoxos, there was the added element that Chibás, in his denunciations of political gangsterism, stealing of public funds, and the like, was trying to combat, in his own way, a strong tendency toward political cynicism. Advancing a social program that dealt with the roots of corruption would entail the risk of losing conservative support. It was easier to try to agitate these increasingly disillusioned people with simple and dramatic denunciations by a leader who was keeping a heterogeneous party together through his personal popular appeal.

This dramatic appeal for administrative honesty was coupled with the promise of Chibás and the Ortodoxo leadership that they would never enter into any electoral or other political pacts with other parties or organizations, thus ensuring that there would be no deals that would prevent the Ortodoxos from implementing their promises. Yet, while Chibás by and large remained faithful to this promise, the lax admission policies of the party compromised much of whatever political honesty might have been gained through the principle of no pacts or agreements. Many traditional politicians were able to enter the party simply by giving lip service to the party's main slogans and supporting its candidates. The well-known landowner Federico Fernández Casas, for example, was allowed to enter the party on the basis of a vague statement of support for some ill-defined agrarian reform program. Thus, while the Ortodoxos did not enter into coalitions with other parties, they did in fact enter into coalitions with powerful individuals.

When asked how the Ortodoxos would actually deal in office with the crucial social problems of Cuban society, Chibás would often answer with long rhetorical outbursts typical of Cuban politics and completely devoid of meaning.[15] At best, he would advocate some mild program of social reform such as giving the right of first option in any voluntary sale of land to those who cultivate it:

> In regard to *Latifundia*, I contemplate a solution on the following bases: (a) indicating a maximum amount for the ownership of lands which are not in production; (b) establishing a progressive scale for compulsory expropriation, with previous indemnification, of idle or semi-idle lands which are in excess of the maximum amount allowed, with the end of proceeding to their eventual distribution among displaced peasants.[16]

In any event, even these vague and mild proposals never became a central part of the political agitation conducted by the Ortodoxo party. There was really only one issue of private property around which the Ortodoxos carried on agitation, and that was their denunciation of public utilities, such as the telephone and electricity companies, and their proposals for nationalizing them.[17] In fact, Chibás served a brief term in jail on charges of contempt of court when he accused some judges of having been bribed by the Cuban Electricity Company (a subsidiary of Bond and Share).[18]

The nascent Ortodoxo party immediately appealed to large sections of the growing middle classes in Cuba and particularly to the professionals and intellectuals. A sizeable number of liberal professors of the University of Havana became important members and leaders of the new party. For some of them, the Ortodoxo appeal was essentially one of pure good government "mugwumpism," without any significant social content. It is perhaps symptomatic of this that the remnants of the ABC party officially voted to dissolve their organization and merge into the Ortodoxo party in July 1947, very shortly after Chibás had founded the new political organization.[19] But aside from this current there was also a more basic dissatisfaction, and even shame, among intellectuals and other elements of the middle sectors over the state of the country and what they rightly considered to be the Auténtico failure. As Claudio Véliz has pointed out, in Latin America this phenomenon was not limited to Cuba alone:

> The intelligentsia ceased to identify itself with the political, so-
> cial, and economic leadership of the urban middle sectors soon after
> the second World War, when it became obvious that the new radical
> plutocrats had abandoned their reformist programmes and were com-
> mitted to a defense of the established institutional structure. This clear
> divergence of goals and attitudes has led to a remarkable situation in
> which a vast urban middle sector has been openly, and rather ig-
> nominiously, abandoned by its own intellectuals. This development is
> not as common as it sounds. The intelligentsia of the rising English
> middle class was definitely identified with its social and political lead-
> ership. Dickens, for instance, as Orwell points out, thought that the
> remedy for the evils he described in English society was bourgeois
> decency not socialist revolt.[20]

The Cuban intelligentsia was not looking toward either "bourgeois decency" or "socialist revolt"; they were hoping for political reform which they thought could be imposed on the capitalists themselves. The more radical sectors of the Ortodoxo intelligentsia helped to propagate a peculiar kind of intransigent political puritanism. This puritanism was more Jacobin than bourgeois; and, while it was vaguely leftist and pro–working class, it was too abstract to have a concrete understanding of Cuban society and its conflicting social classes.

The limits to Ortodoxo radicalism were dictated by the nature of Cuban history since the Revolution of 1933. The Ortodoxo leaders and most of their followers were also the inheritors of the process of moderation that the Auténticos and other nationalists went through in the years after 1935. Although the Ortodoxos had a very wide popular following which included many rural and urban workers, they were even weaker than the Auténticos had originally been in the *organized* working-class movement. For one thing, the Ortodoxos arrived on the political and labor scene after the process of trade-union bureaucratization had reached a very advanced stage of development. Unlike the Auténticos, they were not in existence at

the earlier organization stage when the opportunities for recruitment of organized workers would have been far greater. Besides
this, the ideology of the Ortodoxos was not particularly helpful in
the task of working in the trade unions. Although the Ortodoxos
supported the underdog in regard to welfare measures and in providing *political* support for many strikes, they had not gone beyond
the Auténtico viewpoint in their fundamental approach to the questions of class struggle. As Chibás put it, a class struggle could not be
avoided unless the existing social legislation was applied, using the
influence of government "to create an environment of mutual respect among the various factors of production, as a means of preven-
ing any of them from abusively [i.e., without regard for the rights of
others] going outside their proper bounds."[21]

Yet there is no doubt that Chibás had produced a powerful
revival of the Cuban populist political tradition. Chibás was
explicitly appealing to the tradition of 1933 and identifying his party
with the memory of the martyrs of the "Cuban Revolution" such as
Antonio Guiteras. Chibás's combativeness and outspokenness also
contributed to making him the heir to that tradition. As often happened in Cuba, the youth of the country were particularly receptive
to this moral and political appeal. The success of the Ortodoxo
appeal made the party even more heterogeneous than it had originally been. The potential for divisiveness was very great in a party
that was so large and was precariously held together by the existence of some unique political conditions. There is reason to believe
that there was a section of the Ortodoxo party which had very close
ties with the Cuban Communists (the names of Ortodoxo leaders
Eduardo Corona, Marta Frayde, and Vicentina Antuña have been
mentioned in this connection). The Youth Section of the party often
showed more radical inclinations than the rest of the party,[22] and
Fidel Castro has claimed that, while he was still a member and
secondary leader of the Ortodoxo party, his political consciousness
was already much greater than that of the party which, although it
had sprung from popular origins, had, over a period of years, "been
falling into the hands of landowners and opportunist politicians; that

is, in most of the country its apparatus was in the hands of reactionary and rightist elements." He asserted that he had already begun to work "with the fervent passion of the revolutionary" and had "conceived a strategy for the revolutionary seizure of power." Once seated in Congress, Castro planned to break party discipline by presenting a program that "recognized the most deeply felt aspirations of the majority," one that "would never be approved in a Parliament the great majority of whose members were mouthpieces of the landowners and the big Cuban and foreign businesses." In this way he hoped "to establish a revolutionary platform around which to mobilize the great masses of farmers, workers, unemployed, teachers, intellectual workers and other progressive sectors of the country."[23]

The death of Chibás in August 1951 and the new situation created by Batista's successful coup against Prío in March 1952 — events that will be discussed further in Chapter 7 — were two serious blows that the Ortodoxo party was not able to withstand. Its precarious unity quickly disappeared, and the party divided into many fragments. Yet, in spite of its instability and eventual collapse, the Ortodoxo party showed that there were extensive moral and political resources in the Cuban populist tradition which had failed to reach an appropriate level of political organization and ideological homogeneity. In spite of the great magnitude of popular disappointment in the Auténtico regimes, there was still enough political hope and concern among many Cubans to allow them to respond positively to the Ortodoxo appeal, thus suggesting that the majority of the Cuban people may have been only partly captured by a mood of cynical apathy and were not in fact indifferent to what was taking place in the realm of politics.

It would be very difficult to understand the struggle against the second Batista dictatorship without taking into consideration the legacy, both positive and negative, of the Ortodoxo party and its contribution to the Cuban political tradition. To a great extent, the poverty of the Ortodoxo party was the result of a political leadership that proceeded from the politically inchoate middle classes. The

Ortodoxo leaders were unable to provide a substantial and decisive political alternative because of their own social roots and interests and their lack of significant organized allies such as the working-class movement.

The Working-Class Movement

In the midst of the climate of relative prosperity and civil liberties during the middle and late forties, there was a definite increase in the militancy of Cuban workers. In September 1951 it was reported that, as in previous months, there had been many strikes and acts of violence. During the preceding ten months there had been 120 strikes and 151 demands for salary increases, an all-time record for Cuba. [24]

The split of the trade-union movement in 1947 into two central organizations controlled respectively by Communists and Auténticos contributed to an increase in the militancy of many unions even though its overall effects were distinctly negative for the working class. In many sectors of the working class, the competition between Auténticos and Communists became fierce. The Communists, now in their Cold War period, had lost much of their previous interest in restraining working-class militancy, and the Auténtico labor leaders had to be careful not to appear as mere government tools. The *Report on Cuba* contends that the Auténtico leaders were less experienced in trade-union matters than the Communists they displaced and were regarded by many as political rather than labor leaders. Thus, they were under constant pressure to demonstrate to the rank and file that they could " 'deliver' more for the workers" and could "carry on a 'struggle' with employers even more uncompromising" than that carried on by their former leaders. [25]

Many of the resulting labor conflicts were prolonged, and the Auténtico governments were occasionally forced to use the tool of "intervention" by which a functionary of the Ministry of Labor would take over the enterprise and administer it while the owners retained their ownership rights and continued to receive dividends and profits. Most employers and capitalists strongly disliked the use of "intervention," and this became another factor in the stagnation of the Cuban economy resulting from the fears and restlessness of both capitalists and workers. In fact, native and foreign capitalists were blackmailing the Cuban people and governments to the extent that the latter were forced to make concessions to the former. For example, in June 1949, President Prío lowered electricity rates to their 1944 level. In less than one month, the Cuban Electricity Company announced that its plans to modernize and improve its power plants had been canceled and blamed this action on the presidential decree reducing the rates.[26]

There is no question that the increasing labor militancy of the postwar period placed the Auténtico governments in a very difficult position and undoubtedly contributed to their eventual overthrow by Batista. The often perceptive analysts of *Business Week* made the following assessment of the situation facing the Prío administration:

> As Cuban labor gets more and more politically aware, the government is backed even farther into a corner. . . . If [President Prío] grants labor's demands, say for a wage increase, he risks boosting sugar production costs to the point where Cuba will be partially priced out of the world market. But if he can't keep the workers' standard of living within the political safety zone, he will be tossed out of office willy-nilly. . . . There is no doubt that Cuban labor has put management — particularly foreign management — in a tough spot. Rent laws, import and export duties and wage laws make no bones about discriminating against the foreign businessman. The frequency with which recent strikes have been settled in favor of the workers' claims is a sign of the times. And it is significant that most settlements in the past couple of years have resulted from special government decrees.[27]

It should be pointed out that working-class disillusion with the performance of the Auténtico governments was also a factor encouraging the workers to rely more on their own pressure tactics alone.

The Structure of the Working Class

It was not only its militancy that made the Cuban working class a *potentially* decisive force in society. As a predominantly urban country, Cuba allowed the working class the possibility of exercising a greater weight than that exercised by similar classes in less-developed countries. According to the official definitions of the 1953 Cuban census, Cuba was 57 per cent urban and 43 per cent rural. Donald R. Dyer has examined these figures and found that 36 per cent of the Cuban population in 1953 lived in cities of 20,000 or more inhabitants.[28] This urban predominance was partially the result of the Cuban sugar economy with its "factories in the fields" which created urban units all over the countryside. The sugar economy also created a two-to-one predominance of rural wage workers over peasants. The rural wage earner could and did become associated with the same trade-union movement that organized the workers in the large cities and metropolitan areas.

A balanced view of the Cuban occupational structure will show that it presented serious drawbacks as well as advantages to the organizing of a strong working-class movement. The United States Department of Commerce has provided the following breakdown of the Cuban occupational distribution as adapted from the 1953 Cuban census:[29]

Occupation	*Percentage of Population*
Professional, technical, and kindred workers	4.4
Managers, officials, and proprietors, except farm	4.7
Farmers and ranchers	11.3
Clerical and kindred workers	7.2
Sales workers	6.2
Craftsmen, foremen, operatives, and kindred workers	22.7
Laborers, except farm	4.8
Farm laborers (including unpaid family workers)	28.8
Private household workers	4.0
Service workers, except private household	4.2
Occupation not reported	1.7
	100.0

Here we find, as in so many other countries, a fairly high number of "service" and "tertiary sector" workers who are usually very difficult to organize in trade-unions. We must also add that a large number of the "industrial" workers were employed in Cuba's numerous small plants and were even more difficult to organize than many "service" workers.

Finally, although rural wage workers were easier to organize because of the nature of their collective work situation, this advantage was partly offset by the fact that many of them were temporary rather than permanent workers. These temporary workers worked during the sugar season and then moved on to the cities or to other areas in search of some other form of temporary employment during the rest of the year. In 1946, for example, only 53,693 out of 423,690 agricultural workers were permanent.[30] Thus it is clear that for agricultural workers union membership may often have been more nominal than real.

In spite of what was frequently a purely nominal membership in unions, the bureaucratism and corruption so widespread in Cuban trade unions, and their failure to organize the weaker sections of the working class, Cuban trade unions were *relatively* strong in comparison with those of other Latin-American countries. The United States Bureau of Labor Statistics records that, in the fifties, more than half of Cuba's two million workers were claimed as members of 1,641 trade unions. The organized sectors of the economy included the sugar industry, manufacturing, transportation, communications, electric power, hotel and restaurant operations, banking, and some of the larger retail stores; but union organization remained weak among the smaller commercial enterprises and in cattle raising, coffee growing, and farming on small farms not attached to the sugar industry.[31]

All of these factors, in addition to the relatively effective system of communication and transportation existing on the island, produced a working class that was restless, frustrated, and, under favorable circumstances, quite militant as well. An urban orientation and proximity to the United States made the Cuban worker a

rather unusual example in Latin America. As the United States
Bureau of Foreign Commerce explained,

> The worker in Cuba is self-respecting, intelligent, abstemious,
> and alert. He learns routines with ease and shows aptitude in acquir-
> ing mechanical skills. Ambitious enough to respond to incentive, he
> has wider horizons than most Latin American workers and expects
> more out of life in material amenities than many European workers.
> His health is good and, although his education may be deficient, his
> native intelligence permits him to overcome this obstacle in most
> instances. His goal is to reach a standard of living comparable with that
> of the American worker.[32]

The Militancy of the Workers' Movement

In spite of its actual and potential strength and militancy, the Cuban
working class failed to develop any kind of crystallized ideology or
large mass party. Unquestionably, the class was hostile to the
capitalists and also to the state when the latter was *visibly* inclining
toward the capitalists. The working class was oriented toward pushing back whatever political and economic advances the "enemy" was
trying to make, but it had no thought, even on a theoretical level, of
a revolutionary takeover of the state and a reshaping of society in
accord with working-class interests. In other words, there was too
much class consciousness for the working class to accept a simple
Gomperite philosophy of business-unionism; but this class consciousness was not sufficiently developed into an ideological or organizational mold to provide the working class with a more fundamental approach to society and its problems, let alone a Marxist
ideological perspective. Thus, militant reformism rather than revolutionism (whether theoretical à la German Social Democratic Party
or real), was the central trait of the Cuban working-class movement,
particularly in the forties and early fifties. A kind of class-conscious
pragmatism gained hold of the Cuban workers in which the
methodology of fighting for limited concessions and reforms without
a long-range program was extended into the realm of political action
as well. Charles A. Page has explained one aspect of this trait:

> As a general rule, the Cuban worker makes a nice distinction
> between national politics and syndicate politics. On the national scene

he will vote for the candidate of that one of the almost indistinguishable branches of the PRC [Auténticos] with which he is affiliated. In union elections he will vote for the slate (if he has the option) which has the most promise of increasing his pay; or he may not vote at all, particularly if times are good. That slate may be Communist, *Auténtico*, or the newly resurgent Anarcho-Syndicalist ARG. Neither does the Cuban worker take it amiss that his syndicate leader may have been a Communist in 1939 and an *Auténtico* in 1947. He himself would as quickly change his support again to Communist leadership, should the present *Auténtico* leadership, through its government alliance, cease to "deliver the goods."[33]

Thus, although for partly different reasons, the Cuban working class found itself in a situation similar to that of the Cuban upper and middle classes: it had no ideology or program to offer to the nation as a whole.

The Struggle for Job Security

There is perhaps no better example of the strengths and weaknesses of the Cuban working-class movement than its constant struggle for job security in a situation of high chronic and seasonal unemployment. This was not, as some would claim, an irrational or reactionary attitude of Cuban workers but a perfectly rational although limited response to the fact that they could not have confidence in the economy of a country where the employer class consistently failed to provide an expanding job market. Yet this working-class approach was limited because the employed section of the working class had nothing to offer to the unemployed workers and because the employed workers were unable to deal with such employer tactics as lockouts, rising prices, and the further stagnation of the economy resulting from the stalemate between employers and workers.[34] These problems could not be dealt with by on-the-job militant actions, by pressure-group politics, or through legal and constitutional concessions; instead, much broader political strategies, programs, and alliances were absolutely essential for offering a long-range alternative to capitalist stagnation and unemployment. In the absence of this long-range working-class alternative, and given the peculiar characteristics and weaknesses of the bourgeoisie of a late developing capitalist country such as Cuba, there was further encouragement for a relatively autonomous but definitely capitalist state to assume an increasing role in the actual running of the Cuban economy.

State Intervention and Union Bureaucracy

Increasing state intervention had a detrimental effect on the development of the working-class movement because the unions themselves became a target of official and unofficial state intervention. In Cuba, as well as in other late-developing capitalist countries, class conflict became too threatening to the rulers, and the authorities made sure to intervene in internal union affairs. Thus, the working class was saddled with a double task if it was to retain and develop its power and independence: to organize internally and also to resist the increasingly state-controlled and rigid trade-union apparatus. This, of course, is also true of advanced capitalist countries in the contemporary period of state intervention in the economy; but in an earlier stage of history the working-class had enjoyed relatively greater freedom to organize itself independently from the state. The latter very often tried to suppress or eliminate trade unions altogether; but, by and large, it had not yet penetrated these organizations from within to the extent that it would later on. This provided the working class of those countries with a longer period of autonomous apprenticeship in independent struggles and organization, thus diminishing cooptation and dependence on other classes or on the state.

After 1933, state intervention in the Cuban economy was accompanied by state paternalism toward the unions, as well as by attempts to influence their internal affairs. The Ministry of Labor became a crucial institution in settling all sorts of external and internal trade-union affairs. The Communist-Batista pact of 1938 greatly accelerated this process which had begun with the first Grau government in 1933. The frequent and growing contacts and collusion with government functionaries further encouraged the increasing bureaucratization of the style and functions of trade-union officials in this period. By the late forties, this governmental trend had become so predominant that the *Report on Cuba* even thought it to be more important than collective bargaining itself. It reported, "Ostensible collective bargaining often turns out to be government decrees because the disputed points are taken to the government and settled by an administrative order."[35] This situation only served to strengthen the pressure-group politics and reformism of the Cuban working class, whether under Communist or other auspices. The class fought a protracted trench class war without any overall strategy. Obviously, this placed great limitations on the capacity of that class to take the lead when faced with new crises.

The Communist Party and Cuban "Browderism"

It is impossible to understand the nature of working-class politics in Cuba or the short duration and general weakness of political parties unless we bear in mind the role played by the Cuban Communists, the only durable party, between 1938 and 1948. The international Communist wartime policy of moderation and collaboration with employers and governments was in perfect agreement with the interests and inclinations of the Cuban Communist leadership: their increasing power in the labor and government establishments (they even had members in Batista's wartime cabinet) made them welcome a policy that ensured good relations with their associates and coalition partners. The Cuban Communist party had, in fact, become closely associated with the North American Communist Earl Browder, and the 1945 Duclos letter condemning "Browderism" found it necessary to single out the Cuban Communists as one of the chief representatives of that dangerous deviation.[36] The Cuban party had enthusiastically welcomed the no-strike policy, and changed the name of the party to Partido Socialista Popular (PSP) in 1944. To leave no doubt concerning the party's conciliatory policies, in February 1945, the Executive Committee of the National Association of Cuban Industrialists had a joint luncheon with the Executive Committee of the CTC (Cuban Confederation of Workers) where Lázaro Peña, the Communist head of the CTC, was an honored guest. He delivered a speech revealingly entitled "The Collaboration between Workers and Employers."[37]

Grau's election had momentarily threatened the Communist control of the workers' movement and the whole basis of their moderate policy. But soon Grau came to an agreement with the Communists; the Auténticos' minority status in Congress made Communist help attractive. A number of Auténticos were admitted as new members of the Executive Committee of the CTC, which retained a Communist majority. On their part, the Auténticos helped to elect Juan Marinello, a top intellectual and Communist leader, as vice-president of the Senate. This Grau-Communist agreement lasted from 1944 until 1946. In the 1946 election, the Auténticos obtained a congressional majority and no longer needed to rely on Communist support, which would have become increasingly embarrassing to Grau with the beginning of the Cold War.

Although the 1946 elections showed an increase in the Communist vote,[38] the following year marked the beginning of the end of Communist predominance in the trade-union movement and of a great deal of their influence in Cuban politics. The onset of the Cold War had brought about the international Communist denunciation of Browderism. Blas Roca and the other Cuban Communist leaders were forced to confess their errors and to change their political line, especially in their attitudes toward United States imperialism, but fewer changes were made in domestic policies.[39] The Communist leadership wanted to retain more domestic flexibility so as not to endanger their power and influence beyond what was absolutely necessary in the light of the demands of Moscow and international Communism. But the Cold War period nevertheless witnessed a rapid loss of Communist strength and prestige.

It did not take long for the Auténtico trade-union leaders, with the help of the government and through the use of undemocratic and gangsterlike methods, to oust the Communists from their positions of leadership in the official trade-union movement. As noted earlier, the Communists set up a rival trade-union federation; but their influence quickly declined, and by 1951 the Communists had abandoned their attempts to maintain a rival trade-union organization and were trying to get into the official trade-union movement as best they could. This process of decline continued throughout the fifties and was accelerated during Batista's second regime. (In 1952 Communist party electoral registration was down to slightly more than 50,000; real membership was much lower than that.)

A good part of the Communist loss of influence began with the repeated Auténtico violations of the civil liberties of Communists and the consequent loss of many of the Communist means of propaganda. Thus, the Communist radio station "1010" was confiscated by the Auténtico government, and their daily newspaper *HOY* was continually harassed. More than once government confiscation or harassment was followed by court orders returning the paper and publishing rights to the Communist party. Yet, throughout all these Auténtico attacks, the Communists remained a legal party openly carrying on electoral and political activity. By the time of Batista's coup in March 1952, the Communists still had nine seats in the lower house of Congress. Under different circumstances, these attacks on the Communists and the suppression of their civil liberties might have increased their prestige and elicited sympathy for them among large sections of the Cuban people; but Cold War anti-Communism was very successful and became widely accepted among the large majority of those Cubans who were aware of these restrictions on the freedoms of Communists. Ironically, this anti-Communist reaction was partly a carryover from the pro-Allies ideology of World War II which the Communists themselves had helped to build. Now that the Soviet Union had become the enemy of the Allies, the local Communists were placed in the uncomfortable position of being closely associated with that country in a period when fear of Russia and of Communist takeovers became widespread throughout the non-Communist world. Popular left-leaning magazines like *Bohemia* took strong anti-Communist positions and so did Chibás and the Ortodoxo party. Some of these latter elements protested the curtailment of the Cuban Communists' civil liberties but did not provide political comfort or support for the Communist party. In effect, the party became politically isolated, and at one point it was even reported that many Communist leaders were ready to leave the country.[40]

Given this situation, it was completely out of the question for the Communists to serve as an alternative to the Ortodoxos as the main party of opposition. Not only were the Communists associated with the same kind of electoral politicking that the Ortodoxos were promising to put an end to with their policy of no pacts, but also the Cuban Communists were no longer respectable and were placed in a very difficult position because of their dealings with Moscow. Thus, they got the worst of both worlds: they lacked both clean oppositionist political credentials and Establishment respectability. It is little wonder, then, that the bulk of the opposition to Batista's second regime was to develop in a milieu completely separated from Communist party circles.

To a large extent, the very character of Communist politics and trade-union work had undermined the party's ability to withstand the repression of the Cold War period. The reliance on government favors and the consequent bureaucratization of Cuban trade-unions had strengthened the bread-and-butter reformist approach at the expense of a more serious ideological and political training of the working class. Although Communist trade unionists were generally dedicated and personally honest and were respected as such by many workers, these were hardly sufficient conditions for the development of an *internalized* political consciousness among members of the Cuban working-class, particularly when Communist trade unions were certainly not known for being democratic in the conduct of business. (Communist trade-union leaders were even implicated in the assassination of opposition trade-union leaders, such as Sandalio Junco, an Auténtico and former Trotskyist.)

The Communists dominated the trade unions during a period when Communist political moderation did not encourage the education of Cuban workers in basic Communist principles. Blas Roca complained that the Communist trade-union magazines exaggerated the importance of immediate demands and appeared little concerned about raising the workers' levels of ideological and class consciousness. He added that they carried little propaganda concerning capitalism, imperialism, the oppression suffered by the workers, and "the historic role that the working class is called to play."[41] His was not simply an isolated statement, or an exaggerated complaint spawned by adversity. In good times, Roca had complained about even more basic and elementary flaws in the political education of the Communist party. After the 1942 elections he spoke about how their sympathizers even failed to vote for the Communists:

> Our good cadres who know how to organize a union, a youth club or a peasants' association don't know at the same time how to keep the masses of those organizations, on the day of the elections, from voting for their most open and shamefaced enemies, for those same people who will go to the lower house and use their influence to persecute the unions, to evict peasants, to sabotage National Unity against Hitlerism, and to smash all the popular struggles for their immediate demands.[42]

When the Auténticos came to power and eventually decided to replace the Communist trade-union leaders with those of their own party, the working class did not have the desire, training, or endurance to persist in following their former leaders when these leaders proceeded to form a rival labor federation. Most workers were either cynical about the new operation at the top, where once again one set of leaders was being replaced by another set of leaders more favorable to the current administration in office, or else they shared the new wave of Cold War anti-Communism sweeping the country and its mass media. In 1961, Joaquín Ordoqui, the Communist historian of the Cuban labor movement, summarized the key lesson taught by the experiences of this period when he said that "the heroic resistance offered by working-class sectors to the imperialist-governmental-employer offensive of the postwar period . . . was not more effective because . . . the ideological preparation of the working class [had been] somewhat disregarded."[43]

In the light of the above discussion of the Cuban Communist party and my previous analysis of the nature and role of the Cuban working class, I must seriously challenge a central assumption of Maurice Zeitlin's *Revolutionary Politics and the Cuban Working Class*. Zeitlin explains that even after the Cold War had begun the Communists retained the allegiance of an estimated 25 per cent of the workers and that they had nearly led the workers to power in the abortive revolution of the thirties. Thus, in reality, Zeitlin maintains, the role of the Communists as honest unionists and their role as revolutionary socialist agitators were inseparable. Zeitlin adds, "It is highly likely that procommunism among the workers in prerevolutionary Cuba was permeated with revolutionary socialist values."[44]

Zeitlin's estimate of the number of workers who maintained their allegiance to the Communists is, I think, exaggerated, particularly in view of the sharp decline in Communist influence between 1947 and 1958. Zeitlin also fails to see the qualitative distinction between the nature of Communist influence in the revolutionary period of the early thirties and the quite different kind of influence the Communists were able to exercise as a result of their policies in the 1938–47 period. More importantly, the historical evidence indicates that, although the Communists may have indoctrinated a few workers, the overwhelming majority of Cuban workers, including those who followed Communist leadership, were not seriously reached by basic Communist political education or indoctrination and that, in fact, there was a separation between the role of Communists as trade unionists and the role of Communists as "revolutionary socialist agitators," as Zeitlin calls them. Far more often than not, the incidence of pro-Communism among Cuban workers was based on their belief that Communist trade-union leaders supported reforms and were more *personally* honest and dedicated than rival trade union leaders. This had little to do with whether or not those workers acquired a Communist point of view on more general political questions. In all likelihood those workers were at best "militant reformists," who were far more likely to give political support to Auténticos and Ortodoxos than to the Communists. As a Cuban barber explained to José Yglesias, a pro-Castro novelist, "You understand, that Jesús Menéndez was loved does not mean that the sugarcane workers were Communists. Look at us barbers, we were Liberals, Auténticos, of all political opinions, but our union leaders were Communists and when it came to union matters, we were as one in supporting them."[45]

My objections to Zeitlin's assertions would be relatively less important if they involved only a difference of opinion over the amount and kind of Communist strength and influence within the Cuban working class. However, there is something extremely important at stake here: we cannot understand and explain the strength of the populist politics of the Ortodoxos and Auténticos and the support they elicited at various times among most workers as *individual citizens,* rather than as unionists properly speaking, if we do not grasp the fact that this was possible precisely because there was no significant Communist or revolutionary socialist ideology among the overwhelming majority of Cuban workers. In the absence of any substantial working-class *political* perspective, Chibás and the Ortodoxos were able to appeal to many Cubans on the basis of a very vague program put forward by a heterogeneous, multiclass party which was kept united by the charismatic leadership of Chibás, as well as by the fact that it was the only political alternative visible to most Cubans. A later article by Zeitlin shows how he has indeed seriously misunderstood the nature and trends of Cuban politics between the two revolutions of 1933 and 1959. In it he states that, among the majority of Cuban workers,

> The dominant vision . . . was . . . anticapitalist, antiimperialist, and socialist. Even the essentially reformist and middle-class leadership of the Auténtico (and later *Ortodoxo*) party . . . also clothed its actions and program in a quasi-socialist rhetoric. . . . Most working class struggles, whatever the leadership, and however narrow the economic demands, tended to take on the political slogans of antiimperialism and anticapitalism; it was their one consistent theme.[46]

It is difficult to determine exactly what Zeitlin means by the ambiguous term "quasi-socialist"; but in this context it obscures the fact that the *whole* trend of Cuban politics of this period was away from political anti-imperialism, let alone any social radicalism. Zeitlin's interpretation flies in the face of the well-established fact of the militant but politically limited nature of Cuban working-class struggles which increasingly restricted themselves to immediate demands. The onset of the Cold War period, in particular, practically wiped anti-imperialist politics from the Cuban political scene outside the narrow confines of the Communist party itself. The whole tenor of Zeitlin's analysis seems to be that of an ahistorical sociology of Cuban society which ignores very significant changes (most of them in a socially conservative direction) which took place between the late thirties and the late fifties.

It is only when we fully assess the virtual absence of ideological and political leadership and training in the Cuban middle *and* working classes that we can understand the situation of almost complete organizational vacuum in the anti-Batista opposition in the aftermath of the Batista coup of March 1952. The Ortodoxo coalition collapsed; and the working class, although hostile to the new regime, was not able to provide any significant political leadership for the struggle against Batista, let alone for a "socialist revolution." These are some of the circumstances that help to explain why the Cuban revolution of the fifties was led not by the working class, or by the Communist or Ortodoxo parties, but by a new amorphous and peculiar movement under Fidel Castro. Even Castro himself seems to be in agreement with my analysis of the situation of the Cuban working class when Batista was overthrown. As he told the leaders of the Chilean labor movement, "At the triumph of the Revolution, from the point of view of leadership and cadres, we couldn't count on a tried, awakened workers' movement. We didn't have one. . . . We counted on the support of the workers and farmers — a very broad base — but we didn't have what could be described as a tried, organized, and awakened workers' movement. That's the way things were."[47]

Let us, however, first carefully analyze the second Batista dictatorship and the social processes that helped to bring about the peculiar kind of revolutionary movement that overthrew Batista.

7 | The Second Batista Dictatorship

POLITICAL GANGSTERISM and the rise of the Ortodoxo party were two symptoms of the inadequacy and bankruptcy of the Auténtico administrations. The Auténticos did not prove to be fully adequate substitutes for the eleven years of Batista's Bonapartist rule, even after the latter had mellowed in the years from 1938 to 1944; the beginning of the fifties witnessed a further intensification of the political and moral crisis encouraged by Auténtico rule. The suicide of Eduardo Chibás in August 1951 did not, in the long run, strengthen the forces of moral protest as Chibás had intended;[1] the political and emotional response to the death of the opposition leader could not compensate for the long-run weakening of a party that had lost its most crucial bond of unity.

In the meantime, labor conflict had continued unabated. The discontent of native and foreign capitalists, as well as of ruling elements of United States imperialism, was reflected in the recommendations of the International Bank's *Report on Cuba*, which placed particular emphasis on the need to discipline the Cuban working class and suggested that the government "adopt the system of dismissal wages in use in other Latin American countries" and "make dismissal procedure under existing law simpler, faster and less subject to political pressure."[2] No elected Cuban government, whether Auténtico or Ortodoxo, would have been able to implement these recommendations without considerable difficulty, given the traditional resistance of the Cuban working class to all attempts to solve the stagnation of the Cuban economy at its expense.

Political gangsterism had continued to take its toll of human lives and political confidence. The assassination of the politician Cossío del Pino in February 1952 had been a serious blow to the prestige of the Auténtico administration of Carlos Prío Socarrás. It is little wonder that, in the midst of this situation, there were rumors of massive cabinet changes and of the president's resignation.[3] However, general elections were scheduled for June 1, 1952, and people expected them to be relatively honest and to express the popular desire for change. The Ortodoxos were expected to win the election; and Fulgencio Batista, who had been allowed to return to Cuba in 1948, was supported by a rather mixed bag of politically backward elements and was considered to be the candidate with the least chance of victory.

On March 10, 1952, however, Batista once again emerged as Cuba's strongman through a successful coup supported by the military and some discredited politicians. This coup brought to an end a period of relative stability which had begun in the late thirties. During this period a variety of political concessions and the coming of relative prosperity had somewhat diminished the urgency of those fundamental problems of Cuban society which had not been solved in the period after the Revolution of 1933. The Batista coup of 1952, itself partly a consequence of the lack of viability of Cuban constitutionalism and of the increasingly conservative international climate of the Cold War, was in its turn a crucial cause of the serious aggravation of the unresolved tensions of Cuban society which took place in the fifties. It also proved that the Cuban middle classes, while having expanded as a result of postwar prosperity, were still incapable of consolidating their political influence and power.

Before the coup, the country was sufficiently unstable to create a situation where, on the one hand, many elements, particularly among the upper classes, were yearning for a "strong" government to strengthen "law and order." On the other hand, the Cuban people were too demoralized and disorganized to resist a military coup. On the international scene, a whole series of Latin American dictatorships had come into existence and been granted recognition and support by the United States State Department, a precedent that served as a green light to potential dictators. Batista's coup was followed by prompt United States recognition. The United States saw in Batista a staunch "democratic ally" who would not endanger imperialist interests on the island.

Although it was relatively easy to take power, Batista eventually found that it was much harder to maintain power than it had been in the late thirties and early forties. At that time, the success of Batista's Bonapartist policy depended not only on the weakness of the opposition but also on the support he could obtain from a variety of alliances and deals. In his first period in power, Batista had successfully manipulated the support, or at least the neutrality, of various groups and classes. In the fifties, his new Bonapartist rule relied far more on the weaknesses of his present and potential opponents, and he did not try so hard to obtain their support or acquiescence. That Batista followed this course may have been partly the result of his overconfidence after the great ease with which he took power in March 1952, overthrowing a weak, bankrupt, and discredited administration.

Although the employer classes initially accepted Batista because they expected law and order, as well as the reversal of at least some of labor's gains, his rule did not turn out to be as useful to them as they might have expected. Strikes were greatly curtailed when not completely banned, but no great *legislative* changes were made in the legal rights and social gains of labor. The lack of civil liberties made it increasingly difficult for the working class to carry on its struggles, and workers gradually but continuously lost ground. Yet, their loss was not, at least initially, as great as many employers had hoped it would be. With the passage of time, as the Mujalista labor bureaucracy[4] became increasingly dependent on the government for its very existence and as Batista became more despotic and found it more and more necessary to attract foreign capital, many labor gains were whittled away by government actions (such as the introduction of shipment of sugar in bulk and the increasing use of *"despido compensado,"* or "compensated layoffs").

Batista's relationship to the Cuban ruling classes, however, was based not on firm and organic ties but on temporary convenience. In fact, Batista's increasing reliance on the armed forces and corruption as his sole bases of power eventually alienated most of those upper-class Cubans who had originally accepted and even welcomed his rule. Robin Blackburn has aptly described the precarious social position of Batista's regime in the period 1952–59:

> The Batista machine was politically isolated, since it possessed no real roots in local class formations. It was thus forced to make such internal alliances as it could, within the limits set by the U.S. international and economic policy of the period. The dictatorship remained, of course, the guarantor of the capitalist order in Cuba, but this was because of the context external to it, not because of its class context or ideological orientation. Within the limits of this context, its policy was purely opportunist.[5]

Batista's ability to make internal alliances with various other elements was limited: any understanding with the Communists was out of the question because the Cold War was at its peak, and the support of the Mujalista trade-union bureaucracy was of limited value because it had developed into a clique with very little contact with the rank and file. Thus, as we shall see, on the political level Batista's second dictatorship, while having fewer roots and allies in Cuban society than his first regime, showed greater reluctance to compromise or to give significant concessions to the opposition.

There seems to be little question that Batista was much more self-confident and intransigent during the fifties. Aside from some occasional concessions, such as the general amnesty for political prisoners decreed by his puppet Congress at the peak of his power in 1955, he showed no intention of reaching an accommodation and political solution with the respectable elements of the opposition, such as the SAR (Sociedad de Amigos de la República, discussed later in this chapter). Much of this overconfidence might have been the result of the very conservative international climate of the fifties when Latin American dictators were assured of American support with few, if any, questions asked, and of the confusion and utter disorganization of the domestic opposition in the first four or five years after his 1952 coup.

Cuban oppositionist politics in the fifties, while quite disorganized for a period of time, did indicate that Cuba was too politically advanced to accept Batista's militarist and conservative regime peacefully. The whole post-1933 history had created high expectations which had been encouraged by the struggles and partial gains of the period. As Herbert Matthews described the Cuban situation shortly after Batista's Coup,

> They start the second half of their first century as a republic under a new dictatorship, which is a throwback to the bad old days but with a difference. There had been a taste of democracy between 1940 and 1952; there is an awareness of what good government can be like and how government revenues ought to be spent.
>
> If General Batista goes with the times he will satisfy these Cubans and redeem himself in the eyes of history; if he bucks the trend he is in for a bad time. [6]

As long as the opposition was disorganized and leaderless, Batista was able to stay in power with relatively little active resistance to his rule and on the basis of the support of the armed forces and those few people who benefited from a highly organized, government-sponsored system of corruption far surpassing that of all previous Cuban administrations. As the opposition became better organized and more militant, however, the government decided to rely on sheer brutality to stay in power. Thus, Batista was not willing or able to implement a successful long-term Bonapartist policy as he had done during his previous regime. In the face of the new situation of the fifties, Batista's regime became a gangsterlike and militarist one in which systematic brutality and corruption were the order of the day. The parasitic nature of the regime prevented it from acquiring the relative stability and strength that it could have obtained through the development of truly totalitarian institutions. Its inconsistent and venal policies, as well as its alienation from any class or social stratum outside the army and police, effectively eliminated that possibility. The army and the police had themselves become mercenary and sectarian institutions which were almost completely separated from the rest of society.

The Opposition

Batista's ability to retain power without great use of force in his first four years in office resulted in no small measure from the sorry state of the opposition rather than from his own strength or support. The initial reaction of the opposition was one of complete disorientation and inactivity; the release of long, verbose manifestos was somehow seen as a substitute for a plan of action. This was accompanied by a legalistic approach to the struggle against the government. Thus, as noted in Chapter 6, a large group of well-known opposition leaders introduced a legal suit in the courts challenging the constitutionality of the Batista regime; after a lengthy legal process, the courts rejected the challenge.[7] This did not surprise anybody, but in the meantime valuable time and political resources had been wasted with few political results. This legalistic approach was very much in accordance with the nature and ideology of the established opposition to Batista. The leaders of the Ortodoxos and the Auténticos (who were back in opposition again) had grown too accustomed to the relative peace of the last fifteen years and were not inclined to call for forceful resistance to Batista's militaristic regime. Also, members of the older political generation had internalized much of the constitutional ideology in a manner that prevented them from realizing that, once the Constitution had been thrown out by Batista, there was little hope of effecting change through legal means. Last but not least, the conservatism of middle-class politics in Cuba (with the exception of the student movement) encouraged verbal and legalistic strategies of opposition to the government. In sum, as described in a Fidelista anthology (put out by Castro supporters), the political atmosphere existing soon after the coup was not very conducive to militant resistance. While the press alternated uncertainly between censure and advice, with the usual calls for "reasonableness" and "prudence," very few, among the political leaders of the country, were aware of the dimensions of the consummated act. . . . They tried to patch up legalistic formulas capable of saving the institutional rhythm, even at the high price of whitewashing the coup. . . . Meanwhile, the new situation was consolidating itself with international recognition for the government and [with] the support of the sectors of production and the economy [i.e. big capitalists and landlords, and the labor bureaucracy].[8]

It was a political irony that one of the groups that relatively early advocated forceful resistance to the Batista regime was the group of Auténticos around deposed President Prío, who had originally given up power without any resistance to the military coup. In 1953 Prío was one of the sponsors of the Pact of Montreal which brought together a variety of opposition politicians pledged to fight the Batista government by all necessary means. But the Auténticos were too badly discredited to be able to organize popular resistance to the regime. The Batista coup had in fact liquidated them as a significant political force in the country, bringing to a climax a process that had been going on during the eight years of corrupt Auténtico rule, if not longer.

While the Auténticos were discredited as a result of their previous rule, the Ortodoxos, who had not yet attained national office, were not. It was conceivable that the Ortodoxos might have been able to organize and lead an opposition against Batista along the usual moderate lines of Latin American struggles against dictatorship. Such an Ortodoxo struggle would not have been essentially different from the participation of APRA (Peru), Acción Democrática (Venezuela), and other social democratic and populist parties in Latin American countries in their struggles against military dictatorships. Yet Cuba turned out to be different, and the Ortodoxos completely failed to accomplish such a task; on the contrary, the party split into many factions and virtually collapsed as a crucial political force.

The collapse of the Ortodoxo party was not an unforeseeable event. The death of Chibás had already weakened this political formation, and electoral politics had been left as the key bond keeping the party united. Once the possibility of elections had been removed by Batista, the party had to unite either behind a program of struggle or under a strong leader capable of maintaining party unity in spite of the absence of a clear program. The Ortodoxos did not have such a leader and could not agree on a program. When they tried to do so, the electoral coalition on which the party was based fell apart. Fidel Castro, on the occasion of his definitive break with the remnants of the Ortodoxo party in March 1956, described the major schisms that resulted within the party and pointed to their most crucial consequence:

> The party members entered a state of despair and disorder. . . . I am one of those who firmly believe that when the military coup took place if the Ortodoxo Party — with its firm moral principles, the immense influence that Chibás left on the people, and the good reputation that he enjoyed even among the armed forces (for the propaganda made against the party displaced from power could not be directed against the army) — had stood resolutely against the regime, raising the revolutionary banner, today Batista would not be in power.[9]

I agree with Castro's assessment, and I could add that Castro would not have emerged as a top leader if the Ortodoxo leadership had taken up arms against the Batista regime. Although this lack of Ortodoxo action was not inevitable, it was highly likely given the characteristics of that party. The collapse of the Auténticos and the Ortodoxos almost eliminated the possibility of a more traditional struggle against Batista and was a crucial factor in opening the road for a new and different type of leadership in the person of Fidel Castro. To a considerable extent, the Ortodoxo collapse reflected the behavior of the Cuban middle classes, to which many of this party's members belonged. The middle classes' lack of ideology and of strong organizational autonomy led them to hesitate and to avoid an early confrontation with the Batista regime just as the Ortodoxo leadership did.

The collapse of the established opposition parties took place when the revolutionary groups were small and just barely emerging and had not yet taken the spotlight away from the Ortodoxos and Auténticos. In the meantime, Batista's unpopularity was growing, but no alternative was perceived on the political horizon. This created a kind of political impasse where, as in so many transition periods, there was no lack of despair and confusion. Herbert Matthews said at the time (1953) that, while most Cubans and foreigners seemed to feel no man and no party could lead Cuba out of this impasse if President Batista did not do it, there was simultaneously the feeling that, if there were an election, Cubans would vote for almost anyone who would run against Batista.[10] In late 1954, an observer of Cuban politics was still able to see no possibility of an uprising against the government:

> No one I have talked to in or out of Cuba thinks the present grumbling means the island would rise up against the Government. . . . there is still more apathy than disaffection. Barring economic disaster and the emergence of a more inspiring political opposition, I am inclined to agree with an exiled Cuban who told me, "Batista will be there until he chooses to step down or until he is shot."[11]

The Economic Situation

An important factor influencing the form of popular resistance to the Batista regime was that, unlike the situation during the Machado dictatorship, there was no severe economic crisis. Yet there is no question that the Cuban economy continued to deteriorate and that its chronic problems were further aggravated during the Batista dictatorship. This deterioration expressed itself in two essentially different ways during two periods roughly corresponding to the years 1952–54 and 1955–58.

The period following Batista's takeover in 1952 coincided with a decline in the international sugar market. This was a crucial factor in producing a serious recession in the Cuban economy. From 1952 to 1953, per capita income in Cuba fell by 18 per cent as a result of a drop in production and the deterioration in the terms of trade. This economic relapse almost neutralized the effects of the rather slow growth of the postwar period, as per capita income dipped near the 1945 level.[12]

During 1954 there was little change in the performance of the economy as a whole except that the working class, after two years of a gradual but continually intensifying government and employer offensive to undermine its living standards, lost further ground in its share of the national income. In opposition to those observers who claimed that Batista respected and maintained the gains of the working class, the 1954 *Economic Survey of Latin America* pointed out that substantial changes had taken place during 1954 in the functional distribution of income. Labor's share in net income had fallen from 70.5 per cent in 1953 to 66.4 per cent during 1954; and, on the whole, the average wage rate had decreased. Other sectors were barely able to absorb the additional manpower left idle by the sugar decline. Lack of employment and lower wages represented an overall decrease in salaries and wages of 4 per cent in relation to 1953.[13]

The growing political discontent and restlessness in the country eventually led the Batista dictatorship to implement policies that would improve the economic situation even if such improvement was merely temporary and was achieved at the expense of harmonious economic development. In essence, Batista tried to buy off a part of the population by increasing employment through public works and mostly uneconomical investments which served more to enrich his political associates than to benefit the mass of the Cuban people. By 1955 the effects of this new policy started to be felt in a partial recovery which reached its peak in 1957. "During 1957, Cuba's economic activity attained the highest level registered since the war. . . . If price rises are taken into account, the growth of the gross product in real terms may be estimated at rather over 8 per cent."[14] At this point, a rise in sugar prices on the international market[15] had come to complement Batista's program of public works and had created an economic situation more prosperous than that of the first years of the dictator's second regime.

To be sure, this "improvement" was purely relative and was not even comparable in quality to that experienced by the Cuban people in the immediate postwar period, if for no other reason than that the working class was not now in a position to maximize its gains because it had been deprived of most of its weapons, such as the right to strike and the ability to engage in political activity. More fundamentally, all the chronic ills of the Cuban economy and society remained untouched if not worsened. Serious chronic unemployment was the most crucial feature of a distorted economy which produced a lot of anger and frustration among many Cubans, particularly the young. As the *Economic Survey of Latin America for 1957* pointed out, "during the relatively prosperous interval between May 1956 and April 1957, 16.4 per cent of the labour force [was unemployed]."[16] Regardless of the cyclical variations of the economy in one direction or another, unemployment and general economic stagnation were *permanent* economic grievances of the Cuban people. The various Cuban governments had at best attempted to mollify discontent by employing short-term measures which had few positive long-range effects on the Cuban economy. For example, out of the total bank credits conceded by the Batista dictatorship at the end of September 1957, only 6.1 per cent were destined for agriculture and 29 per cent for industry, while no less than 62.6 per cent were assigned to such relatively unproductive public works projects as the construction of a tunnel under Havana Bay.[17]

Batista's reckless economic policy depleted the foreign exchange reserves, however, and by the time Castro came to power in 1959 only 70 million dollars remained. Furthermore, in spite of all the spending during the last years of the Batista dictatorship, the regime did not achieve its political aims. Political rebellion was by this time rapidly growing and showed little sign of being diminished by the cyclical changes in the economy. In fact, the cyclical improvement in the economy probably increased working-class discontent rather than quieting it, as the government had expected. By and large, however, it was the *political* dynamic of the dictatorship's repression and the opposition to it that were the main factors in dramatically increasing resistance to the regime precisely during those years when there was a certain temporary improvement in the economy.

The civil war that broke out in 1957 did not do much damage

and had a relatively small effect on the Cuban economy. Only during the last months of the Batista dictatorship in 1958 did major disruptions of the economy occur when transportation came to a virtual halt in the eastern half of Cuba.[18] Ironically, some significant United States investments were made during the last two or three years of the Batista dictatorship, all of which were confiscated by Castro within two years after his overthrow of the Batista regime. Batista had instituted giveaway programs to encourage foreign investors and had even raised the rates charged by the foreign-owned telephone company, something other administrations — and even Batista himself — had previously not dared to do. As a result of these policies, economic forecasts for the year 1958 had to take note of "a large increase in direct foreign investment, particularly in electric energy, the telephone services and petroleum," and the *Economic Survey of Latin America for 1957* stated that total private investment had increased from 29 million dollars in 1954 to 46.5 in 1955, and to 58.5 in 1956, and estimated it to have expanded at the same rate in 1957.[19]

The Working Class

It is almost a truism to state that the Cuban working class played no important role in leading the struggle against Batista. Even those who write about the presumed working-class character of the Castro revolution almost always refer to the nature of Castro's movement *after* the latter came to power. Yet unexamined assertions often hide a complicated reality that can be understood only through closer examination.

What in fact was the attitude of the working class toward the Batista dictatorship? In spite of various claims, not a single piece of evidence has been found to show that workers were sympathetic to that regime. The available evidence shows the exact opposite to be true. Initially, the reaction of the working class to the coup was no different from that of the other classes in Cuban society. The overwhelming majority of the Cuban people reacted with surprise and then apathy; only the student movement and a few militants reacted differently. As time went by, anger and indignation against the government increased among the large masses of Cubans, with the difference that various middle-class elements and organizations played a more vocal and leading role than workers did. The reasons for this were as follows: the working class was suffering a double dictatorship, that of Batista in the country as a whole and that of Eusebio Mujal in the trade unions. As a result, workers had no readily available institutions through which they could express or organize their discontent.

It is not a coincidence that those few unions that were under the loosest control of the Batista-Mujal alliance were the militant ones in the struggle against the regime. Thus, the Bank Workers' Union and the Union of Electricity Workers engaged in bitter strikes which had strong overtones of hostility to the dictatorship. The same was true of the 1955 Sugar Strike in the three eastern provinces. Under rather unusual circumstances, independent trade-union leaders such as Conrado Rodríguez and Conrado Bécquer, as well as various Communist trade unionists, were able to play a major political role leading this important strike in which numerous antigovernment demonstrations took place. This antigovernment sentiment was not surprising; the working class continually lost ground during the Batista dictatorship. The huge wave of strikes that broke out immediately after Batista was overthrown was clear evidence of the pent-up economic and political frustrations of the class during the seven years of the Batista regime.

The failure of the two attempts at general strikes against the government has been offered as evidence of the indifference if not sympathy of the working class toward the dictatorship. However, a closer examination of the events in those two strike attempts will show that the primary reasons for these failures were organizational and had little to do with the attitude of the workers. The August 1957 strike was spontaneous; there had been no preparation or organization for it. In spite of this fact, the response was impressive, with many cities all over Cuba becoming almost completely paralyzed during a short period of time.

It was this impressive response to the first general strike attempt that led the leaders of the 26th of July Movement to prepare and organize another general strike attempt.[20] This second attempt took place in April 1958, and it was a complete political and organizational fiasco despite the great response throughout every city in the country except Havana. The Communists had refused to support the strike, and the 26th of July Movement could not have done a worse job of organizing it. Ramón L. Bonachea and Marta San Martín vividly described how the prospects of the strike had been damaged from the very beginning:

> It had been previously agreed that all cadres would start the agitation at noon on April 9. This hour was selected in order to get maximum advantage from siesta time, when the workers went to their homes, and were not back at their jobs until 2 P.M. During these two hours, the Youth Brigade would attack the armory, arms would be distributed, and street fighting would create panic and confusion. Urban transportation would be stopped, and people would be unable to return to their jobs even if they wished to do so. . . . At 11 A.M. the strike order rang loud and clear through clandestine radios and from headquarters to the Youth Brigade. Dismay, outcry and frustration permeated the ranks of the M-26-7 [26th of July Movement] underground when they were forced to move their entire schedule one hour ahead.[21]

Yet, in spite of this, the strike spread very widely, thus showing that the people, both working and middle class, were not indifferent to the political situation in the country. As Jules Dubois described the day,

> The strikes were total in most interior cities, especially Santiago, Camaguey, Cienfuegos, Sagua la Grande (the latter in Las Villas province), Pinar del Rio and other important centers. . . . There was no general strike in Havana. Some factories closed. Some bus lines stopped or offered only limited service. A few stores tried to close, windows were smashed and people rushed to loot the merchandise. The same practices were followed at a few factories. . . . [Batista's] spy service and the counter-measures which he had taken, together with the failure of the rebels to take over and hold any radio stations also helped Batista win the first round of the final battle with Castro.[22]

A crucial reason for the difference between participation in

Havana and in other cities in the country was the fact that the organizational weaknesses of the opposition were far more decisive in the context of an urban metropolitan sprawl like Havana. A city like Santiago de Cuba, for example, had *community* traits that were almost completely absent in the capital. In the former city, hostility to the regime had successfully crystallized because, to a large extent, the traditions and relative compactness of the city greatly facilitated the revolutionary actions of the 26th of July Movement and the civic institutions, even though the latter had failed to create a fully effective apparatus of struggle. In such cities weak factory organizations, for example, were not so much a hindrance because the community itself was better organized, more united, and ready to strike as soon as the word was given. In metropolitan Havana, given the strike organizers' failure to secure any radio stations, only the presence of well-organized factory cells could have provided the organizational framework for the otherwise atomized workers. The abstention of the Communists plus the traditional weakness of the populist Left in serious and organized trade-union work made certain that not many such cells would come into existence; as we have seen, the ones that did exist were made impotent by the organizational failures of the strike leadership.

To sum up what has been implied thus far: (1) the working class did *not* play a crucial role in the struggle against Batista, but (2) the great majority of the working class was hostile to the Batista regime. The key to understanding the apparent contradiction between these two assertions is the realization that workers do not inevitably and effectively act as a class in pursuit of certain goals. There is a double reality in the lives of workers: they are individual citizens and they are workers. As oppressed and abused individuals, the Cuban workers were increasingly hostile to Batista and his cohorts; and, of course, the greatest part of the state of oppression in which they found themselves resulted from their class position. But these facts and conditions did not enable them to respond as a class (i.e., through trade-union or some other form of class action) in opposition to Batista. To have done so they would have had to develop a clandestine union structure in opposition to both the dictatorship and its trade-union puppets; in spite of various attempts, they failed to do this. Their failure did not make them any less hostile to the regime, but their hostility had no institutional vehicles and could not match the relatively greater organizational strength of middle-class "joiners." These latter — students, professionals, small businessmen, and the like — had such institutions as the Instituciones Cívicas, a confederation which included the Bar Association, various professional and religious organizations, and other clubs, to represent their interests in the opposition coalition, although their institutions also turned out to be quite weak and were no match for the strength of Castro's personal leadership.

The failure to make distinctions and to engage in a careful investigation of the behavior of Cuban workers has led a variety of authors of the most diverse — even opposite — points of view to walk into interpretive blind alleys in their attempts to explain the relations between Cuban workers and the revolution against Batista. Thus, Régis Debray implicitly draws an ignorant caricature of a "satisfied" urban proletariat in order to explain the success of the guerrilla movement and the failure of the working-class movement in Cuba.[23] The anti-Castro writer Theodore Draper accepts many of the same premises and explains what he terms the working class's "minor role in the pre-1959 struggle" in terms of its orientation toward trade unionism rather than politics. According to Draper, the trade unions had, over the years, "gained enough concessions and benefits to make their members a relatively privileged class." Another paradox of the Cuban revolution, he asserts, was that, as a result of an upward swing in the Cuban economy, it was won "in conditions of relative prosperity rather than of stagnation or decline."[24]

It is difficult to conceive of a more misleading interpretation of the facts than Draper's. His is based on the false assumption that, because many union members (of which there were more than one million in Cuba) were "relatively" privileged, they were also satisfied. If nothing else, Draper would be hard put to square this assertion with the universally recognized fact that the revolution against Batista had the *political* support of an overwhelming majority of the dissatisfied and angry Cuban population, a majority which, of course, included most of the organized and unorganized working class. It is also important to reiterate that even the better-off trade unionists had lost ground during Batista's regime as a result of a variety of restrictions on trade-union activity, such as the ban on strikes, which seriously curtailed the bargaining power of the organized workers. Although it is quite true that the Cuban economy experienced a relative improvement in 1956 and 1957, it does not follow that stagnation, unemployment, and economic deterioration had been eliminated. And in any event, even if it were proven that there was a clear economic upswing, this would not explain the fact that the Cuban working class played a minor role in the revolution. As we know, relative prosperity is at least as likely to produce an upsurge of militancy and discontent as to produce the opposite results. In fact, the history of the Cuban working class shows that two of its most militant periods were during the depression of the early thirties *and* during the post-World War II economic boom.

No matter what the reasons for the relatively minor role played by the Cuban working class in the struggle against Batista, the fact remains that this seriously reduced the possibilities of at least one political alternative to the Batista dictatorship and facilitated the rise of the particular kind of revolutionary movement Castro was able to build.

The Communist Party

The emergence of a military dictatorship and of a revolutionary situation in Cuba did not reverse the pattern of declining Communist strength which had begun with the onset of the Cold War in the late forties. The old Communist party had little that could attract the new generations of young rebels, while the older, liberal anti-Batista elements would not even consider cooperation with the party of the enemy in the Cold War. This Communist weakness had some significant consequences, not the least being that it contributed to the inability of the working class to take a leadership role in the revolution against Batista. To the extent that the Communists had lost influence among workers, there was also a decrease of politically oriented elements within the working class. This is so even if we fully realize that the party's political influence would have been very negative given the opportunistic nature of its policies and its thoroughly undemocratic character.

After Batista's coup in 1952, there was a short period of uncertainty concerning the position of the Communists vis-à-vis the Batista regime. As Robert Alexander explained, for a short time the Communists hesitated in deciding on an attitude toward the new regime, objecting to their former ally as being "anti-Communist, pro-United States, and anti-democratic"; but they left the door open for patching things up, maintaining that they exercised influence both inside and outside the unions which might prove useful to the dictator. Continued Alexander, "Batista likewise vacillated concerning what position he would take toward his old allies of the P.S.P. [Partido Socialista Popular, i.e., Communist party]." When he at first announced that he did not intend to outlaw the Communist party in Cuba, "a kind of truce seemed to prevail."[25] In his 1960 report to the Eighth National Congress of the PSP, Blas Roca made some admissions that would seem indirectly to confirm Alexander's description of the Communist reaction to the coup:

> All this [the gains of the 1940s] had created a certain amount of pro-Batista sentiment in some parts of the people, even including some backward members of the Party who were not sufficiently developed politically to appreciate duly the changes in the situation of the country and in Batista's orientation, for Batista was turning toward reaction and offering himself as an unconditional vassal of the imperialists if only he could get back to power.[26]

As we know, in Communist jargon, criticism of the "backward elements of the party" is often tantamount to a criticism of previous errors of the party itself. Eventually, the lines were clearly drawn when, in 1952, shortly after the coup, the Batista regime broke diplomatic relations with the USSR and the PSP was outlawed.[27]

The policies and tactics of the Communists varied greatly during the Batista regime. Until 1958, when the Communists finally came around to a position of support for armed revolution and the Castro-led movement, their policies were closer to those of the moderate opposition than to those of the militants. For a long time the Communists maintained a position of electoral opposition to the Batista regime, even when the latter could not possibly be expected to administer honest elections. This electoral tactic led the Communists to invent such slogans as the "negative vote," which referred to a vote of support for the discredited Grau San Martín when the latter ran against Batista in 1954 as a loyal oppositionist. These opportunistic and conservative positions would alternate with theoretically impeccable calls for a "mass struggle" against the Batista dictatorship which would culminate in another "12th of August" (the day Machado was overthrown by a general strike in 1933). The "mass struggle" slogan was often counterposed to the "putschist" strategy and tactics of other revolutionary groups, such as the 26th of July Movement and the Revolutionary Directorate (see Chapter 8), which were often referred to as "petty bourgeois," and so on. Although the Communists were unquestionably making some valid points in their criticisms of terrorism and armed attacks on military barracks as a revolutionary strategy, they offered their strategy of "mass struggle" as an alternative rather than as a complement to armed action. Their theoretical advice carried little weight because it was accompanied by their opportunistic practices and by their inability to produce actual results. Communist participation in the 1955 Sugar Strike, which was perhaps their only important contribution to the struggle against the Batista regime, was not sufficient to make them a fully credible partner in the revolutionary struggle.[28]

It is very clear that the Communist analysis of the Cuban situation was mechanical and unimaginative, as well as opportunistic. The Communists tended to see the Batista dictatorship as a new episode — a downturn — in the cycle of reaction and progress they had witnessed for so many years. They probably figured that

Batista, like most other dictators in Latin America, would eventually be succeeded by some more liberal regime, whether civilian or military. If such a compromise solution was going to be found, the party wanted to ensure that it would be in the strongest possible bargaining position. In that event, it would not help if the party put itself out of the "mainstream" by adopting an insurrectionist attitude. This had been an historic attitude of the Communist movement and, in fact, its pre-1958 position strongly resembled the attitude it took toward Grau and Guiteras in the mid-thirties after the party had abandoned its Third Period policies. The Communist leadership was at the opposite pole from the voluntarism of the revolutionary populist leadership. While the latter would often exaggerate the importance of personal will, sacrifice, and heroism in accomplishing revolutionary goals, the former grossly underestimated the ability of revolutionary action itself to change "objective" conditions and to arouse the people to action. This approach fitted only too well with the theoretical straitjacket of Russian Stalinist "Marxism," where mechanistic scholasticism was substituted for critical revolutionary theory.

By early 1958, it had become obvious that Castro and his 26th of July Movement were the undisputed leaders of the revolution against Batista and that a typical Latin American compromise solution to the increasingly sharp Cuban struggle was unlikely. Accordingly, the Communists started to move in the direction of Castro. By that summer they had reached some form of operational agreement with him, although considerable reservations remained on both sides.[29] The Communists' new policy was spelled out in their program of December 1958 entitled "The Convenient Solution for Cuba" ("La Solución que Conviene a Cuba").[30] This document came out in support of the efforts of the rebel armies and discussed what the program of a new revolutionary government should be. This discussion is highly revealing in showing, among other things, the lack of socioeconomic radicalism in the anti-Batista coalition at the time. Thus, the program is highly defensive in tone when it advocates the nationalization of foreign public utilities and the "revision of colonialist concessions," explicitly reassuring its readers that it is not proposing, for example, "any measures of general nationalization of foreign enterprises" and "that these demands are not, in any way, excessive." It explains at some length that nationalization measures have also been taken in such countries as Mexico, Argentina, and Brazil, and in advanced capitalist as well as Afro-Asian countries.[31] An unspecified program of agrarian reform is proposed without any mention of the requirement of the 1940 Constitution for "previous payment" to the dispossessed owners, a proviso the Communists had openly criticized during the Constitutional Convention itself. Finally, the document proposes that the overthrow of the Batista dictatorship should be followed by the rule of a "democratic coalition" which should include "moderate elements." In this context, "moderate elements" must have meant traditional politicians such as Prío, because at this time nobody, including the Communists, made any distinctions, at least in public, between more and less moderate elements *within* the 26th of July Movement and its auxiliary organizations such as the Civic Resistance.

Perhaps the Communists were responding in this document to rather conservative pronouncements made by Castro earlier in the year regarding his lack of interest in nationalization, which he saw as harmful to economic development.[32] In any event, it is clear that the intended audience for this pamphlet was the anti-Batista coalition in which the Communists desperately wanted to win a legitimate place. To do so, the party had to adapt itself to the predominant tone of militant anti-Batista sentiment combined with a lack of socioeconomic radicalism. Ironically, while trying hard to achieve this goal, the party could not help but remain, as of late 1958, to the "left" of Castro and all the other anti-Batista elements insofar as socioeconomic policy was concerned. The party just barely managed to join the Castro-led coalition a few months before the overthrow of Batista, thus taking a substantial step toward what eventually became a close alliance and fusion after the revolutionary victory took place in January 1959.

The Society of the Friends of the Republic

Batista's 1952 coup, as we have seen, was not immediately followed by great popular resistance. Instead, a somewhat dormant dislike for the dictatorship was the predominant popular response during the first four years of Batista's second regime. This mood was reinforced by a variety of events such as the collapse of the Ortodoxo party. The decline of the Communist party without a revolutionary alternative taking its place, and the increasing bureaucratization and corruption of the official trade-union movement prevented the working class from taking a leading role in the struggle against Batista. Before this relatively resigned mood and political fragmentation were to be converted into support and sympathy for a fairly unified revolutionary movement in early 1957, various other political possibilities had to be eliminated in the course of a very short period of time.

The inability of the electoral parties to provide leadership for the growing opposition to the Batista regime, and their consequent virtual collapse in strength and prestige, did not exhaust all the avenues of peaceful political activity. Gradually, a variety of mostly middle-class organizations, which had behaved with great political indifference in the first few years after the coup, became alarmed at the rising violence and uneasiness in the country and made moves to mediate the conflicts between government and opposition. These efforts reached their peak in May 1955 after Batista, in one of his confident moods, made a few concessions, such as the political amnesty which freed all political prisoners including Fidel Castro and his companions of the Moncada attack (see Chapter 8). At this time, the Society of the Friends of the Republic (Sociedad de Amigos de la República, SAR) had sponsored negotiations between government and opposition delegates in hopes of reaching a peaceful solution to the Cuban crisis. The government showed no willingness to grant any further concessions, and this response considerably hardened the growing oppositionist mood of the middle classes. In the face of the increasing brutality of the Batista regime, these elements eventually found no other place to got but to Castro and the 26th of July Movement.

For a few months the eminently upper- and middle-class SAR, under the leadership of the veteran Colonel Cosme de la Torriente and José Miró Cardona, head of the Havana Bar Association, succeeded in taking the initiative and providing leadership for a disunited opposition "led" by discredited politicians. The moderate SAR succeeded in temporarily placing the revolutionary groups on the defensive. This was clearly shown toward the end of 1955, when the SAR was allowed to hold a huge rally in support of its demands for free elections and full civil liberties. The just-born 26th of July Movement did not endorse SAR's mediation, and all its followers could do was to attend the rally and chant repeatedly "revolución, revolución." Although this was well received by the younger elements in the crowd, it did not succeed in taking the spotlight away from the SAR and the electoral parties which co-sponsored the rally. The next day, Fidel Castro held an indoor meeting in Miami, Florida, to respond to the SAR rally. Castro's meeting received little notice in Cuba while the SAR temporarily monopolized public attention.

The SAR had indeed tried to fill the gap left by the collapse of the electoral parties. Its efforts at mediation were an expression of the increasing alarm of many middle-class elements at the growing political unrest in the country, *and* of their own discontent with the Batista regime. There is little doubt that the elements represented by the SAR were very disturbed about dictatorial rule and corruption and were trying to find a solution in moderate political terms. However, their success was ultimately dependent on Batista's willingness to make use of the face-saving device offered by the SAR and peacefully step down. Batista obviously decided against this, thus virtually liquidating the SAR and its middle-class followers as a decisive force when the inadequacy of moderation was proven in practice. Many of these elements would become followers of the 26th of July Movement and its allied organizations when the latter eventually confronted the Batista dictatorship as its most important adversary. In the meantime, the Cuban middle classes had been deprived of what was probably their best political guarantee that they would be able to control the agenda for a new social and political order after the overthrow of Batista.

The Armed Forces

Although the failure of the SAR virtually eliminated any *political* alternative to a confrontation between the revolutionaries and the Batista dictatorship, this does not mean that all possible alternatives had thereby been exhausted. In mid-1956, shortly after the collapse of the SAR negotiations, a major conspiracy was discovered in the Cuban army. A group of high officers led by Colonel Ramón Barquín, a former Cuban military attaché in Washington, and Major Borbonnet, head of the Cuban parachutists, had been preparing for a military overthrow of the Batista regime in order to install, according to their testimony, some form of liberal democratic regime. It is significant that the chief defense lawyer in their court martial was SAR leader José Miró Cardona. In this trial the accused made serious charges concerning corruption in the armed forces and presented a political defense in which the reestablishment of constitutional government and civil liberties was cited as their main political goal.

Immediately after this conspiracy was discovered, Batista purged the army to ensure its loyalty to the government and to isolate it more effectively from the various middle-class and popular currents of hostility to the regime. His doing so only served to reinforce further the mercenary and sectarian character of the Cuban army and to sever the final ties between the army and the rest of Cuban society, thus making it more difficult for the restlessness and discontent of Cuban society to be transmitted to most of the army officialdom and soldiers.

Later, in the face of the rebels' sharp and violent opposition, the army was not willing and/or able to get rid of Batista but gradually disintegrated through desertion and lack of fighting spirit. Corruption alone was not sufficient to hold this institution together.[33] Because the army rank and file had become so utterly demoralized and was in no mood to resist its elimination, it was relatively easy for the victorious rebels to disband the regular army after the revolutionary victory.

The defeat of the conspiracy also eliminated another possible competitor to the civilian revolutionary leadership. There is no question that the organizers of the conspiracy were sympathetically regarded by a vast majority of the opposition. Thus, the Pact of Mexico signed by the 26th of July Movement and the FEU (University Student Federation) had a more than sympathetic reference to the military conspirators: "The FEU and the '26th of July' regard Colonel Barquín, Major Borbonnet and the other officers who have been dismissed and imprisoned as the worthiest representatives of our army . . . and declare that an army led by these officers, observing the constitution and serving the people, will have the respect and the sympathies of the Cuban revolution."[34]

At the time of the attempted coup, Castro was still in exile in Mexico and his movement was only one year old. Given the favorable popular attitude toward the conspirators, the civilian revolutionaries would have been, initially at least, in a very weak bargaining position vis-à-vis Barquín and his fellow army officers, had their coup succeeded, for the military junta would probably have obtained the support of the more traditional political opposition. That this would have been so is clearly implied by the liberal Rufo López Fresquet, Castro's first Treasury Minister, who in retrospect lamented "the failure of U.S. authorities to help rescue Barquín and other anti-Batista officers from prison in 1957 while there was time to divert public attention from Fidel and his militia to other revolutionaries."[35]

Some pockets of resistance to Batista were still left in the armed forces after the defeat of Barquín and the ensuing purges in the army. In September 1957 a significant Navy rebellion broke out in the port city of Cienfuegos in central Cuba, and the city was actually occupied by the rebels for a couple of days before they had to surrender in the face of constant aerial bombardment by Batista's air force. The Cienfuegos rebellion was a clear symptom of the changing relation of forces within the ranks of the opposition. In this rebellion, the rebel sailors fought side by side with sizable armed civilian contingents of the 26th of July Movement. A rebel victory in Cienfuegos would not have been simply the result of a military coup but would have been a *joint* victory of military insurgents and civilian revolutionaries. By this time, the 26th of July Movement, under the leadership of Fidel Castro, had already experienced a very significant increase in strength and prestige, and the presence of an armed contingent in the Sierra Maestra had captured the imagination of the masses of the Cuban people. Yet, the actual rebel contingents in the mountains were still extremely small, and the navy insurgents also seem to have had close contacts with some traditional politicians of the opposition, such as Tony Varona, a well-known Auténtico leader. Consequently, in the event of a successful navy rebellion, the predominance of Castro and the 26th of July Movement would not have gone uncontested. In any event, the navy was too small to make much of a difference by itself. The success of a navy insurrection would have depended on a simultaneous national civilian uprising throughout the country, which was not too likely, given the existing political conditions.[36]

The behavior of the Cuban army since the Revolution of 1933 and particularly during Batista's second regime (1952–58) puts to the test some past speculations in the field of Latin American studies. Various students of Latin America have had the notion that an increase in the proportion of officers coming from lower- and middle-class backgrounds, greater professionalism, and training in military centers in the United States, which would instill in these officers North American ideas on civil-military relations, would all contribute to making Latin American officers more respectful of constitutional government and more willing to stay out of politics. What happened in Cuba shows that, although these factors may sometimes produce more democratically oriented officers, they are clearly insufficient by themselves. This is to be expected, for all these factors ignore the actual political context in which such professionalization of lower- and middle-class officers takes place.

After the 1933 Revolution, the overwhelming majority of Cuban officers were of lower- and middle-class extraction, but during most of the period from 1933 to 1958 entry into officer training programs was under the control of high army officers, who were not immune to personal and political considerations in making their decisions. Thus, although entry into Cuban military academies usually required participation in competitive examinations, final approval of new entrants was the prerogative of higher officers.[37] This situation contributed to the development of cliques and patron-client relationships between senior and junior officers.

A number of Cuban army officers had received training in military installations in the United States.[38] However, the North American model of civil-military relations probably influenced them much less than the technical aspects of their education and their contact with official United States anti-Communism. In fact, United States military influence served to strengthen the power and morale of precisely those elements in the Cuban army who were the strongest supporters of Batista. Thus, the Inter-American Defense Treaties not only served to train many of Batista's officers in North American military schools but also provided Batista's army with modern weapons for the purpose of "defending the hemisphere against Communist aggression." I remember vividly an ostentatious parade through the streets of Havana of tanks that had just been sent to Batista by "our friends in the North."

Yet there is a grain of truth in the thesis concerning the democratizing influence of professionalization. Most of the officers who supported the Barquín conspiracy were "professional" rather than "political" officers.[39] They resented the use of the army for partisan purposes and particularly for the purpose of supporting and administering the corrupt and repressive politics of Batista. But it must be pointed out that most of the officers who supported Batista and went along with the corruption and brutality of his dictatorial regime were also professionally trained officers of lower- and middle-class background, many of whom had undergone training in United States military academies. Therefore, we must declare this thesis invalid, at least on the solid methodological grounds that a variable effect cannot be explained by a constant cause.

Thus the theories of various students of Latin American society have not been particularly helpful in arriving at an understanding of the nature and behavior of the Cuban army. Although there is very little research available on this important question, I would suggest that the Cuban army can be best understood as an essentially mercenary sect, recruited from among unemployed urban and rural workers and led by an officer corps of middle and low social origins which became a privileged caste. When Barquín and his associates denounced the corruption of the army during their 1956 court martial, they were mockingly called *los puros* ("the pure") by all Batista supporters in the armed forces, thus revealing prevailing army attitudes concerning appropriate behavior. As Ché Guevara suggested, this complicity of soldiers and high officers provided the army with a bond of unity: "The army of Batista, with all its enormous defects, was an army structured in such a way that all, from the lowest soldier to the highest general, were accomplices in the exploitation of the people. They were completely mercenaries, and this gave a certain cohesiveness to the repressive apparatus."[40] However, a unity based on corruption and opportunism is essentially weak and will last only as long as the benefits enjoyed seem to justify the sacrifices demanded. As soon as heavy fighting was required, the Cuban army collapsed. Barquín and his fellow conspirators probably did not have a chance to win, for they could not attract support in an army structured on the basis of corruption. If so, the only alternatives left were total victory for the supporters of Batista or complete elimination of the army.

The Cuban Catholic Church

Yet another important Latin American institution, the Roman Catholic Church, did not and probably could not have played in

Cuba the important role it played in the overthrow of other Latin American dictators such as Gustavo Rojas Pinillas, Juan Perón, and Marcos Pérez Jímenez. The Cuban Catholic hierarchy was fairly conservative and, on the whole, went along with the Batista dictatorship until hostilities reached a high pitch in 1958. At that time, the church appealed to Batista to resign in order to put a stop to the civil war and establish a constitutional government. Batista obviously did not accept the advice of the church, and the latter lost its opportunity to play an important role as a possible mediator. Many individual Catholics and lay groups, such as the small but active Catholic Worker Youth, played an active role in the struggle against Batista but were not able to exercise any great influence on the course of revolutionary developments.

Although a different policy on the part of the hierarchy might have changed and increased the role of the church in the revolution, there were good historical and social reasons for this lessened influence of the Cuban church. The church had sided with Spain during the Cuban struggle for independence, with the result that the newly established Cuban Republic had introduced fairly strict separation of church and state in education, civil law, and other public matters. In addition, the relative weakness of the Cuban oligarchy had its effect on the church as well. The Latin American trinity of upper class, church, and army did not achieve in Cuba a social weight equivalent to that which it has enjoyed in most of Latin America. At the same time, Cuba was perhaps unique in the fact that the church was unable to strike deep roots among the Cuban masses. Most priests were Spanish. Furthermore, the church was urban and middle-class.[41] In the countryside, most peasants infrequently came into contact with priests, except for an occasional baptism. Although the overwhelming majority of Cubans were nominally Catholic, only a small proportion of the population was composed of practicing and committed Catholics.[42]

Batista's power, as we have seen, was not seriously challenged for at least the first four years of his dictatorship because the various existing institutions of Cuban society failed to provide a visible and credible alternative behind which the Cuban people could unite in a struggle against the military regime. Yet the conclusion should not be drawn that the support eventually obtained by the revolutionaries was negative — that the majority of the Cuban people turned to them as a last resort after inspecting all other possible alternatives. That is not the way historical events usually take place. Without a doubt, the support for the revolutionaries was authentic and positive in character. But lack of a credible nonrevolutionary alternative made it possible for the revolutionary alternative to occupy the center of the political stage rather than its left wing. On the basis of their positive appeal, the revolutionaries might have been able to assert themselves even if the army, the SAR, or any of the other alternatives discussed in this chapter had played a more important role; but the *terms* of the revolutionary victory would have been very different from what they eventually were, and Castro and his close associates would have had considerably less freedom of action and political choice.

It can be said that the exhaustion of the various nonrevolutionary alternatives was almost inevitable given the peculiarities of the Cuban social structure. There again, however, these social processes were not predetermined to the extent of precluding a variety of choices and thus a variety of political outcomes. Thus, for example, the nature of the Ortodoxo party placed limits on its ability to act in times of nonelectoral crises but did not predetermine the extent of the very poor response of its leadership. Nor did the fact that the reactionary international climate of the Cold War period encouraged Batista to take a hard-line attitude toward his domestic opponents actually predetermine the extent or degree to which Batista was willing to go in rejecting the compromise solutions offered him by a variety of parties. In fact, when Batista's rule became endangered sometime in late 1957 or early 1958, the United States government, for example, would have been more than happy to work out another one of the classic unprincipled Latin American political deals for the sake of safeguarding North American business and other interests. Batista, after all, was valuable to his North American protectors only to the extent that he could "deliver" law and order. In March of 1958 the United States even placed an arms embargo on the Cuban government in the hope of mending some of its badly damaged political fences with the government that would succeed Batista.

Thus, the attempt at constitutional politics failed and another period of dictatorship began in Cuba. Batista would not and/or could not develop a durable social and political base. The traditional Cuban social and political forces opposed to military dictatorship failed to overthrow Batista. It was up to a nontraditional force to carry out that task.

8 | The Rise of Revolutionary Politics

THE DEVELOPMENT of a revolutionary alternative to Batista's rule was not a sudden and automatic response to the political vacuum created by the exhaustion of the more traditional alternatives discussed in Chapter 7. As a matter of fact, the revolutionary alternative was born immediately after the Batista coup of March 10, 1952, but for several years it was limited to a fairly small minority of the Cuban people; four or five years would pass before it would become a real and desirable choice for the great majority of Cubans. In the meantime, revolutionary actions took a variety of forms — student strikes and demonstrations, armed assaults on military garrisons, terrorism, and the like — all of which were unsuccessful. Yet, although they failed, there is no question that they were indispensable in forming and reinforcing the tradition of struggle essential to preventing the utter demoralization of an oppressed people. Thus, while disillusionment and cynicism dominated the majority of Cubans, a more conscious minority was successful in keeping the revolutionary flame alive.

There is little question that the crucial element in keeping the revolutionary alternative in existence was Cuban youth, and particularly students. The decay and corruption of the Auténtico governments had provoked dissatisfaction and protest among many young people in Cuba, a good part of which had been greatly encouraged by the exhortations of Eduardo Chibás and the Ortodoxo party. These young people had come to realize that, with some exceptions, the "revolutionary" generation of 1933 had failed. This realization was strengthened and confirmed by the inability of the opposition, including the Ortodoxos, to lead the people in a struggle against the Batista dictatorship.[1]

The younger political generation, however, still relied on the positive aspects of the revolutionary tradition of the thirties. Its assessment of that period was mixed and ambivalent rather than purely condemnatory. Youths of the fifties were aware of the heroic struggles and social gains that had taken place in the thirties, and they denounced the members of that political generation precisely because they had failed to keep their promises. Thus, a 26th of July Movement pamphlet published in 1957 praised the "generation of 1930" for having done more in one hundred days, "in spite of its romantic immaturity, . . . in defense of the national interests and of the people than all the governments of the previous thirty years." The pamphlet specifically mentioned, among other things, the abolition of the Platt Amendment and the establishment of an eight-hour working day, the right to strike, and university autonomy as having given the Cuban people "for the first time the feeling of finding itself." Added the pamphlet's authors, "Besides, it was proved that it was possible [for Cuba] to truly exercise the sovereignty of the country without producing a catastrophe."[2]

Thus, the existence of historical precedents of revolutionary struggle was no minor source of inspiration to the rebels of the 1950s. In fact, one of the most important elements of Cuban politics, and one that encouraged revolutionary action in the fifties, was the presence of a Cuban tradition characterized by a high degree of historical and national self-consciousness. The young were helped in their political struggles by their sharp sense of having to live up to their historic duties.

Aside from this, there had also been some organizational ties between the young revolutionaries of the fifties and the minority of the political generation of the thirties which retained its revolutionary enthusiasm and will to struggle. In fact, the earliest revolutionary attempt against the Batista government was not Castro's Moncada attack in July of 1953 but one organized several months earlier by Rafael García Bárcenas, an Ortodoxo professor who was a veteran of the revolutionary movement of the thirties and who organized a group called Movimiento Nacionalista Revolucionario (MNR), with which such revolutionary figures as Armando Hart and Faustino Pérez were originally associated. Even the discredited Auténtico party was still able to contribute its small quota of militant fighters against the regime, notably Menelao Mora, who was one of the leaders of the attack on the Presidential Palace in March of 1957 (see below).[3]

The Populist Tradition

In spite of the continuities listed above, however, it is fair to say that a significant separation existed between the two political generations. Naturally, new political generations never start with a *tabula rasa*. Certain political traditions are inherited and then modified or rejected. However, even when they are rejected, more remains of them than is immediately apparent on a superficial level. These new revolutionary groups definitely belonged to what I call the Cuban populist tradition, although they brought new elements to it.

An important consequence of the lack of strong class consciousness among the Cuban upper and middle classes was that these classes proved incapable of creating a durable party system even by Latin American standards. In its turn, the lack of durable middle- and upper-class parties further hindered the development of strong class consciousness. Instead, there was a recurrence of what I call "populist" politics, usually addressed to an amorphous "people." The "people" were the poor and not the rich, although a small "just and fair" employer might also be included. Many Cubans rallied behind vague but promising programs of social reform which failed to spell out means of implementation or possible implications and consequences. It is striking that a country that witnessed so many social and political struggles never developed major class parties and did not transcend the level of populist movements and electoral machines. At the same time, the peculiarities of United States imperialist domination after 1933 did not encourage the formation of articulate anti-imperialism. There was no direct colonial-type presence which might more easily stimulate the growth of strong anti-imperialist movements and parties. Instead of a visible and obvious American presence, there was a large group of Cuban business and technical personnel who acted as agents for United States capital. This "Cubanization" of foreign-owned businesses was strongly encouraged by the post-1933 labor legislation.

There did exist nationalist sentiment, fused with Cuban populist politics. The strongest brand of Cuban nationalist ideology identified itself with the writings and actions of José Martí, Cuba's major Founding Father, and had an unmistakable Left populist slant. This ideological tradition was used, whether opportunistically or authentically, by practically everyone in the country, including the most conservative elements, but it nevertheless contained a genuine substance. William A. Williams has characterized one Latin American variety of populism as having nonpeasant leaders and attracting participants who have been humiliated by repeated defeats but also conditioned by them to despise the existing government, to be acutely sensitive to criticism, and to anticipate trouble. This brand of populism is not known for original programs or highly integrated ideas but operates instead "with a rather casual, vague, and certainly non-Marxian version of the theory that existing society can only be understood as a class-struggle between the haves and the have-nots." Adds Williams, "Compared with the Russians and their Marxist doctrine as it existed in 1917 (and even more, to the oversimplified and schematic version of it that most commentators work with), the Cubans may indeed seem at first glance to be almost anti-intellectual. But the leaders of the July 26th Movement were not *really* running without *any* ideas on their minds."[4]

The ambiguities of Cuban populism were not inconsiderable. In regard to such a fundamental question as democracy, the attitudes ranged from civil libertarian to frankly authoritarian. Some Cuban populists were friendly to the Perón regime in Argentina while others were hostile. Although there was little sympathy for

Communism, the populist Left was broad enough to encompass both anti-Communism and "fellow-traveling." Attitudes toward crucial domestic questions, such as agrarian reform and nationalization, also varied widely. By and large, however, Cuban populism was reformist and not revolutionary in the social sense of that term. In spite of its uncertainties on the question of democracy, it had become firmly committed to the Constitution of 1940 and its unequivocal civil libertarian assumptions.

Yet policy and program were not the defining characteristics of Cuban populism. More important than these was the personal commitment of the populistic militants who often saw themselves as engaging in heroic acts that would set an example and arouse the masses to militant action. This form of heroism had deep roots in the Cuban political tradition; the key line in the Cuban National Anthem states that "to die for the Fatherland is to live" (*morir por la Patria es vivir*). In this tradition, winning is not the only, or even the main, aim of struggle; it is better to go down fighting than to stay alive and submit to oppression.

Such personal courage frequently produced mindless militancy; organization, program, and planning were often ignored. Thus, during the struggle against Batista, populists spent little time in discussing how best to involve the working class, now suffering under the double dictatorship of Mujal and Batista, in the struggle against the regime.

In many ways, the predicament of the working class under Batista was the result of its own previous, short-range militancy, and there is no question that the spirit of populism hindered the development of a long-range political strategy within this class itself. Also, the organizational weakness of Cuban populism led to an absence of institutions within the Cuban Left. The only exceptions were the student unions and numerous opposition radio hours, which often served as a clearinghouse for protest and as important centers of agitation.

The lack of programmatic clarity prevented the formation of distinct ideological tendencies within the Cuban populist Left.

Radicalism became a matter of militancy in action rather than of social goals and program. While an outside observer might have been able to distinguish various populist wings based on the degree of social radicalism, such a distinction was not clearly established in the minds of the political actors themselves, at least during the forties and fifties. To some extent, the widespread notion that a just Cuban society could be achieved as soon as the Constitution of 1940 was duly enforced helped to limit political and ideological differentiation within Cuban populism. This belief persisted as long as most populists were out of office and while the vague provisions of the Constitution were not put to the test. This undifferentiated constitutionalism facilitated the formation of the socially moderate coalition that made it possible for Castro to overthrow Batista.

The University Students and the Directorio Revolucionario

The student movement was the first significant group to formulate a strategy of militant opposition to the Batista dictatorship. Immediately after Batista's coup in 1952, the Federation of University Students (FEU) began to organize rallies and demonstrations in opposition to the Batista regime, and it continued to maintain revolutionary standards in the midst of an atmosphere of compromise. As the anthology *La Sierra y el Llano* put it, "The FEU . . . immediately realized that those people had arrived to power in order to stay and that they would never voluntarily resign." Declared the president of the FEU, "We are, once more, the standard-bearers of the national conscience. The dramatic circumstances which the Fatherland is undergoing impose on us hard and risky duties. . . . The University continues to be the stronghold and hope of Cuban dignity."[5]

From 1952 until 1956 the university students (with considerable support from their followers in high schools and other public schools) carried the burden of militant opposition to the regime. Even though there were isolated dramatic instances of armed uprisings outside the student movement during this period, they were unsuccessful and lacked the continuity that the student movement, with its connection to institutions where young people met on a day-to-day basis, could provide.

The relative isolation from the rest of society and the greater militancy of the students aggravated within their movement some of the tendencies common to the whole of Cuban populism. The students came to rely even more on terrorism than did such other organizations as the 26th of July Movement. Though abstractly sympathetic to working-class aspirations for a higher standard of living, they displayed little interest in actual working-class problems — not surprisingly, given the middle-class background of most students. Their disinterest was partly a direct result of the trade-union movement's failure to develop a political perspective and program for the working class and the nation as a whole. It is important to note that student populism, while sympathetic to terrorism, was not particularly ascetic or anticonsumptionist in orientation. If anything, they wanted Cubans to have more material comfort *without* the predominant business values of North American society.

The student movement of the fifties did not use its relative isolation from society and its educational advantages to develop a clear set of political ideas or a program for social change. Such factors as the general decline of social radicalism in Cuba since the thirties and the existence of the Cold War had created a climate in which the intellectual level, whether political, social scientific, or artistic, of Cuban revolutionaries was far below that of the period of opposition to Machado's regime.[6]

By late 1956, clashes between students and police had become so frequent and bloody, because of the systematic policy of unmitigated brutality adopted by the Batista dictatorship, that the University Council decided to close the University of Havana, an action that removed a potentially autonomous organizational nucleus for students and their nonstudent sympathizers. A year earlier, the majority of the student leadership had founded the underground Directorio Revolucionario (Revolutionary Directorate) for the purpose of engaging in armed action to overthrow the dictatorship. Although this organization was not restricted to students, it never fully succeeded in reaching beyond the student milieu and so always remained less important than the broader-based 26th of July Movement.

The central strategy of the Directorio was to "strike at the top" which meant, most of all, to assassinate Batista, thus opening the road for the overthrow of the regime. On March 13, 1957, the Directorio, with the help of some militants who had formerly belonged to the Auténtico party, almost succeeded in killing Batista when they attacked the Presidential Palace in broad daylight. The attack failed, and Batista's police force engaged in one of its worse episodes of wholesale repression and murder. The leadership of the Directorio was completely shattered: José Antonio Echeverría, by far its most important and popular leader, was killed in action, and the rest of the leaders were driven into hiding or at least into temporary inactivity.

There is no question that the death of Echeverría, a potential if not an actual competitor to Castro, and the failure of the attack on the Presidential Palace were important factors in shaping the course of Cuban history.[7] By the time the leadership of the Directorio recovered from the serious blow of March 1957 and got around to establishing a permanent base in the mountains of central Cuba in 1958, Castro had already consolidated his political and revolutionary leadership. Thus, although from a purely military standpoint the Directorio was not much weaker than the 26th of July Movement in central Cuba in late 1958, members of the former had to place themselves under the leadership of Castro's emissaries when the latter, accompanied by a relatively small invading column, came to take charge of military operations in that part of the country.

The main problem with the strategy of the Directorio was not, as some might claim, the urban nature of its earlier actions but its emphasis on "striking at the top." In the first place, although the death of Batista probably would have made a significant difference, it was as likely to encourage the establishment of a military junta more stable than Batista's as it was to provoke a successful popular uprising. This approach tended to underestimate the importance of the armed forces as an institutional stumbling block to revolution, an error Castro avoided, at least after 1957. Second, the Directorio's assault on the Presidential Palace was, by its very nature, an all-or-nothing affair, lacking in the tactical flexibility that might have allowed most of the leadership and cadres to survive even if they failed in their assassination attempt. While in the Sierra Maestra, Castro always tried to ensure that all resources would not be invested in a single action, thereby endangering the permanency of the revolutionary base. These precautions did not inevitably follow from the rural nature of his operation any more than the strategic flaws of the Directorio were an inevitable consequence of the pre-1958 urban character of their struggles.

Cuban populism, both in its student and nonstudent forms, was an inadequate vehicle to express the interests of the Cuban middle classes. In the absence of truly durable political parties, the middle classes were at the mercy of outside political actors. In such a political situation some sort of "betrayal" (to use Theodore Draper's term) is not only possible but is almost to be expected. Youth, which was perhaps the only trait common to most active populist revolutionaries, lacked any firm social base in Cuban society. This generational support for Castro, lacking strong and autonomous roots in society, only served to reinforce the organizationally hegemonic role of the Sierra Maestra.

The Emergence of Fidel Castro

The early militant opposition to Batista was not restricted to the student movement at the University of Havana. Former students, activists, members of the youth section of the Ortodoxo party, and the like had come to political conclusions similar to those of the militant students and had joined the latter in a small but young and active part of the Cuban opposition to the Batista dictatorship. One of these activists was Fidel Castro, then a young lawyer and former student leader. He was also a second-rank leader of the Ortodoxo party which had endorsed him as a candidate for Congress in the elections scheduled for June 1, 1952, but prevented by Batista's coup of March 1952. After some initial and unsuccessful attempts to take legal action against the Batista dictatorship,[8] Castro started to organize for an armed uprising against it. His efforts were confined to a small number of people because armed insurrectionist activity, obviously illegal, had to be kept secret. But there were also political reasons for Castro's small number of followers: Castro was practically unknown outside a limited circle of Ortodoxo and student militants. The top leaders of the Ortodoxo party had not yet completely discredited themselves and thus continued to monopolize the attention of those political elements most likely to be receptive to Castro's political message; and disillusionment and fear still dominated the overwhelming majority of Cubans.

In this general political context Castro organized some two hundred followers for an attack on the Moncada Army Headquarters in Santiago de Cuba, the provincial capital of Oriente, on July 26, 1953. Castro conceived of the seizure of these barracks as a means by which the Cuban people would be aroused to take up arms against the Batista regime. He planned to seize a radio station and broadcast Eduardo Chibás's last speech, a dramatic appeal to the Cuban people (*"el último aldabonazo"*). The attack failed, and Castro and several of his followers were eventually arrested and sentenced to prison, where they stayed until their release less than two years later under the terms of a general political amnesty granted by Batista.

Although the politics of the attack on the Moncada barracks showed a strong Ortodoxo coloration, Castro's program was far more radical than anything the Ortodoxos had ever proposed. Castro's proposals were much closer to the politics of Antonio Guiteras in the thirties than to those of Chibás in the forties. Castro's own defense at his trial (*History Will Absolve Me*), as he rewrote it later in prison, spelled out the revolutionary laws he would have implemented in the event of victory. These laws included immediate agrarian reform (with some form of compensation) and the proposal that 30 per cent of business profits go to the workers. In addition to describing such immediate reforms, the document also stated that the revolutionary government would later have implemented a 50 per cent cut in rents and other measures.[9] Undoubtedly, the overall tone of the speech was still within the very broad confines of the Cuban non-Communist political tradition, but it would be a serious mistake to place it in the same category as the more mainstream and traditional forms of Cuban populism. Theodore Draper did so and thus seriously underestimated the radicalism of this document. Wrote Draper, "As Cubans understood it, *History Will Absolve Me* represented a program of radical social reform well within the framework of traditional Cuban left-wing politics. . . . There was virtually nothing in the social and economic program of *History Will Absolve Me* that cannot be traced at least as far back as the 1932 program of the ABC."[10]

Although it is true that Castro explicitly appealed to the political tradition of which the Ortodoxos and other organizations had been a part, none of these organizations would have dared to advocate cutting rents by 50 per cent or giving workers 30 per cent of business profits.[11] Such proposals would have been tantamount to political suicide because they would have alienated large sections of middle-class supporters, particularly within the Ortodoxo party in the forties and early fifties when social radicalism had considerably declined from its peak in the thirties.

Fortunately for Castro's later strategy, *History Will Absolve Me* was a little-known document until after the revolutionary victory of January 1959, when it was virtually disinterred by Castro and those followers who now wanted to turn to the Left. Before his revolutionary victory, Castro disregarded this early document and stressed other later pronouncements of a far more moderate tone and content. The one theme that remained unaltered throughout all of Castro's pronouncements and documents, whether socially moderate or radical, was his unrelenting and militant opposition to the Batista dictatorship. This, and nothing else, was the main basis of his eventual success in gaining the sympathies of the vast majority of Cubans.

History Will Absolve Me had been formally addressed to the Cuban people as a whole, but its real and significant audience was a much narrower stratum of militants who were already receptive to a radical message. Castro was, in fact, addressing himself to a sort of political vanguard among students, militants in the Ortodoxo party, and other such elements who were very confused and disoriented, given the failure and inactivity of the more traditional opposition politicians. It was essential to reach and organize this vanguard if there was to be any hope of reaching the large masses of Cubans. Years later, when Castro, still in the opposition, was able to address himself to the masses, the nature of his message differed significantly from the drastic and potentially divisive proposals of *History Will Absolve Me*.

After the attack on the Moncada, Castro became an important leader of the Cuban opposition to Batista, but he was not yet *the* leader of that opposition. While in jail, he began to widen his appeal. His articles for the popular magazine *Bohemia* (which was still at this point more often than not uncensored) allowed him to strengthen his influence and prestige among a growing circle of oppositionists, particularly the young. All of these articles contained impassioned pleas for militancy with constant references to Martí and other respected revolutionaries of the past.

After Castro's release from prison in 1955, the remaining top Ortodoxo leadership, sensing his growing influence, offered him an important position in the party hierarchy, an offer he refused. After a short stay in Havana, Castro left for Mexico, where he soon founded the 26th of July Movement. Political amnesty and the negotiations between government and opposition had created an unpropitious atmosphere for revolutionary activity in Cuba. During the next sixteen months, Castro traveled through Mexico and the United States propagandizing and promising, in a nearly suicidal but politically very effective slogan, his return to Cuba in 1956 to become either a free man or a martyr. During this period he continued to communicate with the Cuban people through his militant articles in *Bohemia*.

The spirit of political compromise of 1955 gradually disappeared as the SAR failed to obtain any further concessions from Batista, and the latter became progressively more brutal in his suppression of dissent. Cuba was not, as of late 1956, in a fully revolutionary political situation, but there is no question that at least a prerevolutionary political situation existed. Herbert Matthews reported that Cuba was "living through days and weeks of sporadic and isolated violence." His impression was one of tension and suppressed anarchy; but, he added, "there are no signs of popular or organized revolution."[12] It remained for a revolutionary leader to seize this historic opportunity for revolutionary struggle.

The Formation of a Moderate Anti-Batista Coalition

From 1956 to 1959, Cuba witnessed a short period of intense and extremely rapid political change. The year 1956 began with the complete failure of all negotiations between government and opposition; this was followed by the discovery and trial of the military conspirators against the Batista dictatorship. All of this was accompanied by increasingly frequent bombings, student demonstrations and unrest, and wholesale murderous actions on the part of Batista's police. In March 1956, shortly after the negotiations between government and opposition had broken down, Castro made a final break with the Ortodoxo party, while stating that he would continue to follow the political principles originally laid down by Eduardo Chibás.[13] Castro had correctly perceived that the Ortodoxo party and the traditional parties had exhausted their political prestige. A variety of political leaders, such as the popular opposition spokesman José Pardo Llada, had discredited themselves by not adopting a consistent line of militant opposition to Batista as Castro had done. This was the best opportunity to make a new beginning. The 26th of July Movement itself could fill the political vacuum and take the sole leadership of the struggle against Batista.

The year 1956 witnessed the *beginning* of a qualitative change in the attitude of the masses of Cubans toward the Batista regime. In spite of (or perhaps because of) a relative and temporary improvement in the economic situation of the country, popular hostility toward the regime began to increase by leaps and bounds; disillusionment was now replaced by a great increase of anger, although fear increased as well. The arrogance and brutality of the dictatorship were not received with submission or apathy. Castro was not yet able to channel this change in mood toward large-scale support for his cause, whether passive or active. He did return to Cuba before the year was over, but this landing, as well as the Santiago uprising timed to coincide with it, failed. The revolutionary wave had met a temporary setback.

A turning point in the fortunes of Castro and the 26th of July Movement occurred on February 24, 1957, when Herbert Matthews published in the *New York Times* his interview with Castro in the Sierra Maestra, thus proving that Castro was not dead, as the Batista government had claimed and many had believed. This interview also gave the impression that the guerillas were stronger than they were and served to increase Castro's prestige among the Cuban people, who could now envision men in the mountains constituting an antigovernment stronghold.

Also at this time, significant sections of middle-class opinion came to support Castro and the 26th of July Movement. The Civic Resistance Movement was founded in early 1957 as an auxiliary body to the 26th of July Movement. Its members performed a variety of chores ranging from making and collecting financial contributions to smuggling weapons to the Sierra Maestra. According to Jules Dubois, participants in the Civic Resistance Movement "were largely from the middle and upper classes, including businessmen, manufacturers, college professors, teachers, white-collar workers and housewives." The movement was organized in cells of ten persons. Its functions included propaganda, fund raising, and supply.[14]

The first rebel victory took place in La Plata in early 1957.[15] Word of this victory traveled quickly along the rumor grapevine which came into existence after Batista imposed strict censorship. This further enhanced Fidel Castro's reputation as a leader and the 26th of July's standing as the main opposition movement, particularly after the Directorio Revolucionario's unsuccessful attack on the Presidential Palace in March 1957, and the resulting death of José Antonio Echeverría.

Yet Castro's leadership still lacked the respectability, maturity, and middle-class confidence necessary for him to become the leader of an all-inclusive anti-Batista coalition centered around support for him and the 26th of July Movement. This problem was alleviated when two highly respected leaders of the opposition, Felipe Pazos (a top Cuban economist and former president of the National Bank of Cuba) and Raúl Chibás (brother of the deceased Ortodoxo leader Eduardo Chibás) went to the Sierra Maestra and signed a joint "Manifesto of the Sierra Maestra" with Fidel Castro on July 12, 1957. Published in *Bohemia* (during a brief lull between two periods of censorship), this manifesto was read by hundreds of thousands of Cubans.[16] In fact, it became the best-known position paper of Castro and the 26th of July Movement before they came to power. There was a very significant difference between the manifesto and the then little-known *History Will Absolve Me.* The Castro-Chibás-Pazos document was in essence an affirmation of the essentially moderate populist and democratic character of the movement. Although it was very militant in its opposition to the Batista dictatorship, the remedies it proposed were far more moderate than those of Castro's 1953 speech. It demanded the immediate resignation of Batista and the appointment of a new provisional president by the essentially middle-class Instituciones Cívicas (a loose confederation of Cuban civic and professional associations). It also guaranteed that the current army would remain in existence after a purge of those officers and soldiers who had supported the Batista regime.

On the international level, the manifesto opposed any United States intervention in the internal affairs of Cuba and demanded a stop to all arms shipments to Batista, but went no further. General elections were promised within one year of the overthrow of the

Batista dictatorship, and the document declared that the provisional government should "adjust its mission" to a program of government which included the restoration of full civil liberties, union democracy, civil service reform, a campaign against illiteracy, and the establishment of "the bases for an agrarian reform program which shall tend to distribute idle lands and to convert into owners all those . . . who possess [i.e., occupy] small parcels of land, whether they are property of the state or of individuals," this to be done "with previous indemnification to the former proprietors." This promise of agrarian reform was the most "radical" point in the program but was well within the bounds of the spirit and letter of the Constitution of 1940. It was far less radical than the Agrarian Reform Law passed in May 1959, which was still primarily based on the notion of small, individual property. Obviously, neither of these agrarian reform programs bore the slightest resemblance to the program of state ownership of land eventually implemented.

Within a year after the joint manifesto was issued, Castro altered its political demands by declaring that the 26th of July Movement should have the sole right to appoint the president and to reorganize the armed forces. This change was accepted because Castro's own political power within the opposition had increased. It should be noted, however, that *the social content of the program remained unaltered* until after victory had been achieved: for example, the Law of Agrarian Reform decreed in the Sierra Maestra in October 1958 did not depart essentially from the principles laid down in the Castro-Chibás-Pazos manifesto.[17]

Fidel Castro had obviously made a clear choice of strategy in his efforts at building a revolutionary movement against Batista. He accommodated his middle- and even upper-class supporters by adopting a social program that would not frighten them into indifference or opposition. All coalitions necessarily depend, by their very nature, on a compromise between the most radical and the most moderate components; but coalitions also work on the principle that, as the more radical elements become stronger, they can afford to "raise the price" of agreement with the moderates (or vice versa, if the moderates become stronger). Castro chose not to use his increasing strength and unchallengeable popularity to raise the minimum denominator of the revolutionary coalition's social program. He asserted his strength only on the purely executive political level regarding such questions as who would control the president and the army. In fact, Castro later made even more conservative social pronouncements, such as those in *Coronet* magazine repudiating the idea of nationalization.[18]

Castro's coalitionist policies were immensely successful from the point of view of building an enormous following for him during 1957 and 1958. Indeed, at this point, practically the whole Cuban population strongly detested the Batista dictatorship and entered into a veritable honeymoon with Castro and the 26th of July Movement, undisturbed by divisive group or class conflict. Of course, it must be taken into account that there was no important group that offered any social and political perspective to the Left of Castro's program. The Communist party, with its greater social radicalism, might have been an exception, but it was so fearful of offending Castro or the various middle-class forces supporting the revolution and so isolated by the Cold War atmosphere that it could not be of great importance.

In many ways, Castro was following a political logic similar to that of Eduardo Chibás. The latter had also put together a heterogeneous political coalition around one or two laudable aims and slogans, without further specifying his intended policies. Both Chibás and Castro had employed a strategy of postponing the discussion of potentially thorny and divisive political and social issues. The ideological poverty of Cuban politics, particularly after the defeat of the revolutionary wave of 1933–35, allowed them both to follow this course. In addition, the absence of an ideological and/or social challenge from the Batista dictatorship made it unnecessary for Castro to clarify his politics further. The Batista dictatorship, true to its socially parasitic nature, never tried to present any serious ideological defense of its rule aside from the usual platitudes about the free world and anticommunism. For a while, it seemed as if Batista might try to use his wife Marta Fernández as a kind of Cuban version of Evita Perón, but he never did.

The brevity of the actual hostilities between Castro and the Batista regime also favored Castro's strategy because the revolutionary leaders were not forced by time to take actions that displeased either the moderates, or the radicals, or both. The rebels had to administer occupied territory for only a few weeks or months. In spite of some claims made by Ché Guevara,[19] the fact is that the agrarian reform and other measures established in the occupied territories before 1959 were essentially provisional in nature and were so noncontroversial in character that no segment of the revolutionary coalition objected to them.

In conclusion, a new situation had been created in a Latin American country: a nontraditional political figure was leading a struggle against dictatorship supported by the overwhelming majority of the population including the middle classes and most of the traditional opposition politicians. In this situation the traditional politicians and the middle classes were the "guests" of the young nontraditional leader. It was not that Castro and his revolution had become "middle class," but rather that the "middle class" had come to support an outside political leadership which had, at least temporarily, accommodated itself to the values of "middle-class" politics. Castro and most of the *original* cadres of the 26th of July Movement were not part of "middle-class" politics; while they may have made numerous ideological concessions, they remained in control of whatever organization there was in the movement.

Pre-1959 Fidelismo

To achieve a better understanding of these rather unique political events of the late fifties in Cuba, it is necessary to discuss the nature of Castro's appeal and power in greater detail. As we have seen, the appeal of the 26th of July Movement unquestionably was not centered around its ideological or programmatic content. Its statements of social and economic policy were scarce and went largely unnoticed by the vast majority of Castro's sympathizers and followers. What few programmatic documents there were represented the talents of some prominent members of the 26th of July Movement rather than the actual politics of the movement as a whole. Thus, the *Tesis Económica del Movimiento Revolucionario 26 de Julio*, written by two very talented professional economists, Felipe Pazos and Harvard-trained Regino Boti, was a brilliant criticism of conservative economic theory concerning economic development in Cuba. It was definitely not a Marxist document, but rather a critique along the general lines of the Raúl Prebisch school of Latin American economists. Both the *Tesis Económica* and the 1957 document entitled *Nuestra Razón* (written mainly by Mario Llerena) were approved by Castro and issued as official documents of the movement. These documents were more sophisticated and contained a more profound social analysis of Cuban society than that found in the Pazos-Chibás-Castro manifesto, which may explain at least partially why they remained largely ignored during the struggle against Batista while the manifesto, tuned as it was to the political atmosphere and to the needs of the historic moment, and representing as it did the existing state of revolutionary opinion and political sophistication, was read by hundreds of thousands of Cubans.

Theodore Draper has suggested that Castro's originality lay not in his political ideology or program but rather in his conception of the road to power.[20] While there is a substantial element of truth in this observation, it is questionable whether Castro had a sustained and long-range conception of the road to power; and, to the extent that he did, it was very often mistaken. Thus, for example, Ché Guevara has noted some of the strategic and tactical reassessments that became necessary after the disastrous landing in late 1956:

> Before the landing of the *Granma*, a mentality predominated that, to some degree, might be called "subjectivist": blind confidence in a rapid popular explosion, enthusiasm and faith in the power to liquidate the Batista regime by a swift, armed uprising combined with spontaneous revolutionary strikes, and the subsequent fall of the dictator. . . .

After the landing comes the defeat, the almost total destruction of the forces, and their regrouping and integration as guerrillas. Characteristic of those few survivors, imbued with the spirit of struggle, was the understanding that to count upon spontaneous outbursts throughout the island was a falsehood, an illusion. They understood also that the fight would have to be a long one and that it would need vast *campesino* participation. [21]

No, Castro's originality consisted in his unusual ability to seize and understand the psychological dimensions of the political situation at a given moment and to elicit *action* in the direction he desired. His was a tactical rather than a strategic skill. It was accompanied by a persistence and steadfastness of purpose that often led him to "subjectivist" moods. The attack on the Moncada was almost suicidal from any military point of view, but it was well fitted to the political needs of the moment where it was necessary to awaken many Cubans from their disillusionment and political slumber. This was also true of his slogan "In 1956 we will be either martyrs or free men," meaning that he would definitely return to Cuba that year, a slogan that certainly narrowed his freedom of action. Before 1956 was over, he did land in Cuba; his forces met with military disaster, but the fact that he had stuck to his promise *(cumplió su palabra)* provided him with great political capital in a country so used to broken promises and disappointments.

Castro was also in full command of, and had internalized, the political idiom of the Cuban populist tradition, a very important political asset. He made great use of those political appeals that had been historically proven to be very valuable in arousing the idealistic and restless young people of Cuba to action. He knew how to draw on the cult of Martí, both in style and conceptualization. Thus, the exhortations made by Fidel Castro at the time of the attack on the Moncada contained the following typically populist excerpts:

> The *Revolution* declares its love and trust in the virtue, honor, and dignity of our men and expresses its intention of using all those who are truly worthy in the great task of Cuban reconstruction. These men are found in all places and institutions of Cuba, from the peasant hut to the general headquarters of the armed forces. This is not a revolution of castes. . . . If you win tomorrow, the aspirations of Martí will be

fulfilled sooner. If the contrary occurs, our action will set an example for the Cuban people, and from the people will arise young men willing to die for Cuba. They will pick up our banner and move forward. The people of Oriente Province will support us; the entire island will do so. . . . As in 1868 and 1895, here in Oriente we make our first cry of "Liberty or Death!"[22]

Castro knew how to adapt this political tradition to the particular needs and requirements of the current political and military situation. Aware of the background of skepticism that existed among the majority of the Cuban people, Castro established a kind of political puritanism peculiarly suited to Cuban conditions and rooted in the Ortodoxo legacy, which successfully elicited great sympathy (and in some instances active support) from the people of Cuba. As Federico G. Gil explained, curiously ethical, moralistic, almost puritanical overtones pervaded the 26th of July Movement. The rebels treated prisoners humanely, paid for the supplies they requisitioned, and maintained strict discipline and morality in all their camps. "The significance of these factors," according to Gil, "lies in their apparently great popular appeal, in their salutory effect of shaking the rather widespread cynicism among Cubans toward their leaders, and in their kindling the embers of a political crusade in which each citizen saw himself as an active participant in the task of reorganizing the country."[23] Castro never lost sight of the fact that the waging of civil war and revolution was primarily a political and not a military question. It was only after victory that the school of guerrilla warfare was canonized as *the* method adequate for all countries and all situations. Castro handled all questions of political warfare with great shrewdness and was quite self-conscious about the exigencies of such warfare. As he stated in a broadcast of Radio Rebelde in connection with his policy of releasing Batistiano soldiers after they had been captured and disarmed: "Does it seem illogical in the midst of the war to free enemy prisoners? This depends on the war itself and on the concept one has of war. In war one must have a policy for the enemy, just as one must have a policy for the civilian population. War is not merely a matter of rifles, bullets, cannons, and planes. Perhaps that belief has been one of the causes of the failure of the tyranny's forces."[24]

Castro's Political Control

Perhaps Castro's most unique contribution to Cuban politics was that, although he showed great political flexibility and opportunism in accommodating essential middle-class support for his revolutionary coalition, he was far from flexible or permissive on matters that were relevant to his personal control of the movement. Of course, this is a central element of what I have referred to earlier as revolutionary Bonapartism. It was symptomatic that, as Castro's personal prestige and political power increased before the victory of the revolution, he did not demand any substantial programmatic changes in the movement but did demand the sole power to appoint a president and to control the armed forces after the overthrow of Batista. As early as 1954, Fidel Castro had already shown the great importance he attached to personal political control. Thus, in a letter to Luis Conte Aguero, then his close friend, he stated:

> *Conditions which are indispensable for the integration of a truly civic moment: ideology, discipline and chieftainship.* The three are essential, but chieftainship is basic. I don't know whether it was Napoleon who said that a bad general in battle is worth more than twenty good generals. *A movement cannot be organized where everyone believes he has the right to issue public statements without consulting anyone else; nor can one expect anything of a movement that will be integrated by anarchic men who at the first disagreement take the path they consider most convenient, tearing apart and destroying the vehicle.* The apparatus of propaganda and organization must be such and so powerful that it will implacably destroy him who will create tendencies, cliques, or schisms, or will rise against the movement. [25]

Particularly after the 26th of July Movement became the most important revolutionary organization, Castro tried to acquire as much organizational power as possible vis-à-vis other organizations participating in the struggle against the dictatorship. For example, in 1958, when Camilo Cienfuegos was sent from Oriente Province at the head of an "invading column" of the 26th of July's rebel army into the province of Las Villas in central Cuba, an area where other organizations such as the Directorio Revolucionario and the Second Front of Escambray had considerable forces fighting already, Castro directed that "any other force, regardless of its political ideology, which struggles against the mercenary forces of the tyranny and which desires the union of forces to the benefit of the Revolution and a better development of rebel action should accept the command of the Invading Column."[26]

All of this was accompanied by a minimal and rather informal structure *within* the 26th of July Movement and its auxiliary organizations themselves. In such an organizational situation the publicly known leadership inevitably monopolizes power because it is the only body capable of keeping ties with the rank-and-file membership and with the various atomized and fragmented parts of the relatively unstructured movement. In this way, it can act as a spokesperson for the movement without having to be responsible to the members and component parts of the movement in some institutionalized fashion. This was true for the 26th of July Movement before as well as after victory, so the lack of structure cannot be attributed to the original need for secrecy. To a great extent, the movement is cemented by the existence of a presumably great leader who holds together its various components and so keeps the movement alive. Nowhere is this more clearly and strikingly revealed than by Haydée Santamaria, a founder of the 26th of July Movement and a longtime associate of Castro's, as she recalls her reaction after the defeat of the attack on the Moncada barracks:

> I was thinking of Fidel. We thought about Fidel. Of Fidel who couldn't die. Of Fidel who had to be alive in order to make the revolution. Of the life of Fidel who was the life of all of us. If Fidel was alive, Abel and Boris and Renato and the others would not have died; they would be alive in Fidel who was going to make the Cuban revolution and who was going to return its destiny to the people of Cuba.
>
> The rest was a haze of blood and smoke, the rest had been gained by death. Fidel would win the last battle, he would win the Revolution.[27]

In 1957, an incident took place which on close examination throws some light on Castro's modus operandi concerning questions of power and organizational control. As we have seen, the document signed by Castro, Chibás, and Pazos in July 1957 had called for the essentially middle-class civic institutions to nominate the provisional president who was to replace Batista. In November of 1957, representatives of all opposition forces, including the 26th of July Movement (whom Castro would later claim were unauthorized by him to do so) met in Miami and signed a "Document of Unity of the Cuban Opposition to the Batista Dictatorship," which included the establishment of a provisional government, with the understanding that Felipe Pazos would become the provisional president.[28] In an open letter addressed to the signers of the Miami document, Castro promptly repudiated it.[29] In his letter Castro rightly denounced serious omissions in the Miami document, such as the lack of an explicit rejection of foreign intervention in Cuban internal affairs and of a military junta as a replacement for Batista. He also criticized the existence of secret clauses in the Miami document. However, the most salient aspect of the letter from Castro was the fact that he used this objectionable political act commited by other oppositionists to create an opportunity to demand sole authority to nominate the future president and to keep "public order" after the overthrow of Batista. Castro also nominated Manuel Urrutia instead of Felipe Pazos as the future president. Manuel Urrutia had earned the respect of Cubans when, as a magistrate in Santiago de Cuba, he had cast a courageous minority vote supporting the right of revolution against Batista, an action that cost him his job; but otherwise, he had no political record and had far less public prestige than Felipe Pazos. There is no question that Urrutia was a far less powerful figure than Pazos and that as president he would have less independence vis-à-vis Castro. As it turned out, both Pazos and Urrutia broke with Castro and became political exiles in the early sixties, but in the meantime Castro had chosen a relatively powerless personality to occupy the presidency.

After Castro had come to power, political observers such as Jean Paul Sartre, on the basis of their observations concerning the *personal* nature of Castro's rule of Cuban society, concluded that somehow this was a desirable political system or that there was political freedom in Cuba. Apparently, Sartre and others like him could not conceive that the pompous and elaborate bureaucratic organization of East European Communism did not exhaust the varieties of undemocratic rule. Of course, the crucial factor is not the *form* of control but whether various combinations of personal and bureaucratic control and arbitrariness can be checked by free institutional mechanisms through which the masses can control and express disagreement with leaders and authorities. As people of a wide variety of viewpoints ranging from Voltaire to Rosa Luxemburg have pointed out, freedom to agree is no freedom. Castro's structureless movement was in time conveniently discarded and replaced by the familiar institution of the one-party state which controls *all* other political organizations in Cuba.

The Overthrow of Batista

Castro's strategy and tactics were in the end successful. In spite of the temporary setback resulting from the failure of the April 1958 general strike, that year marked the end of the Batista dictatorship. The opposition of practically the whole country was too much for Batista to bear. The most important spokesmen of the middle classes, encouraged by the United States arms embargo and other dramatic events, had in March 1958 openly called for Batista's resignation and for resistance to the regime:

> The Committee of Cuban Institutions believes that this is the only solution which offers Cuba a triumphal escape from chaos at this dramatic juncture. And, conscious of its lack of strength to depose the regime by means of violence, hereby appeals to the entire nation to join in united resistance against the oppression, by exercising the rights granted by the Constitution to free men.[30]

The spirit of resistance was greatly strengthened by the broadcasts of Radio Rebelde which started to function in February 1958. By scrupulously telling the truth about rebel victories and defeats, Radio Rebelde obtained a reputation for veracity sharply in contrast with the ridiculous claims made by spokesmen for Batista's army. By December 1958, the rebels had come to control almost the whole eastern half of Cuba, and this finally caused Batista's flight on December 31, 1958. Faced with the imminent collapse of Batista's regime, the State Department and the emissaries of United States imperialism in Cuba tried to replace Batista with a new government composed of safe conservative elements. This was a continuation of the policy adopted in early 1958, when the United States placed an embargo on all shipments of arms to Cuba although the United States continued to retain its training mission in Batista's army. This final attempt, as was to be expected, met with absolute failure, and Castro's rebel army, which never had more than one or two thousand members, faced little difficulty in taking power away from the remnants of the completely demoralized and disintegrated army.[31]

9 | The Early Development of the Revolutionary Regime

THE DAWN OF 1959 brought forth a massive outpouring of popular joy over the fall of Batista and almost unanimous support for Fidel Castro. Those who had lived through the momentous events of 1933 or had heard or read about them could now see a repetition of the enthusiasm that had greeted the fall of Machado. This similarity was, however, accompanied by a variety of new features which provided significant contrasts with the events of 1933. Thus, while the general strike against the Machado dictatorship had played a crucial role in the latter's undoing, the general strike called by Castro after Batista's overthrow was almost superfluous. In fact, the completely successful 1959 strike was called to ensure the consolidation of the new revolutionary regime and was aimed against no one in particular, because Batista and his cohorts had already fled the country, and no one else dared to challenge Castro. It turned out to be a well-deserved revolutionary holiday for the Cuban working class rather than an instrument of struggle, properly speaking. The role and nature of this 1959 general strike were more than symbolic of the secondary role the Cuban working class had played in this new revolutionary situation which had not been brought about through its own actions.

The popular enthusiasm of 1933 had also expressed itself in such phenomena as widespread looting, and lynchings of well-known representatives and police agents of the Machado dictatorship. In many ways these excesses had provided a partial safety valve, diverting energy and attention from the more fundamental business of social and political change. In 1959, it took only a few hours before this kind of "classic" Cuban revolutionism was brought under firm control by the militias temporarily organized by the 26th of July Movement and other revolutionary organizations.

At the same time, the new revolutionary government promptly meted out a variety of punishments to those responsible for atrocities under the Batista regime. As a result of this policy, several hundred Batistianos were executed under widely varying conditions of due process of law. These measures, which provoked the indignation of many North Americans — their consciences suddenly and unprecedentedly disturbed by the existence of a political struggle in Cuba and its bloody consequences — met overwhelming approval among Cubans of practically all political inclinations (a reaction that was perhaps similar to that aroused by the punishment of collaborators in France in 1945).

The quick introduction of organized revolutionary punishment was not an unexpected response on the part of Castro's revolutionary leadership. As far back as 1957, Castro's letter denouncing the Miami Pact and demanding, among other things, that the 26th of July Movement be the *sole* body responsible for the maintenance of postrevolutionary public order and security argued that postrevolutionary "anarchy" would be the worst enemy of the revolution.[1]

Far more was involved in this issue than the mere question of which was the speediest and fairest way of administering punishment to the Batistiano criminals. Castro's choice of the method of punishment can be fully understood only within the wider context of Castro's whole ideology concerning the *control* of the revolutionary movement. Castro must have given considerable thought to the experiences of the frustrated 1933 Revolution and its aftermath in the forties and fifties, and to the lessons to be learned from these. He probably concluded that the aimless and disorganized violence of so much of recent Cuban history had not only been nonrevolutionary but had in fact often diminished the possibilities for revolutionary change and had instead given further encouragement to political shallowness, and to corruption and gangsterism. But, as I suggested in Chapter 8, he probably also decided that the only alternative to the endless fragmentation of Cuban revolutionary organizations was the creation of a monolithic center of power.

Castro's organizational ideas were put to an early test under what turned out to be extremely favorable circumstances for obtaining popular acquiescence and acceptance of his point of view. During the first days after the revolutionary victory, elements belonging to the Directorio Revolucionario, the only significant revolutionary organization outside the 26th of July Movement, had stolen some weapons from one of the military headquarters; their motives were unclear but may have included resentment and suspicions concerning the political and military monopoly of Castro and the 26th of July Movement.

It goes without saying that most Cubans reacted with great hostility toward this action of the Directorio. The specter of political gangsterism in the university was raised in the minds of the Cuban people even though that phenomenon had ceased to exist at least seven years before. Castro, then at the apex of his prestige and popularity, did not waste this opportunity to drive home the dangers of a multiplicity of "revolutionary" organizations. As he put it in his first triumphal speech in Havana, at Camp Columbia on January 8, 1959,

> We are not that far from the epoch which followed the overthrow of Machado; perhaps one of the greatest evils of that struggle was the proliferation of revolutionary groups which did not take long in starting to shoot one another. And as a consequence what happened was that Batista came and stayed eleven years in power. . . . I am going to ask you a question. Weapons for what? To struggle against whom? Against the revolutionary government which has the support of the people. . . . Today when all liberties exist . . . when all the rights of citizens have been reestablished. When a call to elections is being thought of. Weapons for what? Hide arms for what? To blackmail the president of the Republic, to threaten peace, to create gangster organizations. Are we going to return to gangsterism, with daily shooting in the streets?[2]

Castro promptly rejected any suggestions that the 26th of July Movement share power with other revolutionary organizations. As Castro stated it on the popular television program "Ante la Prensa," on January 9, 1959: "We are remiss to enter into pacts in order to avoid certain problems. I have always thought that the revolution should be made by one movement alone. Our thesis is that one group should not make a revolution, but the people. A small engine gets a bigger engine started."[3]

Aside from the rhetoric about a revolution made by the people, the crucial phrase here is the "small engine." At this time, there was no doubt that the 26th of July Movement was supposed to be the "small engine" but, as we shall see, in the course of the revolutionary regime the 26th of July Movement never meant much as an organization, democratic or otherwise, and it was allowed to deteriorate until it was "merged" into the embryo of what eventually became a new and reconstituted Communist party working along the lines of the misnamed Communist party formula of "democratic centralism."

There was little doubt in the minds of most Cubans and foreign observers that Castro's "engine" was going somewhere; but nobody really seemed to know what the destination would be. During this early period of the political honeymoon, practically all groups and classes of Cubans were talking about the need for agrarian and a variety of other reforms. The terms used had quite different meanings to various groups of people in Cuba; and for the time being Castro was not helping to clarify any specifics. He had been saved from having to commit himself on controversial social issues by the rapid collapse of the Batista regime and the fact that the rebels had to administer liberated areas for only a few weeks before assuming full control. In a sense, he was temporarily prolonging the moderate anti-Batista coalition of 1958, a coalition whose members had little in common other than their intense dislike of the corrupt and brutal Batista dictatorship. Theodore Draper, before his invention of the theory of the "middle-class revolution betrayed," clearly perceived the composition of this coalition:

Long after the rebellion in the Sierra Maestra had taken hold, Castro did not head a homogeneous movement, and the larger it grew, the less homogeneous it became. It included those who merely wished to go back to the democratic constitution of 1940 and those who demanded "a real social revolution." It included some who were friendly to the United States and some who hated it. It included anti-Communists and fellow travelers. . . .

When Fidel Castro entered Havana a conquering hero on January 8 last year, no one knew what he was going to do. It is doubtful whether he himself knew, except in the most general terms.[4]

Some of the confusion among the revolution's adherents had its roots in the Constitution of 1940; contrary to Draper's otherwise penetrating observation, even the "social revolutionaries" paid homage to the majesty of the suppressed Constitution. Conservative Cubans could live with it because, although it emphatically promised agrarian reform, it no less emphatically established a proviso for preliminary compensation for any expropriated land. Furthermore, it is highly doubtful whether the kind of powerful social movement necessary to push for the implementation of the substantive reforms proposed by the Constitution could have coexisted with the procedural safeguards spelled out in that document, to say nothing about the high economic cost of pensioning off large sections of the landed classes.

Yet, despite their desire for land reform, not even the most extreme radical supporters of Castro's revolutionary government would have predicted the massive program of agricultural collectivization undertaken in Cuba in a matter of a very few years. There was no revolutionary social situation in Cuba in the early days of the revolutionary government. This does not mean that the country was not objectively in need of a radical social revolution; what it means is that the prevailing consciousness of even most of the more radical sectors of the population was still eminently reformist. A wave of strikes had broken out in early 1959, and numerous demands had been made by various sectors of the population; but all these expectations were still seen as compatible with a reformed and controlled Cuban capitalism.

This reformist attitude of the early days of the revolution expressed itself not only in the internal affairs of Cuban society but also in the government's relations with the United States. As I have pointed out, the widespread and explicit anti-imperialist sentiment of the early thirties had, for a variety of reasons, undergone a significant decline in Cuba. By the 1950s only members of the Communist party, and very few others, would publicly use the term "imperialism" in referring to the actions and policies of the United States government. Thus, for example, an official pamphlet of the 26th of July Movement published in 1957 discussed this whole issue in polite liberal terms:

> In good political terminology, the term "imperialism" is already inappropriate to the American continent; but there still exist forms of economic penetration generally accompanied by political influence which are very similar to it and which cause irreparable harm to the moral and material welfare of the country which suffers it.
>
> Fortunately, such a situation can be overcome without any legitimate interests being hurt. Through a new treatment of *constructive friendship* Cuba could truly be, as it is advised by many geographical, economic and even political reasons, a loyal ally of the great country of the North and at the same time safely preserve the capacity to orient its own destiny. Through new and just agreements, it can, without unnecessary sacrifices nor humiliating sellouts, multiply the advantages which derive from neighborliness.[5]

In spite of this change in mood and ideology, however, there was still a large reservoir of latent resentment and hostility toward the United States. The revolutionaries had strongly denounced the shipments of arms and ammunition to Batista which continued up to a few months before his overthrow; and the United States military mission, which had remained in the country until the very end of the Batista regime, was immediately ordered out of the country. But these protests and criticisms did not yet go beyond a moderate critique of the North American foreign policy of aiding military dictators. Obviously, although nationalist sentiment existed in the revolutionary ranks and among the Cuban people as a whole, it was not accompanied by a broader condemnation of political and economic imperialism as a system. With the exception of the Communist party, no contemporary political group had developed a political world view that included an anti-imperialist critique, whether Leninist or of some other variety.

The provincialism of Cuban politics had maintained it in virtual isolation from the nationalist and anti-imperialist currents predominant in the Afro-Asian world. However, the situation was significantly different concerning Cuban identification with the rest of Latin America. Thus, the experience of Juan Perón in Argentina and that of Jacobo Arbenz in Guatemala had a significant impact among the most politically aware sections of the Cuban population, particularly among some students, and helped to add new strength to what was becoming a declining anti–United States ideology. It is significant that, after each friction-causing incident between Cuba and the United States, the daily *Revolución* warned that Cuba "will not be another Guatemala."

However, by and large, the opposition to the intervention in Guatemala in 1954 and the initial conflicts with the United States in 1959 were still perceived by most Cubans within the liberal and social-democratic framework of the "mistakes" that the Americans usually make in their dealings with Latin America. Castro's early outburst that any marines landing in Cuba would be shot (a statement he promptly modified) was, at this time, the exception rather than the rule. Still, anti-imperialism was brewing among the Cuban leadership and people and would eventually express itself openly.

In the meantime, domestic and external reformism had allowed the political honeymoon to continue relatively undisturbed. Even the reactionary newspaper *Diario de la Marina* was respectful of Castro's leadership, although it had started to make some politely phrased criticisms of this or that government action. Castro's installation of a very respectable cabinet under the nominal leadership of Manuel Urrutia contributed to a continuation of the 1958 honeymoon, although it was quite clear that the real and ultimate power was always in Castro's hands. Castro could afford to delay and time his actions precisely because he was not faced with an immediately socially explosive situation of the kind that had existed in 1933.

During his first few weeks in power, he consolidated his personal control; and in mid-February, he became prime minister, thus putting an end to the appearance of polycentric power.

Communism and Drift

The unique phenomenon of what eventually turned out to be a Communist revolution, led and sponsored not by a traditional Communist party or even by a leadership that had been associated with "classical" Marxist or socialist politics, has provoked a series of disputes and controversies. Perhaps the best example is the dispute as to whether Castro "was forced" into Communism by the pressures and blockades imposed by United States imperialism or whether he had been for some time a covert Communist or "Marxist-Leninist" and was simply waiting for the best opportunity to reveal his true self and implement his real program of government. Castro's own statements and confessions on this matter are highly ambiguous and can be interpreted variously as, for example, an attempt to establish his credentials vis-à-vis the international Communist movement, with little or no grounding in historical reality, or as a true description of his past. I am referring here in particular to Castro's speech of December 2, 1961, where he first openly announced his profession of "Marxism-Leninism," hinting that he had been a "Marxist-Leninist" or something close to that for some unspecified but significant length of time. Interestingly enough, right-wing Cuban exiles and North American professional anti-Communists who had always regarded Castro as a systematic liar decided that this time he had adhered to the truth and nothing but the truth, thus proving their previous charges of a longstanding Communist conspiracy. Actually, this and other statements by Castro and other revolutionary leaders should be considered as *partial* evidence, and no more than that, in the attempt to understand the Cuban Revolution's evolution toward Communism.

Interpretations of this evolution usually rest on one of two distinctly different assumptions: (1) unrestricted freedom of choice on the part of the revolutionary leadership to establish whatever social system they might have desired for Cuba, or (2) a minimal amount of freedom of choice which led the Castro leadership to choose Communism as an almost purely defensive reaction against American imperialist pressures. Both of these interpretations seriously distort the contemporary Cuban historical record and, furthermore, lead to grave misunderstandings of the ways in which the consciousness of political leaders is formed, the way that consciousness relates to their present and potential followers, and how all of these factors affect the shape of historical developments in Cuba as well as in many other countries.

The evolution toward Cuban Communism can be better understood by making an analogy with a concept developed by David Matza in a very different context. In *Deliquency and Drift*,[6] Matza pointed out that, contrary to those interpretations of delinquent behavior which see the delinquent as being either a completely free agent or a completely determined agent following the values of the delinquent "subculture," what happens to at least a very significant number of delinquents is that the periodic breaking of the bonds tying the delinquent to the society places him or her in a state of "drift" where the commission of a delinquent act is possible but not inevitable. In Matza's own words:

> The periodic breaking of the moral bind to law arising from neutralization and resulting in drift does not assure the commission of a delinquent act. Drift makes delinquency possible or permissible by temporarily removing the restraints that ordinarily control members of society, but of itself it supplies no irreversible commitment or compulsion that would suffice to thrust the person into the act. . . . There is a missing element — an element in the nature of a thrust or an impetus — by which the possibility of delinquency is realized. . . . I wish to suggest that the missing element which provides the thrust or impetus by which the delinquent act is realized is *will*.[7]

Matza would, of course, not deny that restraints on the delinquent still exist, if for no other reason than that he or she has to reckon with the courts, the police, and other agents of repression which restrict freedom of action in a very physical sense. By the same token, I would not deny that there were limits to Castro's freedom of action, such as American imperialism, the rising expectations of the Cuban people themselves, and so on. But it can be stated that the Fidelista leadership was in a state of drift, partly as a result of the elimination of the traditional army and the extreme weakness of traditional conservative forces, such as traditional political parties. At the same time, there was no significant socialist tradition outside of the Communist party nor any new radical or revolutionary group that could fill the organizational vacuum and operate as a potential control on Castro's individual actions.

The available evidence seems to indicate that, at the time of Batista's overthrow on January 1, 1959, Castro himself was not sure of the future course of the Cuban Revolution (perhaps because he had never quite expected such a complete victory) and that he "drifted" for a short while until he *chose* the Communist road for Cuba, probably sometime in mid-1959.[8] This, of course, does not in the least detract from the fact that United States imperialism bears a large share of the blame for the establishment of Cuban Communism; but neither does it prove that a Communist system was the inevitable choice, let alone that it was a choice, inevitable or otherwise, that deserves either admiration or apology. James O'Connor, a student of Cuban society and a supporter of the Castro regime, has aptly summarized and spelled out some of the crucial structural traits that produced a social context within which Castro was able to exercise his will and consolidate his power:

> The liquidation of Cuba's private property system was invariably initiated by the ruling group. The peasantry did not spontaneously seize and cultivate idle lands; with a handful of exceptions, they failed to claim even the small fields in which they labored until the new government formally turned these tracts over to them. . . . Nor did the urban workers and sugar mill laborers independently occupy the factories (this was a sharp departure from the abortive social revolution of 1933); rebel army or militia units at the direction of the central government took possession of Cuba's farm land and industry.
>
> . . . The social revolution was more or less orderly because the political revolution transferred power from one relatively small group of men to another, and because the masses of Cubans at the very least passively supported the social revolution. . . .
>
> The fact that the Cuban farmworker and peasant never had the

political initiative made possible the immediate collectivization of the cattle, rice and sugar sectors of the rural economy.[9]

The Political Structure

A variety of more strictly organizational political factors reinforced the situation described by O'Connor. One of the most crucial factors in the 1959 situation was the virtual absence of political organizations, whether liberal, radical, or conservative. The old Communist party was discredited and was not a powerful political force until it forged close links with the Fidelista leadership. The organizational weakness of the 1933 Revolution had been largely the result of the fragmentation and rivalries of the existing organizations, rather than of the virtual absence of such organizations. As I have previously suggested, the 26th of July Movement was an amorphous group of followers rather than an organization, properly speaking. Many moderate supporters of the 26th of July Movement who had grouped themselves in the Movement of Civic Resistance had even less of an organizational power base, that group having been essentially an auxiliary of Castro's movement. In any event, the Movement of Civic Resistance formally dissolved itself into the 26th of July Movement in late February 1959. Moderate cabinet ministers were in office while Castro found it convenient for them to be there and were quietly and noiselessly replaced when they interfered with Castro's policies, and the Instituciones Cívicas many of them had represented in 1957 and 1958 turned out to be quite insignificant. Even the replacement of President Urrutia in July 1959 was a relatively easy task. The only real political structure was Fidel Castro himself. As C. Wright Mills, speaking as a typical Fidelista, said of him: "Had he not been *here,* and done and said what he did do and say, the history of Cuba would have been different. . . . Many times in those months and years and days just past, he *was* the revolution."[10]

While Mills's assessment of Castro's power may sound exaggerated, it is not. Often sociological conditions maximize the power of given individuals in certain historic situations; such a set of conditions characterized Cuban society in 1959. Karl Marx, in his sociological analysis of Louis Bonaparte, described a similar situation of social and political weakness among the peasantry and deadlock among the bourgeoisie and other social classes in mid-nineteenth-century France. In Cuba, the social and political weaknesses of the middle and working classes, and the lack of a strong oligarchy, combined with the concrete events and developments of the fifties to complete the process of discrediting and disintegrating the pre-Castro political parties. This combination of an absence of political organization and a strong leadership produced an unusual situation in which the Cuban revolutionary leadership was free from most of the controls usually present in Latin American societies to restrict the freedom of action of officeholders, even those who are "revolutionary."

Robin Blackburn, a pro-Castro British analyst of the Cuban scene, has offered a sophisticated interpretation of this phenomenon. He attributes the swift success of so small a revolutionary army to the weakness of its enemy — to the fact that the only resistance came not from a coherent ruling class, not from powerful institutions or respected ideologies, but from "the isolated and opportunistic Batista machine." Blackburn concludes, *"The unprecedented hallmarks of the revolution — its lack of party or an ideology — were the logical product of a pre-revolutionary society which itself lacked any decisive institutional or ideological structures."*[11]

Blackburn's is an impressive analysis which exhibits much sociological insight into Cuban society. Yet it is somewhat schematic, and it ignores the content and varying shades of political life in early revolutionary Cuba. While there was no significant political organization in the Cuba of 1959, there *was* a significant political tradition of radical and democratic populism which was revived in the aftermath of the revolutionary victory by such important elements as the newspaper *Revolución,* the leadership of the new revolutionary trade-union movement, and others of a leftist but noncommunist "humanist" political tendency. One · *Revolución* editorialist even raised the issue of the need for a democratically controlled revolutionary organization at a time when this would have excluded the old Communist party from participation within it.[12] The Fidelista leadership did make organizational choices at given times and under specific circumstances. Thus, by 1961, two years after the victory of the revolution, the revolutionary leadership decided to create a one-party state; but by this time a whole series of objectionable political elements had been either purged, eliminated from political life, exiled, or simply relegated to political oblivion (the fate of the "humanists").

Blackburn's most penetrating insights into Cuban society were, by and large, as true for 1961 as they were for 1959, but they still did not prevent Castro from deciding to form a Communist one-party state in 1961. The explanation of *this* phenomenon lies primarily at a more immediate political level: in 1959, Castro could not have formed a Communist-type party but could have formed only a party of a much broader nature because of the wide diversity of views within the revolutionary ranks at that time. In such a situation it was far more advantageous for Castro to be a maximum leader who could manipulate and suppress various divergent viewpoints until an appropriate level of uniformity was achieved.

Not all tensions and potential divisions had been eliminated by the time the ORI (the embryo of the new Communist party) was established in 1961, but by this time the obstacles that caused Castro to let the 26th of July Movement fall apart had disappeared. Castro's main reason for allowing the movement to fade was explained by the Cuban leaders to Simone de Beauvoir: "The 26th of July Movement, from which the revolution issued, had an apparatus, but a petty-bourgeois one, which could not follow the revolution in the radicalization that has been proceeding since the taking of power; it was not capable of going along with the advance of the agrarian reform. So it was permitted to fall away."[13] Of course, it is very difficult to determine the precise nature of such terms as "radicalization" and "petty bourgeois" in Mme de Beauvoir's or the Cuban leadership's vocabulary. Petty bourgeois could mean anything from hostility to the Communist party and to totalitarianism to the very real phenomenon of middle-class reformism; but, regardless of the precise meaning intended there, the organizational logic of Castro's decision is perfectly clear.

Popular Support

The fact that the Fidelista leadership was in a state of drift where choices could be made relatively freely was the result not only of negative factors, such as the weakness of Cuba's social structure and the elimination of a traditional army, but also of Castro's overwhelming popularity and his considerable political skills. The rather puritanical attitude of the rebel soldiers and authorities in the early stages of the revolution bolstered the new government's widespread support among the masses of Cubans. The announcement made early in the Castro regime that serious cases of misappropriation of funds by public officials might be punished with the death penalty was favorably received in a country that had become extremely cynical about the possibility of public officials ever being honest. In measures like this, one could hear not-too-distant echoes of the climate of public opinion that had provided so much support for Eduardo Chibás and the Ortodoxo party. Cubans of all classes were also pleased by the nonabusive behavior of the brand-new revolutionary police force, many of whose members were former revolutionaries who had great political awareness and had had no time to develop the "professional deformations of character" common to members of all repressive institutions. This latter fact benefited poor people the most because the Cuban upper and middle classes had always been able to obtain greater consideration from the traditional national police in the cities and the Guardia Rural ("rural army police") in the countryside. So, without yet making an appeal to specific "class warfare" themes, Castro was able to obtain a very considerable amount of popular support. Of course, populistic appeals in Cuban politics were naturally associated with Leftist politics, but this still meant, by and large, the kind of reform Leftism of favoring the underdog and improving the general public morals and welfare of the country. It also implied that the rich would not fare particularly well under these new conditions but that most of the middle classes would benefit from a reformist program never, up to this point, spelled out in any kind of serious detail.

Eventually Castro started to take measures that had sharper teeth in terms of the way they affected the grand coalition of 1958, which survived into the political honeymoon of January and February 1959; but at no time during the first six months of 1959 did he implement policies that would make unavoidable a complete break with *all* the more conservative elements still supporting him. He proceeded with some caution and undertook a series of measures throughout 1959 and 1960 which *successively* alienated various sectors of his erstwhile conservative supporters, but in such a manner that they were not able to get together and present a common front against the Castro government. The fact that these various sectors were alienated one at a time rather than all at once, plus the traditional political weaknesses of the upper and middle classes in Cuba, made it relatively easy for Castro to get rid of his gradually increasing number of domestic opponents.

The first serious jolt to the political honeymoon in Cuba came in March 1959, when Castro ordered a radical reduction in rents of up to 50 per cent. This move alienated for the first time a significant section of the Cuban bourgeoisie, but it was nonetheless a very popular measure, and it was unopposed by the many middle-class people who benefited from it. This reform was not a "collectivist" measure in the Communist sense. Rather, it was a radical measure following both the spirit and letter of *History Will Absolve Me*, a document that had just been recalled from obscurity after the socially mellow years of 1956–58, and was part of a very radical populism then being vigorously revived, particularly by the newspaper *Revolución*, official organ of the 26th of July Movement. Interestingly enough, the drastic rent reductions, which had a great impact on the consciousness of the Cuban well-to-do classes, received little notice in the North American press. United States capital had never involved itself in any significant manner in Cuba's housing industry, a very important and growing industry in an otherwise stagnant economy; thus it had remained the preserve of the essentially cautious Cuban capital. After the end of the executions in February 1959, the North American press lost interest in Cuban affairs, a situation that was reversed with the passing of the Agrarian Reform Law in May of 1959.

After the rent-reduction law was passed, Castro continued to reassure and encourage Cuban capitalists by asserting that the products of Cuban industries did contribute to national growth as distinct from the parasitic investors on the housing market.[14] At the same time everybody was talking about the coming agrarian reform, but nobody really knew what it would be like. Until the moment when Castro virtually pulled the law out of a hat in May 1959, discussion about it was so unspecific that the most diverse sectors still supporting Castro could hope that their interests and views would not be hurt and might even be incorporated in the eventual agrarian legislation. This was particularly true of those moderate and conservative elements still supporting Castro, who, having been stunned by the rent law bombshell and having heard various inflammatory speeches, particularly by Raúl Castro and Ché Guevara, were apprehensive about what Castro might come up with next. In this new situation, these elements had relatively little political bargaining power, and they were in fact placing their faith in what they hoped was the relative moderation of Fidel Castro himself.

The radical Agrarian Reform Law enacted in May 1959, although by no means Communist (it emphasized land *redistribution* and referred vaguely to the creation of some form of cooperatives but did not even remotely hint that state farms would become the predominant form of agricultural organization) marked a turning point in the relationship between Castro and his domestic opposition, as well as between Castro and the United States imperialist system, which at this point reentered the anti-Castro fray with great vigor through its press, congressional committees, covert activities, and State Department diplomatic pressure. Domestically, the political honeymoon had now come to an end. Castro continued to enjoy wide support, but now it was a "great majority" rather than "practically all" Cubans who were supporting him. Yet the domestic opposition was still weak and incapable of presenting a serious challenge to the regime. Although practically all upper-class and many middle-class Cubans were now opposed to Castro, significant sections of the middle classes still supported him enthusiastically. The Agrarian Reform Law had, in many ways, been a surprise to most conservative Cubans. Although they had many apprehensions about the regime, they were very much reassured by Castro's trip to the United States in April 1959 and by the anti-Communism Castro had toyed with briefly during the spring of 1959.

There was nothing inevitable about the course Castro chose to take. The assertion that he was driven to drastic action by the powerful pressure of class forces inside Cuba is no more than a myth. As already noted, there were practically no spontaneous land or factory seizures in Cuba. After playing around with various political possibilities (within the usual objective limits, of course), Castro turned to political measures far more drastic than anybody, including the Cuban Communist party, might have predicted. Until the spring of 1959, the Communist party had been to the left of Castro in its social and economic policies. Growing prosperity and the redistribution of wealth, plus other social and political events that took place in the aftermath of Batista's overthrow, had made the overwhelming majority of Cuba's workers and peasants very satisfied with the new regime. Their consciousness was anything but one of impatience and dissatisfaction with Castro's lack of sufficient radicalism during the first months of 1959. To try to read the experience of other revolutionary situations into the Cuban situation of 1959 (such as the problems of dual power, a leadership lagging behind the consciousness of the masses, and so on) is to do serious violence to the actual events.

Although there had been an undeniable move toward the Left in the actions and consciousness of the Cuban masses between January and May 1959, the direction of that shift had been from the leaders to the masses rather than the other way around. The radicalism of the leadership had, in various forms, filtered down to the masses of Cubans, who always remained "behind" the various measures Castro periodically and unexpectedly produced after long night sessions of the revolutionary leadership. While prosperity and popular redistributive policies continued at least until the first shortages were seriously felt in 1961, the leadership was highly successful in selling its revolutionary fait accompli to the great majority of Cubans.

Aside from the mass support produced by the internal political and economic situation of 1959, there had also been a spontaneous growth of anti-imperialist sentiment among the Cuban people. The liberal explanations of well-intentioned American "mistakes" ceased to be accepted by great numbers of Cubans during 1959 and 1960. Whether or not Castro fabricated some accusations in order to exacerbate that sentiment,[15] there was little need for Castro to create artificially a popular reaction among a people awakening and becoming more conscious of its subordination to American imperialism, the reality of which was constantly being proven by the actions of the American power structure itself. Boris Goldenberg, an anti-Castro writer, has described how Washington refused financial support to the Castro regime; demanded rapid and adequate compensation for lands confiscated as part of the agrarian reform; politically supported even the most reactionary Cuban refugees; failed to halt piratical air incursions into Cuban territory; suspended the Cuban sugar quota in reaction to the expropriation of oil companies; and summoned the Mexican ambassador to the State Department to explain the pro-Castro flavor of a prominent Mexican's speech. The autumn 1960 television debates between Kennedy and Nixon fanned the flames of the anti-imperialist fire: "Kennedy upheld the Monroe Doctrine and criticized the economic measures taken against Cuba as 'too little and too late,' recommending collective, direct OAS intervention. Nixon declared such proposals to be irresponsible, while secretly backing the coming invasion attempt."[16]

In the course of a few months, the anti-imperialist spirit of 1933 had regained full force after a long period of decline and the rise of pro-American sentiment in the forties and early fifties. But, unlike the 1933 situation, the Cuban leadership and people were now in a far better position to fight United States imperialism than practically any other country in the history of Latin America. The slate of old Cuban institutions, particularly the traditional army, had been swept clean; there had been relatively little destruction during the fight against Batista. Unlike the 1933 Revolution in Cuba, there was practically no political sectarianism (such as the Third Period policy of the Comintern) in the aftermath of the 1959 Revolution. Finally, and most importantly, there was no Platt Amendment to provide immediate legitimation for a direct military presence in Cuban territory, nor was there, in the absence of the Platt Amendment, a traditional Cuban army that could be used by the United States as they had used the Guatemalan army to overthrow the duly elected government of Jacobo Arbenz.

However, the United States still had a very powerful weapon: its economic ties with and control of crucial sectors of the Cuban economy. Unlike the disorganized and disoriented Cuban bourgeoisie, the United States was able to take the offensive with this powerful weapon and to escalate its economic punishments as Castro expropriated North American investments in the island. In this situation, Castro was not able to attack various North American financial interests one at a time as he had done with the Cuban bourgeoisie. The elimination of the Cuban sugar quota in the summer of 1960 began the American economic squeeze of Cuba, which was soon followed by a more general economic embargo. The Soviet Union stated its willingness to bail Cuba out of this situation of economic emergency. From this fact some have leaped to the conclusion that Castro had no choice but to "go Communist," a fallacious logic that ignores the fact that similar or worse economic crises took place in Sekou Touré's Guinea and Nasser's Egypt, neither of which became Communist in spite of the fact that Russia bailed them out too. As Guevara told the French weekly *L'Express* on July

25, 1963, "Our commitment to the eastern bloc was half the fruit of constraint and half the result of choice."

The first two years of the revolution marked what was in essence a consumers' revolution rather than a developmental revolution. The main subject of talk was *reivindicaciones* (material demands of a more or less immediate kind) rather than economic development as such, although everybody was for the latter as well; there was no serious discussion of how the two were related to each other. The agrarian reform was seen mostly along the lines of social justice and of the improvement of the living standards of agricultural wage workers and peasants. This does not contradict my earlier contention that political radicalization was indeed taking place among the Cuban people; but it was a distinct kind of radicalization which at this time had little, if anything, to do with the state-collectivist ideology and practice eventually established in the country. Castro had at least once expressed his concern with this kind of "redistributive radicalism":

> One of the past epochs is still in the minds of the people. . . . I have found it in rallies, in working-class rallies, for example. I have seen that in these rallies banners and demands are put forward in the same tone that was used when there was a nonrevolutionary Council of Ministers, a nonrevolutionary government. . . . The masses don't realize that this is their government, that this is the government of the people, not at the service of vested interests, that for the first time in our history there is a government which is based on popular majorities. . . . One gets the sensation that they still have in mind the idea that government and people are two different things.[17]

It should be made clear that Castro is not talking here in the fashion of a Kerensky facing Bolshevik-type demonstrations demanding social revolution; rather, he speaks as a popular prime minister in a period of revolutionary change facing what might at times have been "exorbitant" but were still fundamentally trade-union-type demands which had resulted from a combination of the pent-up working-class aspirations held back by the repressive Batista regime and the very political climate Fidel Castro himself had stimulated through his various speeches and early redistributive measures.

In this context, it is easy to understand the complaints in later years of Communist trade-union officials (who were placed in office by Castro after most of the former "Humanista" leadership democratically elected in 1959 had been purged) about the Cuban working-class's low productivity, its absenteeism, and the like. Now, the trade unions had become not the defense organizations of the workers but state organizations, the main purpose of which was to help organize and stimulate higher production. When workers resisted the abolition of pay for Sundays and holidays, Lázaro Peña, a top Communist trade-union leader, complained:

> Under capitalism we struggled for the opposite and we gained it from the employers as one of our then limited material gains. It was like an extra in a miserly salary.
>
> Today we should see its elimination not as something essentially economic, but as [something] political, concerning the revolutionary morality of the working class. Now, no conscious worker should try to collect money unjustifiably without working for it, because, unlike before, it does not affect the profits of any employer but selfishly detracts from the welfare of the whole population.[18]

This was just the beginning of what later became increasing pressures from the official trade-union leaders, party members, and state administrators for "voluntary" work in the canefields, overtime work without pay, repeated "voluntary" collections for a variety of causes, and the imposition of the whole philosophy of "moral" as against "material" incentives about which workers had no choice and over which they exercised no control of any kind.

This is not to say that the revolutionary government had little to offer in the way of material gains to most sectors of the population. Without a doubt, the government scored some very significant successes in raising the standard of living of at least the poorest 25 percent of the population, improving public health, eliminating many racially discriminatory practices, in education and sports and athletics, and extending other social services. On the other side of the balance sheet we have to note important material failures: the inadequate supply of most consumer goods, both Cuban and foreign; the continuing and even increasing economic predominance of sugar; and the shortage and progressive deterioration of facilities, particularly transportation and housing in the urban areas, where more than half of the population resides. As a result, discontent has arisen; of course, this discontent is not necessarily expressed in articulate, organized opposition, but it has produced a situation different from the initial period of almost unanimous support for Castro.

Manipulation and Repression

To understand the Cuban Revolution as it evolved under the leadership of Fidel Castro it is crucial to be aware of the building of an initial fund of overwhelming popular support, but it is no less crucial to understand *how* that popular support was handled and indeed manipulated by the Fidelista leadership. For at least two years, Castro never offered, even to his most ardent followers, any specific program or long-range perspective explaining where he intended to go politically. His method was to make sudden decisions and then present them to the people as faits accomplis. Castro's personal control allowed him to do a considerable amount of political window-shopping during the early stages of the revolution without committing himself to any specific course of action. Thus, for some months after the overthrow of Batista, he did not nationalize the foreign public utilities,[19] even though this had been a classic demand of the Cuban moderate Left dating back to at least the Ortodoxo party in the late forties. Interestingly enough, President Urrutia had shown much greater rigidity and intransigence than Castro on such matters as the abolition of *all* gambling (whether for tourists or for Cubans) and on the granting of safe-conducts to those Batistianos who had obtained asylum in various Latin American embassies. In all these decisions, Castro showed that he possessed a keen pragmatic sense of when and where it was worth making a fight, and that, as much as possible, he would choose the most advantageous issue and moment for each fight.

This personalistic modus operandi clearly had certain advantages from the narrow, tactical perspective of defeating given enemies at a minimum cost, particularly when it was accompanied by the very shrewd tactic of taking one enemy at a time, a tactic Castro pursued during the period of revolutionary consolidation. But, if a political leader is engaged in the task not only of achieving power but of leading a social revolution from below, then such tactics also prevent his ranks and supporters from developing their own political consciousness in an autonomous fashion so that they will, as Marx would put it, cease being the objects and become the subjects of history.

Castro's manipulative philosophy sometimes involved direct misrepresentation, as is suggested by the agrarian reform legislated in 1959 and the quite different one eventually implemented. Whether Castro is or has been a *conscious* liar is of little interest and would in any event be impossible to determine; but misrepresentation, conscious or unconscious, has definitely been a part of his policy. As his staunch supporter Joseph P. Morray has commented:

> The mark of a true revolutionary is that the content of his policy goes beyond his phrases. He must make it effective before it is understood by the guardians of the old order, lest it provoke an inconvenient prevention. . . . Castro has demonstrated this quality. Other Latin American leaders have condemned United States imperialism in phrase and then collaborated with it by seeking aid and loans that have as their principal function the creation of an attractive climate for private investment from the capital-exporting countries. By contrast, Castro's tone was moderate and conciliatory towards the United States. He had dropped the imperialism-baiting of his student days. He was not even identifying foreign private investment with imperialism. Many months would pass before Castro as Prime Minister would join the Communists in hurling the unforgivable epithet "imperialist," which is also a manifesto, at the United States.[20]

This is not to suggest that leaders cannot or should not change policies, given a change in circumstances; but, to take an extreme example, it never would have occurred to V. I. Lenin to pretend he had established the New Economic Policy in the early twenties because he had suddenly been converted to social democracy or capitalism. So we are faced not merely with a question of changing policies but with one of misrepresenting one's politics to both opponents and supporters, which means that the political leader ends up manipulating both.

Such manipulative methods, together with the spying functions of the CDR (Committees for the Defense of the Revolution), the activities of the secret police, the purging of many individuals and groups, and the elimination of all opposition or independent newspapers and magazines (in the summer of 1960, when there was no "clear and present danger" to the government at all), completed the tripod upon which Castro consolidated his power: popular support, manipulation of that support, and repression. When the first two could not be trusted to secure the government's power, the third took over.

At one point, many students of Cuban society (including this writer) underestimated the power of Castro and his immediate inner circle and assumed that the Old Communists, because of their organizational effectiveness and international connections, would eventually achieve a predominant role in the Cuban government. That this did not occur was partly the result of changes in the international situation, particularly the increasing divisions within the international Communist movement, which created more favorable conditions for Castro to increase his bargaining power and control the Old Guard. By the mid-sixties, most of the leading Old Communists had been displaced from the most important positions in the state apparatus. They had retained a declining but still significant representation on the Central Committee (which hardly ever met) and on the Secretariat of the Cuban Communist party (its new name after 1965), but *not* in the crucial Political Bureau which had remained completely Fidelista in composition.[21] Castro did not become a façade or figurehead serving the Old Communist leadership. Castro did not have to follow the old recipes of the Moscow-controlled Communists in Cuba. Nor did he follow the road to power which "classical" Marxism assumed was necessary for victory. Morray has described Castro's revolution in terms that must shake Marx, Lenin, and Trotsky in their graves:

The proletariat took power in Cuba through the conversion to Marxism-Leninism of a government of lawyers. The initiative came from above, not by insurrection from below. . . . Blas Roca, the Secretary General of the Cuban Communist Party . . . declared on November 27, 1961, that the Ministers, despite their bourgeois backgrounds (and, he could have added, despite their non-Leninist pre-October salaries of 600 pesos per month) had become workers and trusted representatives of the working class. He and the other theoreticians of the dissolved Party, writing in *Hoy*, echo and approve Castro's characterization of Cuba as a "proletarian state." . . . One big task still uncompleted, is to convince workers to accept the proffered honor and burden. They are still diffident. They still expect to be told what to do. Through Castro, who is the Cuban Soviet, the workers discover their own interest and participate in the direction of society by ratifying his initiatives.[22]

The Role of Raúl Castro
and Ché Guevara

To comprehend the process by which Castro chose the road of Cuban Communism, it is necessary to understand the role played by Raúl Castro and Ché Guevara, two very powerful figures in the revolution who undoubtedly had great influence on Castro's thoughts and actions. Both Raúl Castro and Ché Guevara had had relations with the international Communist movement and/or its peripheral individuals and organizations. Raúl Castro not only traveled with a student delegation to a "peace congress" in Prague but actually applied for admission to the youth section of the Partido Socialista Popular (Communist party) in June of 1953,[23] although it seems that the Communist party still knew nothing of the preparations for the July 1953 Moncada attack in which Raúl participated. Ernesto "Ché" Guevara was friendly with prominent members of the so-called Latin American democratic Left but also seems to have had the widest acquaintance with Marxist theory of all those in the revolutionary leadership. He participated in the Guatemalan events of 1954; however, he did not join the Argentinian, Guatemalan, or Cuban Communist parties but remained in the vague and often misleading category of "independent Marxist." Guevara was politically more sophisticated than either of the Castro brothers, and his outlook was apparently less narrow than theirs. He seems to have impressed upon the revolutionary leadership the importance of the Guatemalan experience and the lessons to be derived from it in regard to the role of American imperialism and of traditional Latin American armies. In addition his ascetic views had a strong influence on an ideology that would eventually identify socialism with scarcity, not with abundance.

There is no question that although Fidel was and always remained the undisputed maximum leader and could not have been politically challenged by either Guevara or his brother, the latter two did play more than one crucial role. For a while they diverted the apprehensions of the moderates and bourgeois elements toward their own "extremism," particularly after Castro had appointed his brother as successor. But, more importantly, the drastic measures they proposed were always one step ahead of Castro's pronouncements and actions. Whether as a result of a conscious political agreement with Fidel or because of differences of opinion, both Raúl Castro and Ché Guevara remained aloof from Fidel Castro's friendlier approach to the United States in April and May of 1959 and from his short-lived encouragement of "humanism." Many have contended that Raúl Castro's trip to Houston in April of 1959 to speak to his brother on the latter's way to Buenos Aires was mostly the result of Raúl's anger at Fidel's conciliatory gestures toward the United States. Also, at a point when there was still considerable distrust between the Communist Old Guard and Fidel Castro, Raúl and Ché helped to provide a transmission belt of reconciliation and agreement between these two key elements of what would be the future political merger of Old and New Communists.

Morray has accurately described Raúl Castro and Ché Guevara as "the architects and champions of a conscious and proclaimed policy of 'unity' between Communists and non-Communists. . . . They served as a channel of Communist influence on Fidel, neutralizing the petty bourgeois prejudices stimulated by the civilian leadership of the 26th of July Movement."[24] This does not mean that, during 1959 at least, either Guevara or Raúl Castro was making open pro-Communist statements. Even if they had felt like speaking openly on behalf of the PSP, Raúl Castro and Ché Guevara were, unlike the Old Communists, part and parcel of Fidel Castro's government, and at this point they would not have been able to afford or allow such excessive pro-Communism. What Ché and Raúl did was to provide the initial legitimation for the anti–anti-Communist stand initially taken by the PSP and eventually adopted by Fidel Castro himself. A somewhat paradoxical situation resulted in that, while neither Raúl nor Ché was making open pro-Communist statements, they were often in fact more drastic in their pronouncements than the PSP itself. Thus, the PSP would often denounce right-wing anti-Communists while mildly criticizing, without mentioning names, the harm created by leftist extremists who unduly frighten the petty bourgeoisie, and so on. They were referring mostly to Raúl Castro and Ché Guevara, particularly to the latter.[25]

It is important to note that, although Raúl and Ché had a certain following of their own based on their more drastic proposals, neither of them was nearly as charismatic or popular with the Cuban people as was Fidel Castro; therefore, they were highly dependent on Fidel. In a strict technical sense, it could be said that they were much more *influential* than powerful. Also, although their pronouncements were usually more drastic than Fidel's, this was true only on a day-to-day basis. During the first two years of the revolution, Raúl and Ché did not offer a long-range political or programmatic perspective to the Cuban people or even to their own following any more than Fidel did, a fact that can probably best be explained by their dependence on Fidel Castro. The only group that was at this point providing a methodology and a perspective to a sizable number of Cubans who were moving in a revolutionary direction was the PSP, which was thus able to exert an influence way beyond its numbers.

The Role of the Old Communists

The leadership and rank and file of the largely discredited Partido Socialista Popular behaved rather cautiously during the early stages of the revolutionary regime. The contrast with the Communists' behavior during the Revolution of 1933 could not have been greater. By the time of Batista's overthrow, the Communists had become isolated and had dwindled in number,[26] which was sufficient reason for caution. More importantly, unlike 1933, they did not have to follow the sometimes almost suicidal policies of the Comintern's Third Period. In 1959, the policies of the international Communist movement left more elbow room for dealings with other sectors of the Left and with nationalist movements. In early 1959 the Communist press in Cuba followed the usual policy of praising the Soviet Union and the "socialist countries" and attacking the United States in the international field. Domestically it strongly denounced all members of the revolutionary regime, supporters and detractors, who openly expressed anti-Communist sentiment; at the same time it in fact gave the benefit of the doubt to those who might have been anti-Communists but did not make a point of saying so.

As far as Fidel Castro was concerned, at least during the first half of 1959, the Communist party operated as a sort of gentle pressure group trying to move him as far to the Left as possible while avoiding some of the more drastic pronouncements of Ché Guevara and Raúl Castro. This may come as a surprise to those who have accepted the unexamined myth that Castro had *always* been to the Left of the Old Communists, a myth based on a confusion of activism with stands on social questions. There is no doubt that the open and stated policies of the Communists, at least until May of 1959, were more drastic than those of Fidel Castro and the 26th of July Movement. Thus, the Communist party saw its task during this period as one of supporting the revolutionary leadership while pushing it to the Left. As Blas Roca put it: "The key task of this moment *is to defend the revolution and to make it advance.*"[27]

This Communist policy, while full of praise for Fidel Castro and particularly for the early anti–anti-Communist stance of Ché Guevara and Raúl Castro (although sometimes deploring some of their more extreme statements, which might alienate the "progressive" sectors of the middle classes), could not help but bring it into some friction with the revolutionary government. Thus, the Communists openly criticized the six months' no-strike pledge made by the trade-union leadership of the 26th of July Movement, which was fully committed to the revolutionary government, to assure the stability of the regime. As Blas Roca put it in an article in the daily Communist newspaper *Hoy* on February 10, 1959, "Strikes, when they are necessary and just, do not harm the revolution but help it."[28] Without doubt, Roca had scored an excellent point here. However, it was based on a methodology which dictated that, because industry was still owned by the capitalists and because the Communists were neither in control of nor participants in the government, strikes were in order; when the situation later changed so that all industries were nationalized and the Communists were in the government, they of course became the most vehement opponents of any form of strike or trade-union defense actions on the part of the workers (as did Castro and the rest of the revolutionary leadership). In the meantime, however, this Communist position was an irritant to the Fidelista leadership, which was thinking primarily in terms of the stability of a government that had been faced with a wave of strikes in its very early stages.

Along the same lines, more serious friction was caused when it appeared that some Communists had encouraged a few instances of "spontaneous" land seizure. This Communist action provoked Fidel Castro into making some of his strongest anti-Communist remarks of the 1959 period. He had unambiguously stated his position on the question of land distribution in a television interview on February 19, 1959:

> We are opposed to anarchic land distribution. We have drafted a law which stipulates that [persons involved in] any land distribution which is made without waiting for the new agrarian law will lose their

rights to benefits from the new agrarian reform. Those who have appropriated lands from January 1 to the present date have no right to those lands. Any provocation to distribution of lands disregarding the revolutionaries and the agrarian law is criminal.[29]

The Communist party quite cautiously backtracked on what may have been a political experiment on its part, and a few days after Castro's speech it endorsed Castro's land distribution policy. Andrés Suarez pointed out that the PSP had encouraged squatting. However, once Law 87 of February 20 was published in the official *Gazette,* the party nevertheless acknowledged in *Hoy* (February 22, 1959) "that it was necessary to put a stop to the anarchic seizures of land."[30]

From January to May 1959, the Communists had reservations about a possible turn to the Right by the Castro government, reservations that were aggravated by Castro's trip to the United States in April 1959. Thus, the conclusions of the May Plenum of the PSP were even more guarded than previous ones and clearly showed some political pessimism. In spite of all these reservations, however, the Communists continued to support the Castro government. Their patience was rewarded in late 1959 and afterward, when Castro turned so far to the Left that the Old Communists started having serious reservations about his "extremist excesses."

A very important aspect of the activities of the PSP in the early stages of the revolution was the kinds of relationships developed between the party and a variety of non–anti-Communist revolutionaries. In the absence of any other political party (the Directorio had quickly submitted to Castro after the January incident) that could provide a world view to large numbers of militant revolutionaries, and particularly to younger people, there is no question that the PSP, despite its vulgar Marxism and traditional subservience to Russia, was able to exert political influence disproportionate to the number of party members. In a country that was in political motion in a decidedly leftward but diffuse direction, the existence of a political program, both for the long and the short run, and of systematic explanations for various problems facing the country and the world, no matter how opportunistic, crude, and totalitarian, could not help but have significant influence on the minds of many revolutionaries who had not had the time or the inclination to form any crystallized negative attitudes toward Communism. Many of these revolutionaries would pick up the PSP's daily *Hoy* and find that its contents were somehow attractive to them, particularly when many of *Hoy*'s positions were later taken by Castro himself. At the same time, because the Communists were supporting Castro, these revolutionaries were not put in a position of having to choose between Castro and the Communists. Had they been, they would certainly have chosen the former.

By and large, the Communists had adopted what was essentially an ideological and organizational permeationist policy vis-à-vis the revolutionary leadership and rank and file. In pursuit of this subtle policy, the Communist party did *not* engage in any kind of significant recruitment campaign although its membership probably increased during 1959. This policy was not adopted without disagreement within the party leadership itself, however. A minority, led by Aníbal Escalante, had analyzed the Cuban situation in terms of the "Chinese road" (as he called it) in which the party, while acknowledging the leadership and wisdom of Castro, would try to play a vanguard role on its own by vigorously recruiting to its own ranks the most "advanced sectors" of revolutionary opinion (presumably even people like Guevara, Raúl Castro, and/or their followers) and even try to obtain positions of leadership.[31] The party instead adopted the position put forward by Carlos Rafael Rodríguez (the Communist leader closest to Castro) and Blas Roca, which was far more cautious in its bid for influence and power. There is little question that the adoption of this line greatly encouraged Castro's eventual choice of the Communist road, because it was sufficiently flexible and subtle so as not to present an immediate threat to Castro's leadership, which might have made him turn in a quite different political direction. As it happened, the Escalante line retained sufficient strength within Communist circles and eventually presented a threat to Castro after the latter had firmly committed himself to Communism. As we know, Escalante was first purged on March of 1962 when he tried to pack the various positions of state power with Old Communists to the detriment of the younger Communists who were of Fidelista background. Even the well-organized and Russian-backed Cuban Communists could not ignore or set aside the overwhelming power of Fidel Castro's leadership and personal control.

The International Communist Movement

The cautious policy of most of the PSP leadership toward Fidel Castro and their continued support for him, even in April and May of 1959 when they were being attacked by Fidelistas (including Fidel himself), left room for a possible merger of the two forces in a way that did not threaten the hegemony of the Fidelista leadership. At the same time, the development of "polycentrism" in the Communist world permitted the growth and development of the peculiar brand of Cuban Communism shaped and formed by Fidel Castro rather than by the Old Guard of the PSP. As Edward González has pointed out, even the leadership of the pro-Russian PSP was able to exert pressure on the Soviet Union in order to extract greater commitments to the Castro-led revolution.[32] For example, at various times *Hoy* pointedly gave more prominence to the Chinese than to the Russians in their coverage of various international events; thus they were able to make use of techniques that would have been impossible a few years before. As time went by, the ever growing schisms in the international Communist movement provided a setting that helped Castro to become even more independent from the Cuban Communist Old Guard to the point of leaving them in a frankly subordinate position. Thus, from 1960 to 1962 the PSP leadership had been close to being at least an equal partner in the running of the Cuban state apparatus (part of which was undoubtedly the result of their having had more available organizational talents). The Escalante purge of March 1962, which was at least ostensibly supported by the rest of the PSP leadership, marked the beginning of the PSP subordination to Castro and his inner circle of loyal Fidelistas. At the same time, the subordination of the PSP to Castro must have been a popular move which enhanced Castro's prestige with his followers because this move symbolized the fact that he was not going to be a mere puppet of Moscow.

Yet, while Castro could quite easily subordinate the Cuban Communist Old Guard to his wishes, his relations with Moscow were a much more delicate and difficult matter. While he would directly or indirectly criticize Moscow's policies, his great economic dependence on the Soviet Union placed limits on his freedom of action, particularly in the fields of foreign policy and internal economic planning. Castro's encouragement of guerrilla warfare throughout Latin America and his attacks on various Latin American Communist parties did not ingratiate him with Russia; however, it is likely that Castro would have engaged in an even more aggressive foreign policy, particularly in Latin America, if it had not been for Moscow's economic pressure. As far as the Cuban economy is concerned, Moscow's pressure must have been a very weighty factor in Castro's decision to reverse his and Guevara's earlier plans for rapid diversification and industrialization, a policy that had been very badly and irrationally administered by Guevara's Ministry of Industries. This waste infuriated the Russians, who already had other self-serving reasons not to be favorably inclined toward the creation of a diversified and relatively independent Cuban economy. In any event, Castro implemented a policy based, more than ever before in Cuban history, on sugar. He hoped that the production of sugar would bring quicker returns in terms of foreign exchange earnings with which he could start paying Cuba's ever mounting debts to the Soviet Bloc countries that had been virtually subsidizing the Cuban economy. Castro also eventually abandoned his support for guerrilla movements in Latin America and established a foreign policy of friendship with governments in the Western hemisphere that are even slightly independent of the United States State Department (e.g., Panamá, Peru, Venezuela, and most of the former British West Indies), while providing personnel for the implementation of Russian foreign policy goals in countries like Angola.

An Overview

The character of the movement that succeeded in overthrowing the Batista dictatorship was closely related to the character of Cuban society in the years after the Revolution of 1933, which was a watershed in Cuban history. Perhaps the most distinctive traits of this revolution were an active working class and mass participation; both were absent in 1959. Initially, political victories were achieved in the thirties against a weak oligarchy that collapsed in the face of a popular upsurge and the absence of American protection. Yet, this revolution was eventually frustrated, and it failed to resolve permanently any of Cuba's major social problems. It could be said that a half-baked oligarchy had provoked a half-baked social revolution. It was no accident that the 1933 Revolution produced no permanent resolution of any major social question but led first to open counter-revolution and then to a variety of state-capitalist compromises that established the basis for the unstable social and political modus vivendi of the next two decades of Cuban history. No class emerged completely hegemonic after this revolution, and, although capitalism and imperialism strongly consolidated themselves in Cuba, a capitalist *ruling* class of equal strength did not consolidate itself.

This apparent paradox is clarified when we appreciate the importance acquired by the state apparatus in the years after the 1933 upheaval. There was no strong and hegemonic capitalist class capable of dealing with the various crises of the country; rather, a group of powerful but politically inadequate capitalists and their middle-class allies accepted or supported a variety of Bonapartist and liberal political agents which then "faced" these crises on their behalf. It would be hopeless to try to explain all the striking and bizarre twists and turns of Cuban politics in this period only in terms of fundamental class analyses, for the state apparatus and the political system had become somewhat autonomous and separated from the most fundamental social classes. In this period, the Cuban political system deflected as well as reflected the fundamental problems of Cuban society.

This is why the 1933–59 period is primarily characterized by one or another form of Bonapartist rule. The relatively brief attempt at constitutional politics was bound to fail, given the social structural conditions described above. The weaknesses of all social classes had set the framework within which all political parties, reformist as well as traditional, were totally discredited and collapsed not long after Batista's 1952 coup. There were no important and lasting moves toward the creation of an independent non-Communist revolutionary party; the weakness of the working class movement and Castro's opposition would have been decisive obstacles to any such attempts.

As I have pointed out, the opposition to Batista was not led either by any of the older parties or politicians or by working-class, peasant, or middle-class leaders and movements. Instead, an essentially declassé nontraditional leadership organized a heterogeneous coalition which included conservatives, reformists, and revolutionaries. After Batista's overthrow, Castro easily dissolved this coalition, with the eventual aim of creating a fundamentally different power base and social system.

From 1959 to 1960, under Fidel Castro's leadership, the Cuban Revolution turned sharply against capitalism, both native and foreign, and laid the basis for the establishment of a Communist system. These drastic changes were partly a reaction to the resistance offered to earlier revolutionary measures, and partly an act of choice. Native and foreign resistance created problems that had to be solved. Castro and his close associates chose one specific set or system of solutions. This choice was made possible because, while United States opposition to Castro was formidable, internal opposition was weak.

Domestically, Castro's freedom of action was considerable, for there was no important Cuban political alternative to Castro in 1959–60. Such groups as the Auténticos, the Ortodoxos, and the liberal elements of the anti-Batista underground had by this time been completely discredited and/or had organizationally disintegrated.

Bonapartism and populism were the predominant themes in Cuban politics during 1933–59: and both of these were in turn a reflection of weak social classes and weak political organization. In the last analysis this is why the road to the establishment of Communism in Cuba was not through a revolution initially carried out with the active involvement of a workers' or peasants' movement. Cuban Communism was brought about by a unique movement fundamentally different from those that preceded the establishment of Communism in other countries.

Since then, Castro's revolutionary Bonapartism has gradually evolved into a less transitional and more institutionalized Cuban version of the bureaucratic collectivist class societies that currently exist in Eastern Europe and Asia. Whether the newly developing Cuban ruling class would and/or could completely dispense with Castro's revolutionary Bonapartism remains to be seen. This, like other questions concerning present-day Cuban society, is beyond the scope of this book.

Notes

Preface

1. From a speech given by Fidel Castro in October 1965 and originally published in *Política* (Mexico), no. 131 (October 1, 1965); cited in David J. Finlay, Ole R. Holsti, and Richard R. Fagen, *Enemies in Politics* (Chicago: Rand McNally, 1967), p. 196.

2. From a speech given by Fidel Castro on August 23, 1968, quoted in *Granma* (weekly review, Havana), year 3, no. 34 (August 25, 1968), p. 2.

3. K. S. Karol, *Guerrillas in Power*, p. 330.

Chapter 1

1. Ernesto "Ché" Guevara rejected the notion of Cuban "exceptionalism" in his well-known article "Cuba: Exceptional Case?" It is worth noting, however, that even in this article Guevara had to acknowledge such unique Cuban factors as the peculiarities of Batista's army and the fact that Castro enjoyed the advantage of being the first Latin American leader to establish Communism, thus surprising United States imperialists. It should also be pointed out that later pro-Castro writers have been more willing to entertain the notion of Cuban exceptionalism. For example, this seems to have been the predominant assumption of most contributors to a symposium on the theories of Regis Debray (see "Regis Debray and the Latin American Revolution," *Monthly Review*, 20, no. 3 [July–August 1968]). This view seems to be shared by still another pro-Castro writer, Dennis B. Wood, in his article "The Long Revolution."

2. For a comprehensive account of the pre-Castro economy, see James O'Connor, *The Origins of Socialism in Cuba*.

3. The controversies concerning the class nature of the French Revolution illustrate many of the issues raised here. See the excellent discussion in Barrington Moore, Jr., *Social Origins of Dictatorship and Democracy*. See also George Rudé, *The Crowd in the French Revolution* (London, Oxford, New York: Oxford University Press, 1959).

4. Leo Huberman and Paul M. Sweezy, *Cuba: Anatomy of a Revolution*, esp. pp. 56–59, 80–83.

5. Guevara, "Cuba: Exceptional Case?" p. 59.

6. Leo Huberman and Paul M. Sweezy, "Cuba Revisited," esp. pp. 414–15. Years later Huberman and Sweezy adopted a significantly different analysis of the Cuban Revolution. See Huberman and Sweezy, *Socialism in Cuba.*

7. Regis Debray, "Revolution in the Revolution?"

8. Ernesto "Ché" Guevara, *Reminiscences of the Cuban Revolutionary War*, pp. 208–9, 210.

9. Rolando E. Bonachea and Nelson P. Valdés, *Revolutionary Struggle, 1947–1958*, p. 376.

10. Those who took part in Fidel Castro's attack on the Moncada barracks in 1953 or sailed with him to Cuba aboard the *Granma* in 1956, when he returned from exile in Mexico.

11. Hugh Thomas, "Middle Class Politics and the Cuban Revolution," in Claudio Veliz, ed., *The Politics of Conformity in Latin America*, issued under the auspices of the Royal Institute of International Affairs (London, New York, Toronto: Oxford University Press, 1967), p. 261. See also Carlos Franqui, *The Twelve.*

12. Maurice Zeitlin, *Revolutionary Politics and the Cuban Working Class*, pp. 277–78.

13. Ibid., pp. 3–4, 8. I also have serious doubts about the validity of Zeitlin's survey findings. His survey was conducted in 1962, *after* widespread purges of democratically elected trade-union leaders and the introduction of various other repressive measures. A great number of workers undoubtedly supported the revolution at that time, but Zeitlin assumes that he was able to discriminate between those workers who were telling him the truth and those who were merely protecting themselves. This is particularly important when we consider that Zeitlin was officially authorized by the Cuban government to conduct his research. Carmelo Mesa-Lago has also questioned the representativeness of the workers interviewed by Zeitlin. See Carmelo Mesa-Lago, "Availability and Reliability of Statistics in Socialist Cuba."

14. *Granma* (weekly review, Havana), year 5, no. 31 (August 2, 1970), p. 3. This speech was also published in the *New York Review of Books* 15, no. 5 (September 24, 1970).

15. National Agricultural Census of Cuba of 1946, as quoted in Lowry Nelson, *Rural Cuba*, p. 135.

16. For figures on the concentration of workers and size of plants in Cuba, see O'Connor, *Origins of Socialism in Cuba*, p. 141.

17. For a quantitative breakdown of the Cuban occupational structure, see United States Department of Commerce, Bureau of Foreign Commerce, *Investment in Cuba*, p. 183.

18. United States Department of Labor, Bureau of Labor Statistics, Foreign Labor Information, *Labor in Cuba*, p. 3.

19. Theodore Draper, *Castro's Revolution*, p. 10.

20. Theodore Draper, "Cuba: The Runaway Revolution," p. 15.

21. Theodore Draper, *Castroism: Theory and Practice*, p. 133.

22. Karl Marx, *The Class Struggles in France, 1848 to 1850;* and idem, *The Eighteenth Brumaire of Louis Bonaparte.*

23. Marx, *Class Struggles in France,* p. 64.

24. Marx, *Eighteenth Brumaire,* p. 124.

25. Ibid., p. 75.

26. Ibid., pp. 128–29.

27. Hal Draper, "Marx and Bolívar: A Note on Authoritarian Leadership in a National-Liberation Movement."

28. Engels to Marx, April 13, 1866, in Karl Marx and Frederich Engels, *Selected Correspondence, 1846–1895.*

29. Edward Bernstein, *Ferdinand Lassalle as a Social Reformer,* trans. Eleanor Marx Aveling (London: Swan Sonnenschein; New York: Scribners, 1893).

30. Leon Trotsky, *The Revolution Betrayed,* pp. 97–98.

31. Russel B. Porter interview with Fulgencio Batista, *New York Times,* July 5, 1936.

32. Emeterio S. Santovenia and Raúl M. Shelton, *Cuba y su Historia* 3: 225. "Prebends" refers to state revenues appropriated by individual officeholders.

33. Thomas, "Middle Class Politics and the Cuban Revolution," in Claudio Veliz, ed., *Politics of Conformity in Latin America,* pp. 259–61. See also a more recent analysis in Thomas, *Cuba,* chs. 68 and 73, and app. xi.

34. James O'Connor, "On Cuban Political Economy," pp. 236–37, 238, 239.

35. See Leon Trotsky, *The History of the Russian Revolution;* and Crane Brinton, *The Anatomy of Revolution* (New York: Vintage Books, 1965).

Chapter 2

1. Manuel Pedro González and Iván E. Schulman, *José Martí: Esquema Ideológico* (Mexico City: Publicaciones de la Editorial Cultura, 1961), pp. 385–86.

2. Ibid.

3. I should add a comment here on Martí's strong disapproval of racial hatred and discrimination, which had a positive effect on Cuban politics. As C. A. M. Hennessy has written, "Martí's social ideas were permeated by a mystical sense of unity, a secularised version of Christian love, which found one expression in his passionate feeling for the poor, and which embraced the enslaved whom he carefully drew into his revolutionary party. There should be complete racial equality in the new society. 'There is no racial problem', he wrote, 'because there are no races, only humanity' " (C. A. M. Hennessy, "The Roots of Cuban Nationalism," p. 356).

4 Ibid., pp. 349–50, 356.

5. The question of whether Cuba would have eventually defeated Spain without United States intervention has long troubled Cuban historians who have argued among themselves and with foreign historians. Some "revisionists," notably Emilio Roig de Leuchsenring, have claimed that the North American intervention robbed Cuba of its imminent victory. The revisionists rightly renamed the Spanish-American war the "Spanish-Cuban-American War." For a clear exposition and discussion of these polemics, see Robert F. Smith, "Twentieth Century Cuban Historiography," pp. 44–73.

6. The complete text of the Platt Amendment is in Wyatt MacGaffey and Clifford R. Barnett, *Twentieth Century Cuba*, p. 17.

7. Machado "was connected with the public utilities business and had close relations with the Electric Bond and Share and with other American business" (Robert F. Smith, *The United States and Cuba*, pp. 113–14).

Some of the flavor of Cuban politics in this period is conveyed in H. L. Mencken's "Gore in the Caribbees," *The Vintage Mencken*, compiled by Alistair Cooke (New York: Vintage Books, 1958), pp. 57–67. For good summaries of Cuban political and social history up to the early thirties, see Leland H. Jenks, "Cuba Faces a New Deal," in A. Curtis Wilgus, ed., *The Caribbean Area* (Washington, D.C.: George Washington University Press, 1934); and Dennis B. Wood, "The Long Revolution."

8. Sidney W. Mintz, foreword to Ramiro Guerra, *Sugar and Society in the Caribbean*.

9. Robert B. Batchelder, "The Evolution of Cuban Land Tenure and Its Relation to Certain Agro-Economic Problems," p. 243.

10. Ibid.

11. Lino Novas Calvo, "La Tragedia de la Clase Media Cubana," pp. 28–29.

12. An example of this pattern from later in the century would be the case of Angel Castro, a Galician immigrant who became a wealthy landowner in Oriente Province and only one of whose sons, Ramón, followed in his father's footsteps. His two other sons were Fidel and Raúl Castro.

13. Guerra, *Sugar and Society in the Caribbean*, p. 67.

14. Mintz, in ibid., p. xxxviii.

15. Ibid., p. xxvii. Robert Manners and Julian Steward have made similar observations in Puerto Rico. Thus, in comparing workers on the sugar plantations with those on the coffee plantations, they point out that among sugar workers "collective activity through labor unions and political organizations has replaced personal appeals to the landowner as a device to gain economic and political objectives" (Robert A. Manners and Julian H. Steward, "The Cultural Study of Contemporary Societies: Puerto Rico," *American Journal of Sociology* 59, no. 2 [September 1953], reprinted in Lyle W. Shannon, ed., *Underdeveloped Areas* [New York: Harper and Brothers, 1958], p. 168).

16. Mintz, quoting Professor Wallich, in Guerra, *Sugar and Society in the Caribbean*, p. xxxiii.

17. Charles A. Thomson, "The Cuban Revolution: Fall of Machado," p. 254.

18. Ibid., p. 260.

19. Ibid.

20. *Problems of the New Cuba*, report of the Commission on Cuban Affairs (New York: Foreign Policy Association, January 1935), p. 183.

21. Rufo López Fresquet, *My 14 Months with Castro*, p. 5.

22. Ruby Hart Phillips, an observer of the Cuban scene for close to thirty years, many of them as *New York Times* correspondent in Cuba, described this situation as follows: "Realizing that the Cuban people would not support a military government headed by sergeants, they sent out cars and called members of the *Directorio Es-*

tudiantil. The students rushed to the camp, thinking it was their own conspiracy. When they arrived, they decided that, so long as they were in it, they would support the military revolt and everyone shouted: 'Viva la República' " (Ruby Hart Phillips, *Cuba: Island of Paradox*, p. 63).

23. Luis E. Aguilar, *Cuba 1933*, pp. 163–64.

24. United States Department of State, *Foreign Relations of the United States: Diplomatic Papers*, vol. 5, *The American Republics, 1933*, pp. 469–72.

25. Charles A. Thomson, "The Cuban Revolution: Reform and Reaction," p. 268.

26. Aguilar, *Cuba 1933*, pp. 181–82.

27. Ibid., p. 174. Aguilar fails to mention that the practice of compulsory arbitration of labor disputes was also regularized and fully institutionalized at this time.

28. "Support by the students and the lower echelon of the army did not provide a sufficient base to stabilize [Grau's] administration. He needed labor. He offered participation in his cabinet to the Communists, but they turned the offer down and even refused to advise him on social legislation. . . . With continuing United States hostility, the Grau administration proceeded on a deliberate campaign to foster nationalism in labor's ranks; then to accede to labor's demands. When the people massed in the square before the palace to demand some reform, Guiteras would see to it that a presidential decree was signed, sometimes within twenty-four hours" (Charles Albert Page, "The Development of Organized Labor in Cuba," pp. 76–77).

29. Carlos González Palacios, *Revolución y Seudo-Revolución en Cuba* (n.p., 1948), pp. 41–42.

30. *Problems of the New Cuba*, pp. 408–9.

31. Ibid., p. 202.

32. Ibid. It should be noted that this decree added other restrictions as well, all of which virtually eliminated the right to strike. As *Problems of the New Cuba* states on the same page, "The law also placed limitations on the exercise of sympathetic strikes, forbidding propaganda to impede work or foment strikes outside the limits of the labor sector affected by some demand, and prohibited general strikes endangering the public welfare by lack of light, water, telephones, telegraphs, medical service, pharmacies, fire protection, and transport. Employees in these branches were forbidden to suspend activities (Articles 4, 6, 7 and 8)."

33. Ibid., pp. 203–4.

34. "The interior contradictions between the ABC and the central command of the army forced the ABC to leap out of the Government and fall, without prestige or public confidence into opposition. The ABC began immediately to suffer the consequences of the fascistic legislation which it had itself drawn up. The monster was devouring its Frankenstein" (Aureliano Sánchez Arango, "The Recent General Strike in Cuba," pp. 10–15).

35. Thomson, "The Cuban Revolution: Reform and Reaction," pp. 273–74.

36. Ibid., p. 274.

37. "Particularly disconcerting is the fact that a bitter struggle among the politically ambitious has developed, thinly masked behind the veils of political parties and creeds. . . . There are at present no fewer than seventeen left-wing parties and

groups in Cuba, ranging from mild liberals to terrorists" (Frank L. Kluckhohn, reporting for the *New York Times*, March 13, 1935, p. 8).

38. Sánchez Arango, "Recent General Strike in Cuba," p. 13. This analysis is confirmed in its essentials by Charles A. Thomson, a historian of this period.

39. Aguilar, *Cuba 1933*, pp. 133–34.

40. For a more detailed treatment of many of the issues of this period see also Hugh Thomas, *Cuba: The Pursuit of Freedom;* and José A. Tabares, *La Revolución del 30.*

Chapter 3

1. On this point see the interesting article by Maurice Zeitlin, "Political Generations in the Cuban Working Class."

2. Ruby Hart Phillips, *Cuba: Island of Paradox*, pp. 47–48.

3. Ibid.

4. It is impossible to determine accurately the social composition of the ABC. All observers have agreed, however, that it was overwhelmingly middle class in character. Typical is the following description of it: "This interesting organization, composed mainly of young business and professional men, operated secretly during the closing years of Machado's regime and was an important element in his downfall" (Russell H. Fitzgibbon and H. Max Healey, "The Cuban Elections of 1936," *American Political Science Review* 30, no. 4 [August 1936]: 727.

5. Phillips, *Cuba*, pp. 17–18. Charles A. Thomson also refers to Sumner Welles's sympathy for the ABC on account of their social background; see Thomson, "The Cuban Revolution: Reform and Reaction," p. 268.

6. "El Manifiesto del ABC," in Carlos G. Peraza, *Machado: Crímenes y Horrores de un régimen* (Havana: Cultural, S.A., 1933), pp. 215–50.

7. Ibid., p. 243.

8. A group of authors from the generation of 1930 has pointed out the lack of ties between the ABC and the students on one hand and the organized working class on the other hand. They explain it in terms of the essentially middle-class character of both the ABC and the Student Directorate. See José Alvarez Díaz, A. Arredondo, R. M. Shelton, and J. F. Vizcaino, *Cuba: Geopolítica y Pensamiento Económico*, p. 305.

9. "El Manifiesto del ABC," in Peraza, *Machado*, p. 244.

10. Ibid., pp. 244–46.

11. Ibid., p. 246.

12. Ibid., p. 248.

13. Dr. Francisco Ichaso, "Algunos Aspectos del Ideario del ABC," in *Los Partidos Políticos y la Asamblea Constituyente* (Conferencias de Orientación Ciudadana, Club Atenas, February 13–May 15, 1939, Havana), p. 88.

14. For information concerning the Grupo de Avance and analyses of the role it played, see Rosario Rexach, "La Revista de *Avance* publicada en Habana, 1927–1930," *Caribbean Studies* 3, no. 3 (October 1963); Felix Lizaso, *Panorama de la Cultura Cubana* (Mexico City: Fondo de Cultura Económica, 1949), pp. 131–34; Cintio Vitier, *Lo Cubano en la Poesía* (Santa Clara: Departamento de Relaciones Culturales, Universidad Central de Las Villas, 1958), pp. 314–16; and Ambrosio Fornet, "Revaluaciones del Movimiento Cultural del 30."

15. Alvarez Díaz et al., *Cuba*, p. 305. This was not the case for the Ala Izquierda Estudiantil (Student Left Wing), which had a strong working-class orientation. But it was much less significant than the mainstream student movement led by the Directorio Estudiantil.

16. Ambassador Sumner Welles to the Secretary of State, September 16, 1933, in United States Department of State, *Foreign Relations of the United States: Diplomatic Papers*, vol. 5, *The American Republics, 1933*, p. 441.

17. Alvarez Díaz et al., *Cuba*, pp. 303–4. For a sympathetic view of similar movements throughout Latin America, see Robert J. Alexander, "The Latin American Aprista Parties"; and idem, " 'Aprismo' — Is it Socialist?"

18. In the meantime, Grau rejected overtures for a popular front with the Communists, whose international line was changing to the point where Grau was now to be befriended. A student of the Cuban and Chilean Communist parties has described these contacts between the Communists and Grau as follows:

> The Communists have repeatedly drawn attention to their efforts to persuade Grau to join with them in a Popular Front, referring particularly to their visits to him in Miami, in April and May 1935, and again in June 1936, and to cables and letters appealing to Grau for the formation of a Popular Front. According to the Communists, Grau, consistently and sometimes rudely, rejected all Communist overtures. . . . Surprising . . . is the fact that Grau's party, unlike the Socialists in France and Chile, who had also previously been enemies of the Communists, alone refused to make an electoral alliance with them. If Auténtico electoral successes in 1944 and subsequently are any indication, this decision on Grau's part was, in the long run, a sound one." [Stewart Cole Blasier, "The Cuban and Chilean Communist Parties: Instruments of Soviet Policy (1935–48)," pp. 35–36]

19. Thomson, *Cuban Revolution*, p. 271.

20. Rafael Masferrer Landa, *El Pensamiento Político del Dr. Guiteras* (Manzanillo: "El Arte," 1944), pp. 48–49.

21. R. S. de la Torre, "The Situation in Cuba," p. 205. For further information on Guiteras and Jóven Cuba see José A. Tabares, *La Revolución del 30*, pp. 544–53.

22. Torre, "Situation in Cuba," p. 205.

23. Masferrer Landa elaborates more on Guiteras's program in *Pensamiento Político*, pp. 55–56.

24. The absence of accurate figures makes it very difficult to estimate the size of the working class. It is better not to make any numerical estimates lest we provide a deceptive accuracy.

25. For more information on the history of the Cuban working-class movement, see Charles Page, "The Development of Organized Labor in Cuba"; and various standard histories of Latin-American labor movements, such as Víctor Alba, *Historia del Movimiento Obrero en América Latina* (Mexico City: Libreros Mexicanos Unidos, 1964); and Robert J. Alexander, *Organized Labor in Latin America*. Both of these histories are written from a social-democratic point of view. The history of the Cuban labor movement from a Communist point of view is contained in a brief pamphlet by Joaquín Ordoqui, *Elementos Para la Historia del Movimiento Obrero en Cuba*.

26. Comrade Marin (Cuba), "Report to the Seventh World Congress of the Communist International," *International Press Correspondence* 15, no. 52 (October 10, 1935): 1301.

27. Robert J. Alexander, *Communism in Latin America*, p. 21.

28. *The Communist* 13, no. 11 (November 1934): 1157.

29. Ibid.

30. For an attack equally hostile to both Grau and Guiteras, see Joaquín Ordoqui, "The Rise of the Revolutionary Movement in Cuba," *The Communist* 13, no. 12 (December 1934): 1258–59.

31. Alexander, *Communism in Latin America*, p. 272.

32. Fabio Grobart, "The Cuban Working Class Movement from 1925 to 1933," p. 99.

33. Marin, "Report to the Seventh World Congress," p. 1302.

34. Blas Roca, "Forward to the Cuban Anti-Imperialist People's Front," report to the Seventh Congress of the Communist International by the general secretary of the Cuban Communist Party, *The Communist* 14, no. 10 (October 1935).

35. Phillips, *Cuba*, p. 14.

36. These old traditional politicians, true to their past, could not help but engage in their petty intrigues, even in situations where the interests of their own class were at stake. Charles A. Thomson has described some of the petty wranglings that took place within the Mendieta administration: "Within the cabinet patronage had proved a serious bone of contention; meetings ran to interminable lengths while representatives of rival factions discussed plans for distributing municipal appointments — important in relation to the conduct of the coming elections." (Thomson, "Cuban Revolution: Reform and Reaction," p. 271.)

37. This lack of visibility was reinforced by the fact that Cuban labor laws would limit the number of Americans able to work in Cuba, thus creating a situation where almost the entire technical staff and supervisory personnel, as well as workers in North American concerns, would be Cubans. As far as Cuban workers were concerned, there would be relatively few situations where Americans would be giving *direct* orders to Cubans working for them.

38. Robert F. Smith, *The United States and Cuba*, pp. 158–59.

39. Phillips, *Cuba*, pp. 87–90.

40. Ibid.

41. Thomson, "The Cuban Revolution: Fall of Machado," p. 258.

42. Welles to Cordell Hull, October 5, 1933, United States Department of State, *Foreign Relations of the United States: Diplomatic Papers*, vol. 5, *The American Republics, 1933*, p. 473.

43. Welles to Cordell Hull, November 6, 1933, ibid., p. 515.

44. Thomson, "Cuban Revolution: Reform and Reaction," pp. 274–75.

45. Ibid.

Chapter 4

1. J. D. Phillips, "Batista Links His Destiny with Cuba's," interview with Batista in the *New York Times Magazine*, October 14, 1934, p. 3.

2. Jorge Mañach, "El Septembrismo," appendix to Jorge Mañach, *El Militarismo en Cuba* (collection of articles originally published in the Havana daily "Acción"; Havana: Seoane, Fernández y Cia., Impresores, Compostela 661, 1939), p. 18.

3. Charles A. Thomson, "The Cuban Revolution: Reform and Reaction," pp. 274–75.

4. Russel B. Porter interviews Fulgencio Batista, *New York Times*, July 5, 1936.

5. Ibid.

6. Russell H. Fitzgibbon and H. Max Healey, "The Cuban Elections of 1936," p. 733.

7. Ibid., pp. 733–34.

8. Guillermo Martínez Marquez, "Semblanza de Pablo," in Pablo de la Torriente Brau, *Pluma en Ristre*, compiled by Raúl Roa, prologue by Carlos Prío Socarrás, President of the Republic (Havana: Publicaciones del Ministerio de Educación, Dirección de Cultura, 1949), p. xx.

9. Juan Rivas, "Signs of Bankruptcy of the Cuban Military Dictatorship," *International Press Correspondence* 16, no. 33 (July 18, 1936): 883.

10. Blas Roca, *Las Experiencias de Cuba*.

11. Throughout this period the Communists engaged in profuse pro-Batista apologetics. See, for example, the Communists' pamphlets of the period such as *El Recibimiento al Coronel Batista* (1938), and Fulgencio Batista, *Estoy con el Pueblo* (Havana, 1939).

12. Guillermo Martínez Marquez, "If There is a Free and Sovereign Constituent Assembly, I Will Return," interview with Ramón Grau San Martín in Miami, January 24, 1937, *Bohemia*, year 29, no. 4.

13. Report by "Juan Reporter" on Auténtico assembly in Havana, in *Bohemia*, year 29, no. 33 (August 15, 1937), p. 34.

14. Ramón Grau San Martín, *La Revolución Cubana ante América*.

15. Martínez Marquez, "Semblanza de Pablo," p. 43.

16. Guillermo de Zéndegui, *Fundamentos Doctrinales para una Nueva Constitución del Estado Cubano*.

17. For an interesting, although one-sided, report of the Batista-Auténtico contacts and the subsequent Auténtico split, see Rubén de León, *El Origen del Mal*, pp. 320–30.

18. José Antonio Guerra y Debén, "Recent Evolution of the Sugar Industry," appendix to Ramiro Guerra *Sugar and Society in the Caribbean* (New Haven: Yale University Press, 1964).

Chapter 5

1. The composition of the Constitutional Convention after the elections were held was as followed: Opposition: Partido Revolucionario Cubano (Auténticos), 18; Partido Demócrata Republicano, 17; Partido Acción Republicana, 6; Partido ABC, 4. Government: Partido Liberal, 17; Partido Unión Nacionalista, 9; Fusión Unión Revolucionaria-Comunista, 6; Conjunto Nacional Democrático, 3; Partido Nacional Revolucionario, 1 (Gustavo Gutierrez Sánchez, *Constitución de la República de Cuba*,

Sus Antecedentes Históricos, Su Espíritu, Estudio Crítico sobre sus mas Fundamentales Principios [Its historic antecedents, its spirit, critical study of its most fundamental principles] [Havana, Cuba; Editorial Lex, 1941]).

2. For a detailed report on the proceedings of the Constitutional Convention, see Cuba, Convención Contituyente, 1940, *Diario de Sesiones de la Convención Contituyente*, vols. 1–2.

3. For a translation of many excerpts and articles from the 1940 Constitution, see Maurice Zeitlin and Robert Scheer, *Cuba: Tragedy in Our Hemisphere*, pp. 224–36. For a brief summary of constitutional provisions, see Emeterio Santovenia and Raúl M. Shelton, *Cuba y su Historia*, vol. 3, 2d ed., p. 131 ff.

4. Translated in Zeitlin and Scheer, *Cuba*, p. 234.

5. Rufo López Fresquet, *My 14 Months with Castro*, pp. 6–7.

6. *Business Week*, October 12, 1940, p. 64. It is also worth noting the following brief but suggestive analysis: "In Cuban neocolonial society, the irreconcilable antagonistic forces — revolution and reaction — remained in an impotent equilibrium. Neither was able to smash its opponent. They had no alternative but to coexist and to make some mutual concessions. The world situation sealed that peculiar status. The 1940 Constitution legally countersigned the forced equilibrium" (José A. Tabares, *La Revolución del 30*, p. 624).

7. See the interesting discussion of this in Boris Kozolchyk, "Law and Social Change in Latin America," especially p. 496.

8. Edmundo Desnoes, *Inconsolable Memories*, pp. 28–30. Other contemporary Cuban novels that also describe very well the prerevolutionary social climate are Lisandro Otero's *La Situación* and *En Ciudad Semejante*, and Guillermo Cabrera Infante's *Tres Tristes Tigres* (also *Three Trapped Tigers*, English translation by Donald Gardner and Suzanne Jill Levine, in collaboration with the author).

9. See, for example, Lino Novás Calvo, "La Tragedia de la Clase Media Cubana," p. 76.

10. Juan F. Carvajal, "Observaciones sobre la Clase Media en Cuba," in *Materiales Para el Estudio de la Clase Media en la America Latina* (Washington, D.C.: Pan American Union, 1950), p. 44.

11. For an excellent critique of theories about Latin American societies and about the middle classes in Latin America, see José Nun, "A Latin American Phenomenon," pp. 55–91.

12. G. D. H. Cole, "The Conception of the Middle Classes," pp. 283–84.

13. International Bank for Reconstruction and Development, *Report on Cuba*, p. 6. For an excellent description and analysis of the Cuban economy in this period, see James O'Connor, *The Origins of Socialism in Cuba*.

14. International Bank, *Report on Cuba*, p. 52; and *New York Times*, January 3, 1951, p. 86.

15. *New York Times*, ibid.

16. "Some Aspects of the Recent Evolution of Cuba's Economy," in *Economic Review of Latin America*, special issue (Bogotá, Colombia: United Nations, Economic Commission for Latin America, August 1955), p. 52.

17. Ibid.

18. Eugene Staley, *The Future of Underdeveloped Countries*, rev. ed. (New York: Harper & Brothers, for the Council of Foreign Relations, 1961), pp. 16–17.

19. "Cuba's Great Expectations," in *Business Week*, December 18, 1948, pp. 117–18; and United States Department of Commerce, Bureau of Foreign Commerce, *Investment in Cuba*, p. 124.

20. International Bank, *Report on Cuba*, chs. 24, 25.

21. Robin Blackburn, "Prologue to the Cuban Revolution," p. 59.

22. Theodore Draper, *Castroism: Theory and Practice*, p. 114.

23. Gino Germani, *Estrategía para Estimular la Movilidad Social: Aspectos Sociales del Desarrollo Económico en la América Latina* (Paris: UNESCO, 1962).

24. Carlos Raggi Ageo, "Contribution to the Study of the Middle Classes in Cuba."

25. One who did so was Lowry Nelson in his book *Rural Cuba*.

26. "Changes of Employment Structure in Latin America, 1945–1955," *Economic Bulletin for Latin America* (United Nations, Economic Commission for Latin America) 2, no. 1 (February 1957): 37.

27. International Bank, *Report on Cuba*, p. 476.

28. Novás Calvo, "La Tragedia de la Clase Media Cubana," p. 29.

29. J. B. Stuart, "Cuba's Elections: Background and Analysis," *Fourth International* 5, no. 7 (July 1944): 205.

30. Rubén de León, *El Origen del Mal*, pp. 333, 343. Rubén de León describes in further detail on pages 330–43 this process of entry of traditional and professional politicians into the Auténtico party.

31. William S. Stokes, "The Cuban Parliamentary System in Action, 1940–1947," p. 354.

32. Carlos González Palacios, *Revolución y Seudo-Revolución en Cuba* (n.p. 1948), p. 16.

33. Louis A. Perez, Jr. "The Rise and Fall of Army Preeminence in Cuba, 1898–1958," pp. 211–13.

34. *El Primer Mensaje del Presidente Dr. Ramón Grau San Martín al Congreso Cubano* (Havana: Ministerio de Defensa Nacional, Dirección de Propaganda de Guerra, 1944).

35. Stokes, "Cuban Parliamentary System," p. 355.

36. Ibid., p. 356.

37. William S. Stokes, "The 'Cuban Revolution' and the Presidential Elections of 1948."

38. Blackburn, "Prologue to the Cuban Revolution," pp. 69–70.

39. Merle Kling, "Towards a Theory of Power and Political Instability in Latin America," pp. 136–37.

40. Robert Michels, *Political Parties* (New York: Free Press; London: Collier-Macmillan, 1962), pp. 107–8.

41. Claudio Véliz, "Obstacles to Reform in Latin America," pp. 24–25. Edwin Lieuwen also tends to support Véliz's analysis. See Edwin Lieuwen, *Arms and Politics in Latin America*, rev. ed. (New York, Washington, London: Frederick A. Praeger Publishers, for the Council on Foreign Relations, 1961), p. 48.

42. In Cuba, for example, I would modify this thesis by pointing out that the urban middle classes "reached the sources of political power" only in the loose sense of the Auténticos' having been drawn originally from the middle classes. As we shall see, the formation of the Ortodoxo party is evidence of the fact that the urban middle classes were not fully in power yet. Finally, the Auténticos did not become "sedate and technically minded" but rather conservative and corrupt.

43. Harry Kantor, *The Ideology and Program of the Peruvian Aprista Movement*, p. 98.

44. Ruby Hart Phillips, interview with Ramón Grau San Martín, *New York Times*, May 12, 1940, p. 18. Also highly revealing in this connection is the following statement by the second Auténtico president, Carlos Prío Socarrás, who was a student leader during the 1933 Revolution: "Time has gone by and circumstances have changed. It occurs to me to think that without our red-hot war cry of 'Down with imperialism and death to its national accomplices!' we wouldn't have shaken the American conscience and with it that of Franklin Delano Roosevelt, chief of a new policy which banished from our hemisphere the humiliating and enslaving practices which we lived under" (Carlos Prío Socarras, "Prólogo," in Pablo de la Torriente Brau, *Pluma en Ristre*, compiled by Raúl Roa [Havana: Publicaciones del Ministerio de Educación, Dirección de Cultura, 1949], pp. xiv–xv).

Chapter 6

1. Ruby Hart Phillips, *Cuba: Island of Paradox*, p. 219.

2. From an article written by Fidel Castro in December 1955, in Rolando E. Bonachea and Nelson P. Valdés, eds., *Revolutionary Struggle, 1947–1958*, p. 299.

3. William S. Stokes, "National and Local Violence in Cuban Politics," pp. 59–60. See also the excellent and very informative article by Nelson P. Valdés and Rolando E. Bonachea, "Fidel Castro y la Politica Estudiantil de 1947 a 1952."

4. Boris Goldenberg, *The Cuban Revolution and Latin America*, p. 149, n. 2.

5. Charles Page, "The Development of Organized Labor in Cuba," pp. 173–74, n. 58.

6. Ibid.

7. E. J. Hobsbawm, *Primitive Rebels*, pp. 52–53.

8. Luis Conte Aguero, *Eduardo Chibás: El Adalid de Cuba*, pp. 229–33. See also *Bohemia* (Havana), January 10, 1937.

9. A good example of this was Chibás's vigorous defense of Finland's right of self-determination at the time of the 1939 Russian invasion. During the sessions of the 1940 Constitutional Convention, Chibás debated the Communist delegates who were defending Russia's actions in Finland. See Conte Aguero, *Eduardo Chibás*, pp. 272–76.

10. Ibid., pp. 497–98.

11. Ibid., p. 581.

12. Ibid., pp. 718–19.

13. *Hispanic American Report* for February 1952 (published March 1952), 5, no. 2, p. 16.

14. See, for example, Eduardo Chibás, "Roosevelt: Paladin Mundial de la Democracia," *Bohemia*, December 6, 1936, pp. 38–39.

15. For a good example of this, see Mario Llerena's interview with Eduardo Chibás, quoted in Conte Aguero, *Eduardo Chibás*, pp. 678–80.

16. Quoted in ibid., p. 729.

17. Ibid., pp. 688–89.

18. Ibid., pp. 602–3.

19. Ibid., p. 516.

20. Claudio Véliz, "Obstacles to Reform in Latin America," pp. 28–29.

21. Conte Aguero, *Eduardo Chibás*, pp. 730–31.

22. In 1949 the National Commission of the Youth Section of the Ortodoxo party wrote a manifesto that showed a clear Marxist (but non–Communist party) influence in its analysis of Cuban society and politics. See Comisión Nacional Organización de la Sección Juvenil del P.P.C.(O), *El Pensamiento Ideológico y Político de la Juventud Cubana* (Havana, 1949).

23. Interview with Fidel Castro in *Playboy*, January 1967, pp. 63–64.

24. *Hispanic American Report* for September 1951 (published in October 1951), 4, no. 10, p. 16. For more information on the strike situation in Cuba at this time, see the *New York Times*, January 3 and 4, 1951.

25. International Bank for Reconstruction and Development, *Report on Cuba*, pp. 365–66.

26. *Hispanic World Report* (former name of *Hispanic American Report*, published by the Stanford University Hispanic American Program) for June and July 1949 (published respectively in July and August 1949), 2 no. 7, p. 32, and no. 8, p. 33.

27. *Business Week*, December 18, 1948, p. 117.

28. Donald R. Dyer, "Urbanism in Cuba."

29. United States Department of Commerce, Bureau of Foreign Commerce, *Investment in Cuba*, p. 183.

30. National Agricultural Census of Cuba for 1946, as quoted in Lowry Nelson, *Rural Cuba*, p. 135.

31. United States Department of Labor, Bureau of Labor Statistics, Foreign Labor Information, *Labor in Cuba*, p. 3.

32. United States Department of Commerce, *Investment in Cuba*, p. 24.

33. Page, "Organized Labor in Cuba," pp. 172–74.

34. "It is instructive to compare the attitude toward new ventures of Cuba's capital with the attitude of labor. Labor's reactions to the relative stagnation and great instability of the Cuban economy have taken the form of an almost pathological insistence on security — in the form of job tenure — and at times a strong resistance to mechanization. Similarly, Cuban capitalists and investors have reacted to the same factors in their own way with a craving for excessive liquidity and a reluctance to invest at home" (International Bank, *Report on Cuba*, p. 528).

35. Ibid., p. 360.

36. From 1935 on, there were frequent conferences of leaders of individual Latin American Communist Parties with Browder and other United States Com-

munist leaders in the New York Party headquarters. . . . Apparently, Browder's vice-royalty included the Caribbean parties and those of the West Coast of South America, including the Chilean Party" (Robert J. Alexander, *Communism in Latin America*, p. 38). Earl Browder was for many years the top leader of the Communist party in the United States during its most conservative period. The 1945 Duclos letter, written by French Communist party leader Jacques Duclos, not only condemned Browder but served as a mouthpiece for Stalin, conveying to the world Communist movement his new Cold War policy.

37. Lázaro Peña, *La Colaboración entre Obreros y Patronos*. This edition of Peña's speech also contains a defense of it; see the introduction by Blas Roca, general secretary of the Cuban Communist party (at this time called Partido Socialista Popular).

38. The party reached a peak in this election: 197,000 provincial votes. This was more than 10 per cent of the total votes cast, and an increase of 67,000 votes over the 1944 total; further, it represented an excess of 43,000 votes over the 1946 party registration of 154,000. It should be pointed out that the membership of the party was always only a fraction of its legal registration, the latter being necessary to keep the party on the electoral ballot. Thus, it has been estimated that in 1946 party membership was 37,000. See Wyatt MacGaffey and Clifford R. Barnett, *Twentieth Century Cuba*, p. 157. The source of the previously cited figures is Blas Roca, *El Triunfo Popular en las Elecciones*.

39. See the pamphlet by Blas Roca entitled *Al Combate ¡Por la Economía y el Bienestar Popular!* which contains the proceedings of the Third National Assembly of the Partido Socialista Popular (Communist party) on January 24–28, 1946, and features Roca's confessions and denunciations of Browderism. It is perhaps the only Cuban Communist pamphlet that shows open disagreement among various leaders of the party about the mistakes of the past and the course to be followed in the future.

40. *Hispanic American Report* for August 1950 (published September 1950), 3, no. 9, p. 15.

41. Blas Roca, "La Ideologia de los Cetekarios," *Fundamentos* (Havana), year 11, no. 107 (February 1951): 113.

42. Blas Roca, *15 de Marzo; Analisis y Perspectivas*, pp. 19–20. Charles A. Page also noted the same thing, as quoted elsewhere in this chapter.

43. Joaquín Ordoqui, *Elementos para La Historia del Movimiento Obrero en Cuba*, p. 37.

44. Maurice Zeitlin, *Revolutionary Politics and the Cuban Working Class*, pp. 3–4, 8.

45. José Yglesias, *In the Fist of the Revolution*, p. 25.

46. Maurice Zeitlin, "Cuba: Revolution without a Blueprint," p. 41.

47. Speech by Fidel Castro to the leaders of the Central Organization of Workers (CUT) in Santiago, Chile, November 23, 1971. *Granma* (weekly review, Havana) December 5, 1971, p. 14.

Chapter 7

1. Chibás shot himself at the end of a radio broadcast that had been cut off because he went over his allotted time. In the broadcast, Chibás tried to rally support

for accusations he had made against a government minister, the validity of which had been questioned by opponents and sections of the press.

2. International Bank for Reconstruction and Development, *Report on Cuba*, p. 388.

3. "Prio scotched rumors that he intended to resign, although four days later, on September 24, the Cabinet resigned en masse to permit the President a free hand at reorganization. Several days later, Roberto Agramonte, Presidential candidate of the Partido del Pueblo Cubano (Ortodoxos), spoke in answer to the President's speech and charged that there was a crisis of authority in Cuba precisely because the people had lost confidence in a government overloaded with graft and corruption" (*Hispanic American Report* for September 1951 [published October 1951], 4, no. 10, p. 16).

4. Eusebio Mujal was a top Auténtico labor leader, who later went over to Batista.

5. Robin Blackburn, "Prologue to the Cuban Revolution," p. 71.

6. Herbert L. Matthews, "Republic with No Citizens," p. 47.

7. By this time, Fidel Castro had also introduced a lawsuit challenging the constitutionality of the regime; however, Castro's court case was little known while the court challenge introduced by the group of opposition leaders led by Ramón Zaydin, Pelayo Cuervo, and others attracted a great deal of public attention.

8. Casa de las Américas, *La Sierra y el Llano* (Havana: Casa de las Américas, 1961), pp. 20–21.

9. Rolando E. Bonachea and Nelson P. Valdés, eds. *Revolutionary Struggle, 1947–1958*, pp. 315–16.

10. Herbert Matthews reporting for the *New York Times*, October 24, 1953, p. 6.

11. Oden Meeker, "Cuba under Batista," p. 23.

12. United Nations, Department of Economic and Social Affairs, *Economic Survey of Latin America for 1953*, prepared by the Secretariat of the Economic Commission for Latin America (New York: U.N. Department of Economic and Social Affairs, 1954), p. 17.

13. United Nations, Department of Economic and Social Affairs, *Economic Survey of Latin America for 1954* (New York, 1955), p. 161.

14. United Nations, Department of Economic and Social Affairs, *Economic Survey of Latin America for 1957* (New York, 1959), p. 177.

15. Ibid.

16. Ibid., p. 183.

17. Ibid. This economic approach was a practice of long standing in Cuba. Thus, in 1955 the Economic Commission for Latin America had already made the following comment: "It is evident that when the Government distributes its capital expenditure as it does, it creates in the short run a larger volume of employment than that which would result if investment were channeled towards agriculture or industry . . . it might be tentatively stated that the types of public investment usually made in Cuba tend to augment or maintain the level of income and the volume of employment when not financed by taxes, but they do-not alter the structure of production of goods. That is to say, these investments tend to rise or maintain effective demand without modifying the import coefficient." See also "Some Aspects of the Recent Evolution of Cuba's Economy," *Economy Review of Latin America*, special issue

(Bogotá: United Nations Economic Commission for Latin America, August 1955), p. 55.

18. *New York Times,* January 14, 1959.

19. United Nations, *Economic Survey of Latin America for 1957,* pp. 178, 181–82.

20. The 26th of July Movement was founded by Fidel Castro in 1955 in Mexico, where he went after being released from jail under the general amnesty decreed by Batista's puppet Congress. See Chapter 8 for further details.

21. Ramón L. Bonachea and Marta San Martín, *The Cuban Insurrection, 1952–1959,* pp. 211–12.

22. Jules Dubois, *Fidel Castro,* pp. 252, 254.

23. Regis Debray, "Revolution in the Revolution?"

24. Theodore Draper, *Castroism: Theory and Practice,* p. 77.

25. Robert Alexander, *Communism in Latin America,* pp. 292–93.

26. Blas Roca, *Report to the Eighth National Congress of the Popular Socialist Party of Cuba* [Communist party], p. 9.

27. In *Communism in Latin America,* Alexander maintains that at this point the Cuban Communists adopted the policy of "Dual Communism," creating a Communist group that supported Batista while the party as a whole opposed him. I do not find Alexander's thesis convincing. In the absence of supporting evidence, it is very hard to understand the purpose and rationale that would have led the party to adopt such a dangerous policy. Alexander himself does not satisfactorily explain why the party would have done so.

28. It should also be noted here that the Communists were, on the whole, less persecuted than other opposition groups. Far fewer Communists than members of other groups were murdered by the Batista regime. But there is no evidence to support the contention of authors like Ramón Bonachea and Marta San Martín that the Communist party frequently collaborated with Batista's forces and turned in other oppositionists to the government. The case of Marcos Rodríguez, a Communist who turned out to have been an informer, seems to have been an isolated case rather than the rule.

29. For a more detailed exposition of Castro-Communist relations during this period, see Draper, *Castroism,* pp. 26–34.

30. Partido Socialista Popular, "La Solución que Conviene a Cuba" December 10, 1958 (fifteen mimeographed pages). This pamphlet obviously was clandestinely produced. It is available in the New York Public Library, which has a valuable collection of Cuban Communist publications.

31. Ibid., p. 8 ff. This document, in its great effort to show that some degree of nationalization is quite a normal thing in almost all countries, omits the well-known criticisms of nationalization within a capitalist economy which are commonplace in the Communist, socialist, and even the liberal literature on the subject.

32. Andrew St. George, "A Visit with a Revolutionary," interview with Fidel Castro, *Coronet* (February 1958).

33. By 1958, corruption in the army had reached fantastic proportions. Army supplies would be misappropriated for the purpose of obtaining private profit for important officers. Very often the bonuses due to combat soldiers would not reach

them but were stolen by their superiors. It is no wonder that the intelligent political warfare and humane behavior of the rebel army were highly successful in causing a complete loss of the will to fight on the part of so many soldiers.

34. Quoted in Boris Goldenberg, *The Cuban Revolution and Latin America*, p. 155, n. 1. The whole text is reprinted in *13 Documentos de la Insurrección* (Havana: Organización Nacional de Bibliotecas Ambulantes y Populares, December 1959), pp. 37–39.

35. Rufo López Fresquet, *My 14 Months with Castro*, p. 35.

36. It has been established that the navy insurgents had naval support outside Cienfuegos. Many navy officers and sailors throughout Cuba were also involved in the rebellion, but lack of coordination left the Cienfuegos insurgents acting on their own.

37. Coronel Pedro A. Barrera Pérez, "Por Qué el Ejército no Derrotó a Fidel Castro," *Bohemia Libre*, July 10, 1961.

38. "Since 1937, the Military Academy of El Morro had produced a new cohort of officers. Of the 1,200 officers of the Cuban army more than 1,000 were graduates of the academy and several hundred of them had taken special courses in the military academies of the Panama Canal Zone and Mexico, and in Fort Bering and Fort Briggs and other important academies of the U.S.A." (Jose Suárez Nuñez, *El Gran Culpable* [Caracas, 1963]).

39. Colonel Barreras has pointed out that there were three ways in which promotion could take place in the Cuban armed forces: through seniority, competitive examinations, or executive appointment. Barreras maintains that Batista made most frequent use of the last-mentioned method. See Barrera Pérez, "Por Qué el Ejército no Derrotó a Fidel Castro"; and Louis A. Perez, Jr., "The Rise and Fall of Army Preeminence in Cuba, 1898–1958," p. 249.

40. Major "Ché" Guevara, "Cuba: Exceptional Case?"

41. In 1959 there were two hundred parishes served by seven hundred priests, most of whom were Spanish. Cuban nationals numbered only about one-fifth of the total, hardly an asset. See Wyatt MacGaffey and Clifford R. Barnett, *Twentieth Century Cuba*, p. 243.

42. Mateo Jover Marimón, "The Church," in Carmelo Mesa-Lago, ed., *Revolutionary Change in Cuba*, pp. 399–403.

Chapter 8

1. "In fact, it seemed the rebel youths were just as angry with the old political parties as they were with the Batista government. One man, whom I had known since the days of the 1933 revolution, told me ruefully that his son had remarked that he, the boy's father, would have to be eliminated from the political life of the nation when Castro's revolution won." (Ruby Hart Phillips, *Cuba: Island of Paradox*, p. 296).

2. From the 1957 pamphlet *Nuestra Razón: Manifiesto-Programa del Movimiento 26 de Julio*, reprinted in Enrique González Pedrero, *La Revolución Cubana* (Mexico City: Escuela Nacional de Ciencias Políticas y Sociales, 1959), p. 98.

3. The political platform of the MNR and the views of other early revolutionary

groups and individuals are reprinted in *13 Documentos de la Insurrección* (Havana: Organización Nacional de Bibliotecas Ambulantes y Populares, December 1959).

4. William Appleman Williams, *The United States, Cuba, and Castro*, pp. 50–51.

5. Casa de las Américas, *La Sierra y el Llano*, pp. 21–22. For a useful account of the history of the Cuban student movement see also Jaime Suchlicki, *University Students and Revolution in Cuba, 1920–1968.*

6. Carleton Beals, "The New Crime of Cuba." For an illuminating discussion relevant to this question, see also Roberto Fernández Retamar, "Hacia una Intelectualidad Revolucionaria en Cuba," *Casa de las Américas*, and Roque Dalton et al., "Diez Años de Revolución: El Intelectual y la Sociedad," *Casa de las Américas*, year 10, no. 56 (September–October 1969).

7. For a more detailed account of the Directorio Revolucionario and of these events, see Ramón L. Bonachea and Marta San Martín, *The Cuban Insurrection, 1952–1959*, pp. 49–60, 106–33.

8. As previously mentioned, Fidel Castro had gone to court challenging the constitutionality of the Batista regime. See Jules Dubois, *Fidel Castro*, pp. 26–30.

9. "History Will Absolve Me," in Rolando E. Bonachea and Nelson P. Valdés, eds. *Revolutionary Struggle, 1947–1958*, pp. 164–221.

10. Theodore Draper, *Castroism: Theory and Practice*, p. 6.

11. It is highly revealing that when Theodore Draper summarizes the contents of "History Will Absolve Me" he does not mention these two radical proposals. See Draper, *Castroism*, pp. 5–6.

12. Herbert Matthews, *New York Times*, November 4, 1956.

13. Draper, *Castroism*, pp. 10–11.

14. Dubois, *Fidel Castro*, p. 213.

15. Ernesto "Ché" Guevara, *Relatos de la Guerra Revolucionaria* (Buenos Aires: Editora Nueve 64, 1965), p. 30.

16. *Bohemia*, July 28, 1957. It has been translated in Bonachea and Valdés, *Revolutionary Struggle*, pp. 343–48.

17. Nor did it differ from two other moderate documents of the 26th of July Movement: the *Tesis Económica del Movimiento Revolucionario 26 de Julio*, reprinted in Fidel Castro, *La Revolución Cubana: Escritos y Discursos*, ed. Gregorio Selser (Buenos Aires: Editorial Palestra, 1960); and *Nuestra Razón*.

18. Andrew St. George, "A·Visit with a Revolutionary," interview with Fidel Castro, *Coronet*, February 1958. I would also like to note a small but revealing incident which shows the direction of Castro and the 26th of July Movement's socioeconomic program. In 1957, a small group of 26th of July exiles in Costa Rica printed various radical extracts from "History Will Absolve Me." *The Nation*, in its edition of November 20, 1957, reprinted these extracts, implying that this was part of the current program of the 26th of July Movement. After this happened, Mario Llerena, Castro's representative in the United States, stated that "Castro's views were 'much more moderate' than those circulated by the Costa Rican group or than those described in a pamphlet published in Mexico City entitled *Nuestra Razón* (Our Cause)," (*Hispanic American Report* 10, no. 11 [November 1957]: pp. 596–97). It is

indeed ironic that Llerena himself had written most of Nuestra Razón (see Draper, *Castroism,* p. 12), a document which was not really "radical," and that all of the extracts quoted by the Costa Rican group had been written by Castro himself.

19. While Guevara has made a good case for the contention that Fidel Castro and his friends had changed their *attitude* toward the peasantry, he has failed to show that the rebel army did anything radical about it before their victory in January 1959. See Ernesto "Ché" Guevara, "Proyecciones Sociales del Ejército Rebelde," speech of January 27, 1959, reprinted in Castro, *La Revolución Cubana.*

20. Draper, *Castroism,* pp. 21–26.

21. Ernesto "Ché" Guevara, "Notes for the Study of the Ideology of the Cuban Revolution," originally published in *Verde Olivo,* October 8, 1960; reprinted in *Che Guevara Speaks: Selected Speeches and Writings* (New York: Merit Publishers, 1967), p. 21.

22. Bonachea and Valdés, *Revolutionary Struggle,* pp. 158, 159.

23. Federico G. Gil, "Antecedents of the Cuban Revolution," *Centennial Review* 4, no. 3 (summer 1962): 387.

24. Radio Rebelde broadcast of August 19, 1958, in Bonachea and Valdés, *Revolutionary Struggle,* p. 409.

25. Luis Conte Aguero, *26 Cartas del Presidio,* p. 73. These letters were published before Conte Aguero's break with Castro. The emphasis is Castro's.

26. "A las Fuerzas Revolucionarias de la Zona Norte de las Villas," Camilo Cienfuegos, Commander of the Invading Column "Antonio Maceo" of the 26th of July Revolutionary Army, 1958, reprinted in Casa de las Américas, *La Sierra y el Llano,* p. 277.

27. "Relato de Haydée Santamaria," in *La Sierra y el Llano,* p. 40.

28. Reprinted in Dubois, *Fidel Castro,* pp. 188–90.

29. For a translation of this letter, see Bonachea and Valdés, *Revolutionary Struggle,* pp. 351–63. For a detailed account of the whole incident see Bonachea and San Martín, *Cuban Insurrection,* pp. 161–72.

30. Quoted in Dubois, *Fidel Castro,* p. 228.

31. There was a half-hearted attempt on the part of Barquín and other freed army officers to take over the command of the armed forces, but nothing came of it. For details of United States attempts to install a government to the liking of North American interests, see Earl E. T. Smith, *The Fourth Floor,* pp. 164–67; and 86th Cong., 2d sess., 1960, *Communist Threat to the United States through the Caribbean, Hearings before the Subcommittee to Investigate the Administration of the Internal Security Act and Other Internal Security Laws of the Committee on the Judiciary,* pt. 10, testimony of William D. Pawley, September 2, 1960 (Washington, D.C.: Government Printing Office, 1960), pp. 738–39. See also Bonachea and San Martín, *Cuban Insurrection,* pp. 322–25, 407, which is particularly informative on the role of the CIA within the opposition to Batista.

Chapter 9

1. Rolando E. Bonachea and Nelson P. Valdés, *Revolutionary Struggle, 1947– 1958,* pp. 357–58.

2. Fidel Castro, *Discursos para la Historia*, bk. 1, pp. 11, 15–16. See also the account of these events in Jaime Suchlicki, *University Students and Revolution in Cuba, 1920–1968*, p. 88.

3. Castro, *Discursos para la Historia*, bk. 1, p. 20.

4. Theodore Draper, "Cuba: The Runaway Revolution," pp. 15, 16.

5. Movimiento Revolucionario 26 de Julio, *Nuestra Razón: Manifiesto-Programa del Movimiento 26 de Julio*, p. 124 (italics as in the original).

6. David Matza, *Delinquency and Drift* (New York: John Wiley and Sons, 1964).

7. Ibid., p. 181 (Matza's emphasis).

8. It goes without saying that, unlike the delinquents studied by Matza, once a Communist system had been established in Cuba, Castro would have found that his freedom was curtailed by the creation of a social structure that could not be easily destroyed or dismantled, even by a strong leader like himself. Some of Matza's findings would thus be clearly inapplicable to the situation we are currently analyzing, as when Matza states (p. 26): "Delinquency is a status and delinquents are incumbents who *intermittently* act out a role. When we focus on the incumbents rather than the status, we find that most are capable of conventional activity. Thus, delinquents intermittently play both delinquent and conventional roles. They play or act well in both situations" (Matza's emphasis). Some of this might have applied to the behavior of the Castro leadership *before* they made a commitment to building a communist society in Cuba rather than afterward. It should also be clear that Communists acquire state power, while delinquents do not. For this and other reasons it is obvious that no conclusions can be derived from this limited analogy in terms of remedial action, or the like.

9. James O'Connor, "On Cuban Political Economy," pp. 236–37, 238, 239.

10. C. Wright Mills, *Listen, Yankee* (New York: Ballantine Books, 1960), p. 123 (Mills's emphasis).

11. Robin Blackburn, "Prologue to the Cuban Revolution," pp. 81–82 (Blackburn's emphasis).

12. *Revolución*, February 16 and April 15, 1959.

13. Quoted from *France Observateur*, April 7, 1960, in Theodore Draper, *Castro's Revolution*, p. 24.

14. For examples of some of the numerous occasions when Castro encouraged the development of Cuban national industry under capitalist auspices, see Castro, *Discursos para la Historia*, bk. 1, pp. 108–9, 124–25, 142–43; and bk. 2, pp. 40–41.

15. For example, Carlos Luis, in a sensitively written article, "Notes of a Cuban Revolutionary in Exile," casts serious doubts on the veracity of Castro's charges that bombings by American-based planes, rather than Cuban antiaircraft fire, had caused a number of civilian casualties in an important episode that took place in October 1959.

16. Boris Goldenberg, *The Cuban Revolution and Latin America*, p. 347.

17. Fidel Castro in an "Ante la Prensa" interview of February 19, 1959, in *Discursos para la Historia*, bk. 2, p. 121.

18. *Trabajo* (first fortnight of October 1962), p. 48.

19. Castro was also unwilling at this time to nationalize the Shell Company which had had major responsibility in the British sale of arms to Batista after the American embargo in early 1958. See Castro's speech to the Shell workers in *Discursos para la Historia*, bk. 1, p. 79.

20. Joseph P. Morray, *The Second Revolution in Cuba*, p. 38.

21. "It is instructive to make comparisons between the National Directorate of the ORI [Organizaciones Revolucionarias Integradas] and the PURS [Partido Unido de la Revolución Socialista] and the Central Committee of the new PCC [Communist party]. The former consisted of twenty-five members: the latter has one hundred. . . . The participation of 'old Communists' has also decreased, considerably from 40 per cent to 18 per cent. . . . As has been said, the PCC follows the model of Communist organization, and thus we must assume that its decisive organs are the Politburo — which the ORI and the PURS lacked — and the Secretariat. In the former, consisting of eight members, there is no 'old Communist'; and in the Secretariat there are the familiar names of Roca and Carlos Rafael Rodríguez" (Andrés Suarez, *Cuba: Castroism and Communism, 1959–1966*, pp. 227–28).

22. Morray, *Second Revolution in Cuba*, p. 165.

23. For the very convincing evidence concerning Raúl Castro's political background, see Hugh Thomas, "Middle Class Politics and the Cuban Revolution," p. 258.

24. Morray, *Second Revolution in Cuba*, p. 61.

25. See, for example, the statement of the May 1959 Plenum of the PSP, as quoted in Edward González, "The Cuban Revolution and the Soviet Union, 1959–1960," p. 414; a summary of the points developed at greater length in this work is contained in idem, "Castro's Revolution, Cuban Communist Appeals, and the Soviet Response." See also Blas Roca's reference to the danger of "exceptionalism" (probably referring to Guevara) at the PSP Plenum of October 1959, quoted in Suárez, *Cuba*, p. 39.

26. Membership estimates for January 1959 range from seven to twenty thousand members.

27. Francisco Calderio (Blas Roca), *29 Artículos Sobre la Revolución Cubana* (Havana: February 1960), p. 14 (Roca's emphasis). This was the formulation adopted in the January [1959] Theses of the PSP.

28. Reprinted in ibid., p. 203.

29. Castro, *Discursos para la Historia*, bk. 1, p. 137.

30. Suárez, *Cuba*, p. 49. This incident modifies somewhat O'Connor's assessment of the question of land distribution in revolutionary Cuba, although the latter remains fundamentally correct. We have to bear in mind that after the Communists backtracked on this issue, there was no significant political group in Cuba which gave political encouragement to land seizures.

31. This position was put forward by Aníbal Escalante as early as January of 1959. For evidence concerning this and other differences of strategy and tactics within the PSP leadership at various points during the revolution, see Edward González, "Cuban Revolution and the Soviet Union," pp. 343–46.

32. Ibid., p. 564 ff.

Selected Bibliography

Books and Pamphlets

Aguilar, Luis E. *Cuba 1933: Prologue to Revolution*. Ithaca, N.Y., and London: Cornell University Press, 1972.

Alexander, Robert J. *Communism in Latin America*. New Brunswick, N.J.: Rutgers University Press, 1957.

———. *Organized Labor in Latin America*. New York: Free Press, 1965.

Alvarez Díaz, José; Arredondo, A.; Shelton, R. M.; and Vizcaino, J. F. *Cuba: Geopolítica y Pensamiento Económico*. Miami, Fla.: Colegio de Economistas de Cuba en el Exilio, 1964.

Bonachea, Ramón L., and San Martín, Marta. *The Cuban Insurrection, 1952–1959*. New Brunswick, N.J.: Transaction Books, 1974.

Bonachea, Rolando E., and Valdés, Nelson P., eds. *Revolutionary Struggle 1947–1958. The Selected Works of Fidel Castro*, vol. 1. Cambridge, Mass., and London: MIT Press, 1972.

Cabrera Infante, Guillermo. *Tres Tristes Tigres*. Barcelona: Editorial Seix Barral, 1967. Also *Three Trapped Tigers*, translated from the Cuban by Donald Gardner and Suzanne Jill Levine, in collaboration with the author. New York: Harper and Row, 1971.

Casa de las Américas. *La Sierra y el Llano*. Havana: Casa de Las Américas, 1961.

Castro, Fidel. *Discursos Para la Historia*. Bks. 1–2. Text of speeches by Dr. Fidel Castro from January 1, 1959, to May 1, 1959. Havana: Imprenta Emilio Gall, 1959.

Casuso, Teresa. *Cuba and Castro*. Translated from the Spanish by Elmer Grossberg. New York: Random House, 1961.

Conte Aguero, Luis. *Eduardo Chibás: El Adalid de Cuba*. Mexico City: Editorial JUS, 1955.

———. *26 Cartas del Presidio*. Havana: Editorial Cuba, 1960.

Desnoes, Edmundo. *Inconsolable Memories.* Translated by the author. Foreword by Jack Gelber. London: André Deutsch, 1968.

Draper, Theodore. *Castroism: Theory and Practice.* New York: Frederick A. Praeger, 1965.

————. *Castro's Revolution: Myths and Realities.* New York: Frederick A. Praeger, 1962.

Dubois, Jules. *Fidel Castro: Rebel — Liberator or Dictator?* New York: New Bobbs-Merrill Company, 1959.

Dumont, René. *Cuba: Socialism and Development.* New York: Grove Press, 1970.

Foreign Policy Association. *Problems of the New Cuba.* Report of the Commission on Cuban Affairs. New York: Foreign Policy Association, January, 1935.

Franqui, Carlos. *The Twelve.* Translated by Albert B. Teichner. New York: Lyle Stuart, 1968.

Free, Lloyd A. *Attitudes of the Cuban People toward the Castro Regime, in the Late Spring of 1960.* Princeton, N.J.: Institute for International Social Research, 1960.

Goldenberg, Boris. *The Cuban Revolution and Latin America.* London: George Allen and Unwin, 1965.

González Palacios, Carlos. *Revolución y Seudo-Revolución en Cuba.* N.p., 1948.

Grau San Martín, Ramon. *La Revolución Cubana ante América.* Mexico City: Ediciones del Partido Revolucionario Cubano (Auténtico), 1936.

Guevara, Ernesto "Ché." *Ché: Selected Works of Ernesto Guevara.* Edited and with an introduction by Rolando E. Bonachea and Nelson P. Valdés. Cambridge, Mass., and London: MIT Press, 1969.

———— *Reminiscences of the Cuban Revolutionary War.* Translated by Victoria Ortiz. New York: Monthly Review Press, special edition for Merit Publishers, 1968.

Gutíerrez Sánchez, Gustavo. *Constitución de la República de Cuba: Sus Antecedentes Históricos, su Espíritu, Estudio Crítico sobre sus mas Fundamentales Principios.* Havana: Editorial Lex, 1941.

Hobsbawm, E. J. *Primitive Rebels.* New York: W. W. Norton, 1965.

Huberman, Leo, and Sweezy, Paul M. *Cuba: Anatomy of a Revolution.* New York: Monthly Review Press, 1960.

————. *Socialism in Cuba.* New York and London: Monthly Review Press, 1969.

Kantor, Harry. *The Ideology and Program of the Peruvian Aprista Movement.* University of California Publications in Political Science, vol.

4. Berkeley and Los Angeles: University of California Press, 1953.

Karol, K. S. *Guerrillas in Power: The Course of the Cuban Revolution.* Translated from the French by Arnold Pomerans. New York: Hill and Wang, 1970.

Kozolchyk, Boris. *The Political Biographies of Three Castro Officials.* Santa Monica, Calif.: Rand Corporation, 1966.

Lenin, V. I. *What is to be Done?* Little Lenin Library, vol. 4. New York: International Publishers, 1929.

León, Rubén de. *El Origen del Mal.* Coral Gables, Fla.: Service Offset Printers, 1964.

Lipset, Seymour Martin. *Agrarian Socialism.* Berkeley: University of California Press, 1950.

López Fresquet, Rufo. *My 14 Months with Castro.* New York: World Publishing Company, 1966.

MacGaffey, Wyatt, and Barnett, Clifford R. *Twentieth Century Cuba.* Garden City, N.Y.: Doubleday Anchor Books, 1965.

Marx, Karl. *The Class Struggles in France. 1848 to 1850.* Moscow: Progress Publishers, 1965.

———. *The Eighteenth Brumaire of Louis Bonaparte.* Moscow: Foreign Languages Publishing House, n.d.

———, and Engels, Friedrich. *Selected Correspondence, 1846–1895.* Translated by Dona Torr. New York: International Publishers, 1942.

Mesa-Lago, Carmelo, ed. *Revolutionary Change in Cuba.* Pittsburgh: University of Pittsburgh Press, 1971.

Mills, C. Wright. *Listen, Yankee.* New York: Ballantine Books, 1960.

Moore, Barrington, Jr. *Social Origins of Dictatorship and Democracy.* Boston: Beacon Press, 1966.

Morray, Joseph P. *The Second Revolution in Cuba.* New York: Monthly Review Press, 1962.

Movimiento Revolucionario 26 de Julio. *Nuestra Razón: Manifiesto-Programa del Movimiento 26 de Julio.* Reprinted in Enrique González Pedrero, *La Revolución Cubana.* Mexico City: Escuela Nacional de Ciencias Políticas y Sociales, 1959.

Movimiento Revolucionario 26 de Julio. *Tesis Económica del Movimiento Revolucionario 26 de Julio.* Reprinted in Fidel Castro, *La Revolución Cubana: Escritos y Discursos.* Edited by Gregorio Selser. Buenos Aires: Editorial Palestra, 1960.

Nelson, Lowry. *Rural Cuba.* Minneapolis, Minn.: University of Minnesota Press, 1950.

O'Connor, James. *The Origins of Socialism in Cuba.* Ithaca, N.Y., and London: Cornell University Press, 1970.

Ordoqui, Joaquín. *Elementos para la Historia del Movimiento Obrero en Cuba.* Havana: Comisión Nacional de Escuelas de Instrucción Revolucionaria, 1961.

Otero, Lisandro. *En Ciudad Semejante.* Colección Esta America. Buenos Aires: Ediciones de Crisis, 1974.

———. *La Situación.* Colección Concurso. Havana: Casa de las Américas, 1963.

Partido Socialista Popular [Communist party]. *La Solución que Conviene a Cuba.* Havana(?): n.p., December 10, 1958.

Peña, Lázaro. *La Colaboración entre Obreros y Patronos.* Havana: Ediciones Sociales, 1945.

Phillips, Ruby Hart. *Cuba: Island of Paradox.* New York: MacDowell, Obolensky, 1959.

Roa, Raúl. *La Revolución del 30 Se Fué a Bolina.* Ediciones Huracán. Havana: Instituto del Libro, 1969.

Roca, Blas. *Al Combate ¡Por la Economía y el Bienestar Popular!* Proceedings of the Third National Assembly of the Partido Socialista Popular, January 24–28, 1946. Havana: Ediciones del Partido Socialista Popular, 1946.

———. *Las Experiencias de Cuba.* Report to the Mexican Communist party's Seventh National Congress, February 1939. Havana: Editorial Páginas, 1939.

———. *15 de Marzo: Análisis y Perspectivas.* Report of Blas Roca, General Secretary of URC [Unión Revolucionaria Comunista] at the URC Executive Committee meeting of March 28, 1942. Havana: Editorial Páginas, 1942.

———. *Report to the Eighth National Congress of the Popular Socialist Party of Cuba.* Report made by General Secretary Roca in August 1960. New York: New Century Publishers, 1961.

———. *El Triunfo Popular en las Elecciones.* Report to the meeting of the National Executive Committee of the Partido Socialista Popular on June 22, 1946. N.p., 1946.

———. *29 Artículos Sobre la Revolución Cubana.* Havana: Comisión de Educación y Propaganda del Comité Municipal de la Habana del PSP, February 1960.

Rodríguez Quesada, Carlos. *David Salvador: Castro's Prisoner.* New York: Labor Committee to Release Imprisoned Trade Unionists and Democratic Socialists, 1961.

Rojo, Ricardo. *My Friend Ché.* Translated from the Spanish by Julian Casart. New York: Grove Press, 1969.

Rosell, Mirta, ed. *Luchas Obreras contra Machado.* Ediciones Políticas.

Editorial de Ciencias Sociales. Havana: Instituto Cubano del Libro, 1973.

Santovenia, Emeterio S., and Shelton, Raúl M. *Cuba y su Historia*. Vol. 3. 2d ed. Miami, Fla.: Cuba Corporation, 1966.

Smith, Earl E. T. *The Fourth.Floor*. New York: Random House, 1962.

Smith, Robert F. *The United States and Cuba: Business and Diplomacy, 1917–1960*. New Hayen, Conn.: College and University Press, 1960.

Suárez, Andrés. *Cuba: Castroism and Communism, 1959–1966*. Foreword by Ernest Halperin. Translated by Joel Carmichael and Ernest Halperin. Cambridge, Mass.: M.I.T. Press, 1967.

Suchlicki, Jaime. *University Students and Revolution in Cuba, 1920–1968*. Coral Gables, Fla.: University of Miami Press, 1969.

Tabares, José A. *La Revolución del 30: Sus Dos Últimos Años*. Havana: Editorial de Arte y Literatura, Instituto Cubano del Libro, 1971.

Thomas, Hugh. *Cuba: The Pursuit of Freedom*. New York and London: Harper and Row, 1971.

Trotsky, Leon. *The History of the Russian Revolution*. Ann Arbor: University of Michigan Press, 1932.

———. *The Revolution Betrayed*. New York: Merit Publishers, 1965.

Williams, William Appleman. *The United States, Cuba, and Castro: An Essay on the Dynamics of Revolution and the Dissolution of Empire*. New York: Monthly Review Press, 1962.

Wood, Bryce. *The Making of the Good Neighbor Policy*. New York: Columbia University Press, 1961.

Yglesias, José. *In the Fist of the Revolution: Life in a Cuban Country Town*. New York: Random House, Pantheon Books, 1968.

Zeitlin, Maurice. *Revolutionary Politics and the Cuban Working Class*. Princeton, N.J.: Princeton University Press, 1967.

———, and Scheer, Robert. *Cuba: Tragedy in Our Hemisphere*. New York: Grove Press, 1963.

Zéndegui, Guillermo de. *Fundamentos Doctrinales para una Nueva Constitución del Estado Cubano*. Introduction by Enrique De la Hoza. Havana: Publicaciones del Buró de Propaganda Auténtica, Partido Revolucionario Cubano (Auténtico), April 1939.

Articles and Periodicals

Alexander, Robert J. " 'Aprismo' — Is It Socialist?" *Modern Review* 1, no. 9 (November 1947).

———. "The Latin American Aprista Parties." *Political Quarterly* 20, no. 3 (July–September 1949).

Batchelder, Robert B. "The Evolution of Cuban Land Tenure and Its Relation to Certain Agro-Economic Problems." *Southwestern Social Science Quarterly* 33, no. 3 (December 1952).

Beals, Carleton. "The New Crime of Cuba." *The Nation*, June 29, 1957.

Bergman, Arlene Eisen. "More Revolution." *The Movement* 4, no. 10 (November 1968)

Blackburn, Robin. "Prologue to the Cuban Revolution." *New Left Review*, no. 21 (October 1963).

Cambridge Opinion (Cambridge, Eng.), no. 32.

Carvajal, Juan F. "Observaciones sobre la Clase Media en Cuba." In *Materiales para el Estudio de la Clase Media en la América Latina*. Washington, D.C.: Pan American Union, 1950.

Castro, Fidel. Speeches of August 23, 1968, and July 26, 1970, in *Granma* (weekly review), year 3, no. 34 (August 25, 1968), and year 5, no. 31 (August 2, 1970).

Cole, G. D. H. "The Conception of the Middle Classes." *British Journal of Sociology* 1, no. 4 (December 1950).

Cronon, E. David. "Interpreting the New Good Neighbor Policy: The Cuban Crisis of 1933." *Hispanic American Historical Review* 39, no. 4 (November 1959).

Debray, Régis. "Revolution in the Revolution?" *Monthly Review* 19, no. 3 (July–August 1967).

Draper, Hal. "Marx and Bolivar: A Note on Authoritarian Leadership in a National Liberation Movement." *New Politics* 7, no. 1 (winter 1968).

Draper, Theodore. "Cuba: The Runaway Revolution." *The Reporter*, May 12, 1960.

Dumont, René. "The Militarization of Fidelismo." *Dissent* 17, no. 5 (September–October 1970).

Dyer, Donald R. "Urbanism in Cuba." *Geographical Review* 47 (April 1957).

Fernández Retamar, Roberto. "Hacia una Intelectualidad Revolucionaria en Cuba." *Casa de las Américas*, year 7, no. 40 (January–February 1967).

Fornet, Ambrosio. "Revaluaciones del Movimiento Cultural del 30." *Casa de las Américas*, year 7, no. 40 (January–February 1967).

González, Edward. "Castro's Revolution, Cuban Communist Appeals, and the Soviet Response." *World Politics* 21, no. 1 (October 1968).

Grobart, Fabio. "The Cuban Working Class Movement from 1925 to 1933." *Science and Society* 39, no. 1 (spring 1975).

Guevara, Ernesto "Ché." "Notes for the Study of the Ideology of the Cuban Revolution." Originally published in *Verde Olivo*, October 8, 1960.

Reprinted in *Ché Guevara Speaks: Selected Speeches and Writings.* New York: Merit Publishers, 1967.

Guevara, Major "Ché." "Cuba: Exceptional Case?" *Monthly Review* 13, nos. 3 and 4 (July and August 1961).

Hennessy, C. A. M. "The Roots of Cuban Nationalism." *International Affairs* 39, no. 3 (1963).

Huberman, Leo, and Sweezy, Paul M. "Cuba Revisited." *Monthly Review* 12, no. 8 (December 1960).

Kling, Merle. "Towards a Theory of Power and Political Instability in Latin America." *Western Political Quarterly* 9, no. 1 (March 1956). Reprinted in John H. Kautsky, ed., *Political Change in Underdeveloped Countries: Nationalism and Communism.*

Kozolchyk, Boris. "Law and Social Change in Latin America." *Hispanic American Historical Review* 44, no. 4 (November 1964).

Luis, Carlos. "Notes of a Cuban Revolutionary in Exile." *New Politics* 2, no. 4 (fall 1963).

Masó, Calixto. "Obrerismo y Política ¿Cuales deben ser sus Relaciones?" In *Cuadernos de la Universidad del Aire del Circuito CMQ.* (Tercer Curso.) *Actualidad y Destino de Cuba,* no. 15. Havana: Talleres de Editorial Lex, March 1950.

Matthews, Herbert L. "Fidel Castro Revisited." *War/Peace Report,* December 1967.

———. "Republic with No Citizens." *New York Times Magazine,* May 18, 1952.

Meeker, Oden. "Cuba under Batista: More Apathy Than Disaffection." *The Reporter* 2, no. 4 (September 14, 1954).

Mesa-Lago, Carmelo. "Availability and Reliability of Statistics in Socialist Cuba." *Latin American Research Review* 4, no. 1 (winter 1969), and no. 2 (spring 1969).

———. "The Revolutionary Offensive." *Trans-Action* 6, no. 6 (April 1969).

Mintz, Sidney. Foreword to Ramiro Guerra, *Sugar and Society in the Caribbean.* New Haven, Conn.: Yale University Press, 1964.

Novás Calvo, Lino. "La Tragedia de la Clase Media Cubana." In *Bohemia Libre,* January 1, 1961.

Nun, José. "A Latin American Phenomenon: The Middle Class Military Coup." In *Trends in Social Science Research in Latin American Studies: A Conference Report.* Berkeley: Institute of International Studies, University of California, 1965.

O'Connor, James. "On Cuban Political Economy." *Political Science Quarterly* 79, no. 2 (June 1964).

————. "The Organized Working Class in the Cuban Revolution." *Studies on the Left* 6, no. 2 (March–April 1966).

Organización ABC. "El Manifiesto del ABC." In Carlos G. Peraza, *Machado: Crímenes y Horrores de un Régimen.* Havana: Cultural, S.A., 1933.

Pazos, Felipe. "Comentarios a dos Artículos sobre la Revolución Cubana." *El Trimestre Economico* (Ciudad de México), 29, pt. 1, no. 113 (January–March 1962).

Pensamiento Critico (Havana), no. 39 (April 1970).

Raggi Ageo, Carlos, "Contribution to the Study of the Middle Classes in Cuba." In *Materiales para el Estudio de la Clase Media en la América Latina.* Washington, D.C.: Pan American Union, 1950.

"Régis Debray and the Latin American Revolution." *Monthly Review* 20, no. 3 (July–August 1968).

Sánchez Arango, Aureliano. "The Recent General Strike in Cuba." *Three Americas* (Mexico City), 1, no. 4 (June 1935).

Smith, Robert F. "Twentieth Century Cuban Historiography." *Hispanic American Historical Review* 44, no. 1 (1964).

Stokes, William S. "The Cuban Parliamentary System in Action, 1940–1947." *Journal of Politics* 2, no. 2 (May 1949).

————. "The 'Cuban Revolution' and the Presidential Election of 1948." *Hispanic American Historical Review* 31, no. 1 (February 1951).

————. "National and Local Violence in Cuban Politics." *Southwestern Social Science Quarterly* 34, no. 2 (September 1953).

Thomas, Hugh. "Middle Class Politics and the Cuban Revolution." In Claudio Véliz, ed., *The Politics of Conformity in Latin America.* Issued under the auspices of the Royal Institute of International Affairs. London and New York: Oxford University Press, 1967.

Thomson, Charles A. "The Cuban Revolution: Fall of Machado." *Foreign Policy Reports* 11, no. 21 (December 18, 1935).

————. "The Cuban Revolution: Reform and Reaction." *Foreign Policy Reports* 11, no. 22 (January 1, 1936).

Torre, R. S. de la. "The Situation in Cuba." *New International* 2, no. 6 (October 1935).

Torres, Simón, and Aronde, Julio. "Debray and the Cuban Experience." In *"Régis Debray and the Latin American Revolution." Monthly Review* 20, no. 3 (July–August 1968).

Valdés, Maxine, and Valdés, Nelson P. "Cuban Workers and the Revolution." *New Politics* 8, no. 4 (1971).

Valdés, Nelson P., and Bonachea, Rolando E. "Fidel Castro y la Politica Estudiantil de 1947 a 1952." *Aportes* (Paris), no. 22 (October 1971).

Vásquez Candela, Euclides. "La Revolución Humanista." In Festival Popular de Divulgación Revolucionaria, *Temas en Torno a la Revolución.* Havana: Editorial Tierra Nueva, 1959.

Véliz, Claudio. "Obstacles to Reform in Latin America." *World Today* 19, no. 1 (January 1963).

Wood, Dennis B. "The Long Revolution: Class Relations and Political Conflict in Cuba, 1868–1968." *Science and Society* 34, no. 1 (spring 1970).

Zeitlin, Maurice. "Cuba: Revolution without a Blueprint." *Trans-Action* 6, no. 6 (April 1969).

————. "Political Generations in the Cuban Working Class." *American Journal of Sociology* 71, no. 5 (March 1966).

Public Documents

Cuba. Convención Constituyente. *Diario de Sesiones de la Convención Constituyente.* Vols. 1–2, February 9–July 4, 1940. Havana: P. Fernández, 1940.

International Bank for Reconstruction and Development. *Report on Cuba.* Findings and recommendations of an economic and technical mission organized by the International Bank for Reconstruction and Development in collaboration with the government of Cuba in 1950. Francis Adams Truslow, chief of mission, Washington, D.C. Baltimore, Md.: Johns Hopkins University Press, 1951.

United States Department of Commerce, Bureau of Foreign Commerce. *Investment in Cuba.* Washington, D.C.: Government Printing Office, 1956.

United States Department of Labor, Bureau of Labor Statistics. Foreign Labor Information. *Labor in Cuba.* Washington, D.C.: Government Printing Office, May 1957.

United States Department of State. *Foreign Relations of the United States: Diplomatic Papers,* vol. 5, *The American Republics, 1933.* Washington, D.C.: Government Printing Office, 1952.

Unpublished Material

Cole Blasier, Stewart. "The Cuban and Chilean Communist Parties: Instruments of Soviet Policy (1935–1948)." Ph.D. diss., Columbia University, New York, 1956.

González, Edward. "The Cuban Revolution and the Soviet Union, 1959–1960." Ph.D. diss., University of California, Los Angeles, 1966.

Page, Charles Albert. "The Development of Organized Labor in Cuba." Ph.D. diss., University of California, Berkeley, 1952.

Perez, Louis A., Jr. "The Rise and Fall of Army Preeminence in Cuba, 1898–1958." Ph.D. diss., University of New Mexico, Albuquerque, 1971.

Index

ABC party, 22, 39, 40, 68, 79, 186; and Batista-Mendieta regime, 45–47, 57, 58, 243n.34; and conflicts with student movement, 50; and Constitutional Convention of 1940, 94; decline of, 57–59; dissolves into Ortodoxo party, 58, 126; ideology of, 52; Ichaso on, 56; influence of fascism on, 59; and lower middle class, 63; manifesto of 1932, 54–56; negotiates with Welles, 37; opposes Grau-student government, 41, 57; structure and composition of, 53, 56–58, 244n.4

Acción Democrática, 114, 151

Acción Revolucionaria Guiteras (ARG) in labor movement, 120–121, 135

Agramonte, Roberto, 123

Agrarian reform, 102, 205, 206, 215, 219, 221; and Agrarian Reform Law of 1959, xviii, 191, 217–218, 224, 230–231; Auténtico program of 1939 on, 89; Castro-Chibás-Pazos document on, 191; Castro's manipulation of, 25, 225; Communist party and Castro clash over, 230–231, 259n.30; Communist party program of 1958 on, 165; Constitution of 1940 on, 95, 191; under Grau-student government, 43; ignored by Batista, 81; in rebel-occupied areas, 191, 193, 257n.19; role of peasants and workers in, 6

Agrarian Reform Law of 1959; xviii, 191,224; and Castro, 217–218, 230–231

Agricultural wage workers, xiv, xix, 212, 213; and Castro's agrarian re-

form, 221; and "factories in the fields," 6, 13, 132; and unionization, 133. *See also* Economy; Sugar industry

Aguilar, Luis E., 42–43

Ala Izquierda Estudiantil. *See* Student Left Wing

Alexander, Robert, 62; on Communist-Batista relationship, 162

Alma Mater (student newspaper), 43

Almeida, Juan, 9

American Federation of Labor, 65

Anarchism and anarchists, 12, 55, 120; influence in working class, 65; in Havana Federation of Labor, 65

Angola, 234

"Ante la Prensa," 205

Anti-Batista coalition, 23–24, 188–193, 205–206, 216, 236

Antuña, Vicentina, 128

APRA (Peru), 61, 62, 89; and Auténticos, 114, 115, 151

Arbenz, Jacobo, 208, 220

Argentina, 65, 102, 103, 165, 208, 226

Armed Forces of Cuba, xiii, 47, 61, 174, 184, 195; attempted Barquín coup, 168–172; under Batista's regimes, 20–22, 40, 42, 48, 62, 71, 74–76, 79, 80, 149, 150, 168–173, 239n.1; under Céspedes regime, 38; and Chibás, 152; Cienfuegos rebellion, 169–170, 255n.36; Communist party influence on, 75; corruption in, 21, 22, 168–169, 254n.33; and coup of 1952, 146; and Grau, 108, 118; Guevara on, 172; Hotel Nacional battle, 74; and Machado,

Armed Forces of Cuba (*cont.*)
73–74; professionalization of officers
in, 170–171; during Republican
period, 72–73; and revolution of
1959, 4, 211, 215, 220 (*see also*
Rebel army); Sergeants' Revolt,
20–22, 40, 74; trained by U.S., 22,
72, 73, 171–172, 201, 255n.38;
Welles and, 74–75
Auténtico party, 20, 21, 63, 64, 77,
83–85, 91, 93, 94, 114, 135, 138,
170, 178, 183, 236; abstentionist
period, 87; opposition to Batista, 62,
150–153; and Communist party, 67,
69, 87–90, 120, 130, 138–139, 141,
243n.28; corruption in, 107–113
passim, 118, 122, 151, 176; degeneration of, 106–108, 112–114, 116,
117, 122, 150–153; formation of,
61–62; Grau administration of, 105,
109–112; ideology of, 89; and labor
movement, 120, 130–131; and middle class, 110–112, 115–116,
250n.42; and Ortodoxo party, 122–
124, 127–129; and political gangsterism, 117–122, 145; Prío administration of, 109–111, 129, 131, 146,
151, 165; the "Realists" of, 90, 124;
reformist nature of, 88–91; reorganization of, 87–88; on U.S. imperialism, 115–116; and working
class, 134–135, 142–143, 243n.28

Bank Workers' Union, 157
Barquín, Ramón, Col., 257n.31; coup
against Batista, 168–169, 171, 172
Batchelder, Robert B., on communal
land system in Cuba, 32
Batista y Zaldívar, Fulgencio: as
Bonapartist conservative, 20–22,
78–81, 90, 109; early years, 78–79;
exile, 108, 146; overthrown, 200–
201; political philosophy of, 81; on
U.S.-Cuba relations, 79
Batista y Zaldívar, Fulgencio: first regime of, xvii, xviii, 3, 9, 12, 15, 20,
23, 24, 58, 82, 85, 86, 91, 111, 119–
121, 124, 136, 145, 229; and armed
forces, 21–22, 40, 42, 48, 62, 71,
74–77, 80, 239n.1; and Auténticos,

62, 88, 90; as Bonapartist regime,
78–81; and Communist party, 21,
83–87, 89, 93, 136; and elections of
1940, 106; and elections of 1944,
108–109; "normalizations" under,
81–83, 93; second regime compared
to, 147; students join, 59
Batista y Zaldívar, Fulgencio: second
regime of, 15, 22, 23, 25, 121, 129,
139, 144, 145–196 passim, 199–203,
205, 207, 220, 221, 223, 235, 236;
alliance with Mujal, 147, 148, 156–
157, 180; and armed forces, 148–
150, 168–173; Auténtico and Ortodoxo opposition to, 149–153; Barquín conspiracy, 168–172; Batistianos executed, 203; Castro-
Chibás-Pazos document on, 190;
Castro's early opposition to, 184–
188; Cienfuegos Navy rebellion,
169–170; and Communist party,
162–163; compared to first regime,
147; coup of 1952, 132, 139, 144,
146–147, 149, 166, 185, 236;
economy during, 147–148, 153–156,
161, 189, 253n.17; and labor, 147,
159–161; and Ortodoxos, 129–130;
overthrow of, 200–201, 257n.31; and
political gangsterism, 121; and ruling class, 147–148; and SAR, 166–
168; and student movement, 181–
182; and working class, 155
Batista, Marta Fernández de, 193
Batista-Communist alliance. *See* Batista, first regime; Communist Party
Batista-Mendieta regime, 58, 63,
246n.36; and ABC, 46, 47, 58; and
labor, 45–46; and Law of National
Defense, 46, 243n.32; recognized by
U.S., 45; and U.S. imperialism, 71
Becquer, Conrado, 157
Berle, A. A., 60
Blackburn, Robin, on Batista's
second regime, 148; on Cuban
landed oligarchy and *nouveaux
riches,* 104; theory of Castro's rise to
power, 213–214
Bohemia, 139, 187, 188, 190
Bolívar, Simón, 19, 28, 29
Bolsheviks, 19, 221

Bonaparte, Louis Napoleon, 17–20, 78, 213
Bonaparte, Napoleon, 197
Bonapartism, 16, 149; and Auténtico regimes, 112; Batista as Bonapartist conservative, 20–22, 78–80, 109; Castro as Bonapartist revolutionary, 23–27, 197–200, 212–213; and Cuban politics 1933–1959, 235–237; Marx's theory of, 17–19; and peasantry, 18; and populism, 27
Borbonnet, Major, 169; coup against Batista, 168
Boti, Regino, 194
Brazil, 102, 165
British West Indies, 234
Browder, Earl, 137, 251n.36. *See also* Communist party
Bureaucrats. *See* State bureaucracy of Cuba
Business Week, on 1940 Constitution, 97; on Prío administration, 131

Caffery, Jefferson, 41, 47, 49, 71, 74. *See also* Welles, Benjamin Sumner
Camagüey, 158
Camp Columbia, 204
Carbó, Sergio, 90
Cárdenas, Lázaro, 86
Carvajal, Juan F., 100
Castro-Chibás-Pazos document, 8, 190, 191, 194, 198
Castro, Fidel, xii, xvii, 4, 20, 22, 100, 122, 150, 155, 170, 174, 190, 242n.12; and agrarian reform, 6, 185–186, 217–218, 230–231; as Bonapartist revolutionary, 17, 23–27, 197–200, 212–213; and Castro-Chibás-Pazos document, 8, 190–191, 194, 198; coalitionist period, 189–193, 205–206; compared to Chibás, 192–193; and Communism, 209–215, 224, 258n.8; and Communist party, 163–165; on Czechoslovakia, xiii; and the economy, 185–186, 190–191, 206, 216–219, 221–223, 230–231, 234, 236, 256n.18; emergence of, 184–188; exile of, 169, 187–188; and "La Sierra y el Llano" theory, 8–10;

leadership style of, 199–200, 223–225; and Miami document incident, 199, 203; and middle class, 4, 14–16, 21–24, 100, 101, 186, 189, 190–193, 197, 198, 216–218; role in Moncada attack, 185–186; on nationalization, 165; and Ortodoxo party, 128–129, 152–153, 184–188; and the peasantry, 5–6, 15, 217–219, 221, 257n.19; on political control, xiii–xiv, 197–200, 203–205; on political gangsterism, 118–119; and populist tradition, 195–196, 215–216; on revolution, 204–205; as "the revolution," 212; rise to power, 23–26, 193–201, 208–209; and SAR, 166–167; speech of 1970, xiv, 12; and the 26th of July Movement, 187–188, 191–198 passim; and the upper class, 25, 191, 216–218; on war, 196; and working class, 5–7, 10–15 passim, 144, 160, 161
Castro, Fidel, early regime of, 6; and Agrarian Reform Law of 1959, 216–219, 230–231; Bonapartist quality of, 23–27, 197–200, 212–213, 235–237; and Castro, Raúl, 226–228; and Communism, 209–212, 233–234, 258n.8; and Communist party, 225–226, 229–233; consolidation of power, 202–205, 211–212; economic policies of, 206, 216–219, 221–223, 230–231, 234; Escalante purge, 233; and Guevara, Ernesto "Ché," 220–221, 226–228; political conditions under, 223–226; political structure of, 212–215; reformist period of, 205–209; and revolution of 1933, 235–236; and strike of 1959, 202; support of, 215–217; trade unions under, 222; and U.S., 219–221; and U.S.S.R., 233–234; relation of workers to, 10, 226. *See also* Revolution of 1959; 26th of July Movement
Castro, Manolo, 119
Castro, Raúl, 9, 217, 242n.12; "anti-anti-communist" position, 228–230; political background, 226; role in early Castro regime, 227–228
Catholic Church and Bastista regime,

Catholic Church & Batista (*cont.*) 173; weakness of, 172–173, 255n.41

Catholic Worker Youth, 173

CDR. *See* Committees for the Defense of the Revolution

Census of Cuba, 1953, 104

Céspedes, Carlos Manuel de, and regime of, 37, 40, 50; ABC participates in, 57; abolishes Machado Constitution, 38; dissolves Congress, 38; fall of, 77

Chibás, Eduardo, 139, 143, 176, 190, 250n.9; background of, 122–123; and Castro, 185, 188, 192, 215; on class struggle, 128; death of, 129, 145, 151–152, 252n.1; on land reform, 126; politics of, 123–125. *See also* Ortodoxos

Chibás, Raúl, 190

Chile, 102, 103

China, 232, 233; Revolution, 25

Cienfuegos, 158; navy rebellion, 169–170, 255n.36

Cienfuegos, Camilo, 197

Civic Resistance, 165, 189, 212

Cold War, 123; and Communist party, 130, 138–140, 142, 161, 192, 251n.36; effect on labor movement, 11, 120, 141; effect on political climate, 144, 146, 174, 182

Cole, G. D. H., on "middle class" versus "bourgeois," 101

Colombia, 103

Colonos, 33–34, 91

Committee of Cuban Institutions, 200

Committees for the Defense of the Revolution, 225

Communism, xii; Chibás' attitude toward, 123; condemned by ABC, 56; criticized in Auténtico program, 89; and democratic control, xiv; populists' attitude toward, 179–180; and revolution of 1959, 236, 239n.1

Communist party of Cuba, xiii, 36, 49, 50, 63, 83, 106, 121, 123, 124, 135, 161, 163, 166, 192, 205, 207, 211, 212, 214, 215, 218, 222, 224, 245n.18; and ABC, 55, 57; alliance with Batista (1938), 11–12, 21, 84–87, 89, 93, 136, 247n.11; and Au-

ténticos, 69, 88–91 passim, 120, 130; and "Browderism," 137–144, 251n.36, 252n.38; bureaucratization of, 66–67; and Céspedes regime, 38–39; and Constitutional Convention of 1940, 94–95; early years of, 64–67; during Cold War, 130, 138–142, 157–159, 161, 162, 192, 207–208, 251n.36; failure to educate rank and file, 140–141; and general strike of 1933, 68, 229; and general strike of 1935, 48, 68–69; and general strike of 1958, 8, 158–159; Grau-Communist agreement (1944–1946), 138; growth of, 67, 85; and the "Llano," 8–9; opposes Grau government, 41–44, 243n.28; as an opposition party, 113–114; and Ortodoxos, 128; Popular Front, period of, 48, 67–69, 83–88, 115, 229, 245n.18; program of 1958, 164–165, 254n.30, 254n.31; role of Old Communists in early Castro regime, 225, 229–234, 259n.21, 259n.31; and second Batista regime, 161–165, 254n.27, 254n.28; Third Period of, 12, 38–39, 41, 48, 64, 67–69, 85–88, 115, 164, 220, 229; and Zeitlin's theory of working class, 11–14, 142–144

Conservative Party, 36

Constituent Assembly of 1901, 30

Constituent Assembly of 1940. *See* Constitutional Convention of 1940

Constitution of 1901, 30–32. *See also* Platt Amendment

Constitution of 1940, xviii, 16, 88, 106, 150, 165, 191; article 90 of (agrarian reform), 95; *Business Week* on, 97; and Cuban political development, 97–98, 206, 248n.6; and populism, 180–181; provisions of, 94–95; social legislation in, 96–97; unenforceability of, 95, 96–98

Constitutional Convention of 1940, 86, 88, 89, 93–94, 106, 165, 250n.9; composition of, 247–248n.1

"Convenient Solution for Cuba, The," 164

Córdoba Movement, 66

Corona, Eduardo, 128
Coronet (Magazine), 192
Cortina, José Manuel, 110–111
Cossío del Pino, Alejo, 146
Creole artistocracy of Cuba, 28
CTC. *See* Cuban Confederation of Workers
Cuban Communism (1959 and after), 2, 226, 236; versus Communism in other countries, 237; and Communist "polycentrism," 233; theories of Castro's road to, 209–213, 258n.8; and U.S. economic embargo, 220–221. *See also* Castro, Fidel; Communist party of Cuba
Cuban Confederation of Workers (CTC), 106; and Communist Party, 65–66; pro-Auténtico (CTC[a]), 120–121
Cuban Congress, 95, 109
Cuban Electrical Company, 126, 131
Cuban Revolutionary party. *See* Auténtico party
Cuban War of Independence (Spanish-Cuban-American War), 29, 33, 56, 73, 82; U.S. intervenes in, 30–31, 241n.5

Dance of the Millions (or Fat Cows), 35
De Beauvoir, Simone, 214
Debray, Régis, 239n.1; on "La Sierra y el Llano" theory, 7; on urban working class, 160
De la Torre, Haya. *See* Haya de la Torre, Víctor Raúl
De la Torre, Oscar, 57
De la Torre, R. S., 63
De la Torriente Brau, Pablo, 82
De la Torriente, Cosme, Colonel, 167
De León, Rubén, 90, 106, 107
Delinquency and Drift (Matza), 210
"Democratic Socialist Coalition" of 1944, 108
Desnoes, Edmundo, 99
De Zéndegui, Guillermo, 89
Diario de la Marina, 100, 208
Directorio Estudiantil. *See* Student Directorate
Directorio Revolucionario, xviii, 163,

182, 197, 231; attacks Presidential Palace, 178, 183, 184, 190; steals arms from 26th of July Movement, 204; strategy criticized, 183–184
Document of Unity of the Cuban Opposition to Batista Dictatorship. *See* Miami Pact
Draper, Hal, 19
Draper, Theodore, 14, 15, 16, 104, 184, 186, 205–206; on Castro's rise to power, 194; on Cuban trade unions, 160–161
Dual Power, 26
Dubois, Jules, 158, 189
Duclos letter, 137, 252n.36

Echeverría, José, Antonio, 183, 189
Economic Commission for Latin America, 102–103, 105
Economic Survey of Latin America, 154–156
Economy of Cuba, xix, 112; during Batista's regimes, 147–148, 153–156, 161, 189, 253n.17; *Business Week* on, 131; capitalist development, 91–92, 98–99, 135–136, 251n.34; and Castro, 185–186, 190–191, 206, 211, 216–219, 221–223, 230–231, 234, 236; and Constitution of 1940, 95–97; and crisis of late 1930's, 81; and government intervention, 91–92, 130–131; effects of Great Depression on, 36, 40, 49, 64–65, 93, 101; Guevara on, 234; latifundia, 32, 33, 55, 126; misuse of prosperity, 102–104; post-World War I prosperity, 35; and Spanish-Cuban-American War, 33; stagnation of, 135–136; Trade Reciprocity Treaty, 71–72; and U.S., 72, 103–104, 200–201, 207, 219–220; and U.S.S.R., 233–234; post-World War II, 101–106; and working class, 131–134. *See also* Sugar industry
Eighteenth Brumaire, The (Marx), 80
Eighth National Congress of P.S.P., 162
Eisenhower, Dwight D., xix
Engels, Frederick, xii, 19
Escalante, Aníbal, 232–233

"Factories in the fields," 13, 132
Federación Obrera de la Habana, 50
F.E.U. (University Student Federation), 169, 181
Fernández Casas, Federico, 125
Fidelismo, 193–197
Fidelistas, xiv, 3, 9–10, 17, 211–212, 214, 215, 223, 225, 230, 233, 234
"50 percent decree," 44–45
Fitzgibbon, Russell, 82
France, 203
Frayde, Marta, 128

García Bárcenas, Rafael, 178
General strike of 1933, 37, 65. *See also* Revolution of 1933; Working class of Cuba
General strike of 1935, 79, 84, 87; and armed forces, 76; and Communist party, 69; failure of, 47–49; role of students in, 48–49. *See also* Revolution of 1933
General strike of 1959, 202
Georges Sorel School for Leadership, 120
Germani, Gino, 104
German Social Democratic party, 113, 134
Germany, 65, 113
Gil, Federico C., 196
Goldenberg, Boris, 219
Gómez, Miguel Mariano, 76, 82, 94
González, Edward, 233
González, Manuel Pedro, 29
González Palacios, Carlos, 108
"Good Neighbor" policy, 36, 71, 83, 117; Prío on, 250n.44
Granma (newspaper), 240n.14
Granma (yacht), xviii, 24, 194–195
Grau-student government (1933), 45, 50, 62, 63, 68–70, 78, 90; and ABC, 57, 59; and Communist party, 42, 43, 68–69, 243n.28; decrees of, 43; ideological differences in, 41–42; isolation of, 60–61; students in, 50, 59–61; Welles on, 41–42, 60, 74–75; and working class, 43–45. *See also* Revolution of 1933
Grau San Martín, Ramón, between regimes (1934–1944), 124, 163, 164;

condemned by Communists, 67; and Constitutional Convention of 1940, 94; and elections of 1940, 94; and elections of 1944, 108; founds Auténticos, 61–62; leads "Orthodox" majority of Auténticos, 90; militancy declines, 88–89; rejects Popular Front, 69, 245n.18; as symbol of Cuban revolution, 107–108. *See also* Auténtico party
Grau San Martín, Ramón, second administration of (1944–1948), 107, 108; abandons anti-imperialism, 115–116; characterized, 109–111; corruption of, 110; failure of, 111–114; Grau-Communist agreement (1944–1946), 138; Ortodoxos oppose, 122–123; and political gangsterism, 117–118; and state bureaucracy, 110. *See also* Auténtico party
Great Depression, 36, 40, 49, 64–65, 93, 101
Grupo de Avance, 57, 66, 244n.14
Guantánamo Bay Naval Base, xviii, 30, 46, 71
Guardia Rural, 215
Guatemala, 208, 220, 226–227
Guerra, Ramiro, 33–34
Guevara, Ernesto "Ché," xiv, 172, 193–195, 220–221; "anti-anti-Communist" position of, 227–230; and early Castro regime, 217, 227–228; on Cuban exceptionalism, 239n.1; on "La Sierra y el Llano" theory, 7–8, 9; on peasants of Sierra Maestra, 5–6; political background, 226–227
Guiteras y Holmes, Antonio, 68, 75, 117, 128, 164, 185, 243n.28; in Grau administration, 41, 42; role in Joven Cuba, 62–64, 69

Hart, Armando, 9, 178
Havana, 45, 158, 159, 171, 187, 204, 206
Havana Federation of Labor, 37, 65
Havana University Student Federation, 119
Haya de la Torre, Victor Raúl, 61
Healy, Max H., 82

Hennessy, C.A.M., 30
Hermida, Ramón, 58
History Will Absolve Me (Castro), 14, 185–187, 190, 216; Theodore Draper on, 186
Hobsbawm, E. J., 121–122
Hotel Nacional, battle of, 74
Hoy (Communist daily), 139, 226, 230, 232, 233
Huberman, Leo, 14, 15; theory of Cuban revolution, 5–7
Humanistas, 214, 222, 227
Humildes, Los, 123
Hungary, 103

Ichaso, Francisco, on ABC, 56
Iglesias, Aracelio, 123
Intelligentsia of Cuba, 49, 82, 127, 129; Grupo de Avance, 57, 66, 244n.14; and political parties, 56–57, 126–127
Inter-American Defense Treaties, 171
International Communist Movement (after Communist International), 225–227, 233–234
Instituciones Civicas, 160, 190, 212
Italy, 65, 113
Izquierdo, José, 37

Joven Cuba, 84, 88; and Communist party, 69; decline of, 64; de la Torre, R. S., on, 63; program of, 62–63
Junco, Sandalio, 40, 65, 140

Kantor, Harry, 115
Karol, K. S., xiv
Kennedy, John F., 219
Kerensky, Alexander, 26, 221
Kling, Merle, 112, 119
Korea, Korean War, 102, 122, 123

La Plata, 189
"La Sierra y el Llano," 7–10
Las Villas (province), 197
Labor movement in Cuba, 35, 42, 106, 132, 133, 166, 182, 213, 236; and Batista-Mendieta regime, 45–46; and Batista-Mujal alliance, 147, 148, 156–157, 180; and Céspedes regime, 38–40; Communist party gains in, 85–86, 138–140; Communist-

Auténtico split in, 120–121, 130; and Communist-Batista alliance, 11–12, 21, 84–89, 93, 136, 247n.11; and Constitution of 1940, 94–97; during early Castro regime, 221–222, 230; and general strike of 1935, 47–49; and Grau regime, 43–45, 243n.28; in late 1940's and early 1950's, 13, 130–131, 134–137; and Ortodoxos, 127–128; and recession of 1952–1954, 154; and revolution of 1933, 37, 39–40, 47–49, 50, 64–65; and second Batista regime, 147, 159–161; state involvement in, 91, 96–97. *See also* Communist party of Cuba; Working class of Cuba
Land reform. *See* Agrarian reform
Laredo Bru, Federico, 93
Latifundia, 32, 55, 126; proletarianizing effect of, 33
Latin America, 3, 4, 29, 98, 99, 101, 111, 116, 123, 164, 179, 213, 220, 227, 234, 239n.1; armed forces in, 170–172; Catholic Church in, 172–173; Cuban identification with, 208; economic growth in, 102–103; economic role of state in, 112; intelligentsia in, 127; middle classes in, 104–105, 114–115
Law of National Defense, 46
Left-Wing Communism: An Infantile Disorder (Lenin), 124
Lenin, V. I., xii, 124, 224, 225
Leninism, 89
"Leninist levy," 19–20
L'Express (French newspaper), 220
Ley de Coordinación Azucarera, 91
Liberal party, 36, 94, 143
Ligas Campesinas (Peasant Leagues), 35
Lipset, Seymour Martin, 34–35
Llerena, Mario, 194, 256n.18
López Fresquet, Rufo, 40, 95, 96, 169
Lumpenproletariat, 18
Luxemburg, Rosa, xii, 200

Maceo, Antonio, 28
Machado, Gerardo, and regime of, xvii, 20, 36–38, 49, 50, 71, 76, 84, 93, 117–118, 122, 182; ABC and

Machado, Gerardo (*cont.*)
Student Directorate oppose, 52; and American business, 31, 242n.7; and Communist party, 68; and middle classes of Cuba, 56–57; and Sergeants' Coup, 73–74; and worker revolt, 64–65
Mafia, E. J. Hobsbawm on, 121–122
Maine, U.S.S., xvii
Mañach, Jorge, 80
"Manifesto of the Sierra Maestra," 190
Marinello, Juan, 138
Márquez Sterling, Carlos, 94
Martí, José, 61, 123, 179, 187; Castro on, 195–196; importance in Cuban history, 30; political philosophy of, 29–30, 241n.3
Martínez Sáenz, Joaquín, 58
Martínez Villena, Rubén, 66
Marx, Karl, xii, 17–19, 78, 80, 213, 224, 225
Masferrer, Rolando, 121
Matos, Hubert, 9
Matthews, Herbert, on Batista's coup of 1952, 149, 153; on Cuba, 1956, 188; interview with Castro, 189
Matza, David, 210, 258n.8
Mazzini, Giuseppe, 29
McCarthyism, 123
Mendieta, Carlos, 45, 46, 71. *See also* Batista-Mendieta regime
Menocal, Mario G., 94
Mexico, xviii, 25, 103, 165, 169, 187
Miami Pact, 198–199, 203
Michels, Robert, 113
Middle class of Cuba and ABC, 4, 25, 52, 53, 56, 58, 244n.4; and armed forces, 170–172; and Auténticos, 61, 111–112, 126, 127, 143; and Batista, 146, 150–151, 157, 166–168; and anti-Batista coalition, 23, 24, 189–193, 205–206, 236; and Castro, 4, 21–24, 100, 101, 186, 189–193, 197, 198, 215–218, 236; and Civic Resistance Movement, 165, 189, 212; conservatism of, 106, 111, 114–116, 150, 250n.42; and the economy, 33, 63, 102–105; and Joven Cuba, 63; and Ortodoxos, 126–127, 129, 135, 143, 146, 150, 152, 157; and populism,

184; rural, 33–34, 91, 105; and SAR, 166–168; weakness of, 63, 98–102, 104–105, 129, 135, 144, 152, 173, 178, 250n.42
Mills, C. Wright, 57, 212
Ministry of Education, 110
Ministry of Labor, 43, 44, 46, 85, 121, 136; under Auténticos, 130
Ministry of Industries under Guevara, 234
Mintz, Sidney W., 32, 34, 35
Moncada barracks attack, 9–10, 24, 166, 177, 187, 195, 198, 226, 240n.10; Castro's role, 185–186
Monroe Doctrine, 219
Mora, Menelao, 178
Morray, Joseph P., 224, 225, 227
Movement of Civic Resistance. *See* Civic Resistance
Movimiento Nacionalista Revolucionario (MNR), 178
Movimiento Socialista Revolucionario (MSR), 120
Mujalista trade union bureaucracy, 147, 148, 157, 180

National Association of Cuban Industrialists, 137
National Bank of Cuba, 95, 190
National Confederation of Labor, 37
Nationalization of property, xii–xiii, 25, 180, 192, 223, 259n.19; Castro on, 192; Communist party on, 164–165, 254n.31; critique of Huberman and Sweezy on, 6–7; O'Connor on, 211; Ortodoxos on, 126
Nazi-Soviet Pact, 86
New Deal, 123
New Economic Policy (NEP), 224–225
New York Times, The, 189
Nixon, Richard M., 217
Nouveaux riches of Cuba, 104; Desnoes on, 99–100
Novás Calvo, Lino, 33, 105
Nuestra Razón (document of July 26th Movement), 194, 256n.17

Occupational structure of Cuba, 132–133
O'Connor, James, on nationalization,

O'Connor, James (*cont.*)
25, 211–212
Official Gazette, 231
Ordoquí, Joaquín, 141
Organization of American States
(OAS), 219
ORI (Organizaciones Revolucionarias
Integradas), 214, 259n.21
Oriente province, 62–63, 185, 196, 197
Ortodoxo party, 117, 119, 139, 140,
142, 144–146, 174, 176, 178, 184,
190, 223; ABC merges with, 58, 126;
and Auténticos, 122–124, 127–129;
and Batista, 150–153, 166, 177; and
Castro, 185–188, 215; collapse of,
129–130, 150–153, 236; founded,
122; and intelligentsia, 126–127; and
middle class, 126–127, 129, 135,
143, 146, 150, 152, 157; populist
tradition of, 128, 129; program of,
124–126, 251n.22; weakness of,
125–128
Ostrogorski, M., 113

Pact of Mexico, 169
Pact of Montreal, 151
Page, Charles A., 120; on working
class politics, 134–135
Panama, 234
Pardo Llada, José, 188
Partido del Pueblo Cubano. *See* Or-
todoxo party
Partido Revolucionario Cubano (PRC).
See Auténtico party
Partido Socialista Popular (PSP). *See*
Communist party of Cuba
Partido Unión Revolucionaria, 85
Pazos, Felipe, 190, 194, 199
Peasantry of Cuba, xiv, 13, 18, 85, 211,
235, 236; attitude of early Castro re-
gime toward, 217–219, 221,
257n.19; and Auténticos, 61; Gue-
vara on, 5–6; Huberman and Sweezy
on, 5–6; lack of organization of, 35;
and theory of "La Sierra y el Llano,"
7–9. *See also* Agrarian reform in
Cuba
Peña, Lázaro, 137, 138, 222, 252n.37
Pérez, Faustino, 178
Pérez Jímenez, Marcos, 173

Perón, Evita, 193
Perón, Juan, 173, 179, 208
Peru, 114, 234
Petty bourgeoisie, 160
Phillips, Ruby Hart, 70, 113, 250n.44,
255n.1; on Sergeants' coup, 73–74,
242n.22; on talk with Ambassador
Welles, 53–54
Pinar del Río, 158
Platt Amendment, xvii, xviii, 30–32,
177, 220, 242n.6; abolition of,
46–47, 71
Poland, 103
Political Bureau of Cuban Communist
Party, 225
Political gangsterism, 125, 138, 145,
146, 204; and Auténticos, 117–118,
120–122; Batista ends, 121;
Hobsbawm on, 121–123; and labor
movement, 120–121; and student
movement, 119–121
Popular Front. *See* Communist party
of Cuba
Populism and populist groups in Cuba,
24, 52, 66, 67, 87, 114, 159, 164,
180, 186, 190; and ABC, 59; and Auténticos, 61–62, 89, 117; and
Bonapartism, 27, 236–237; Castro
appeals to tradition of, 195–196,
215–216; and Chibás-Ortodoxos,
123, 128–129; and Constitution of
1940, 97, 180, 181; and Cuban nationalism, 179; and Grau-student
government, 59; and army, 75; and
Martí, 30; and political gangsterism,
118–119; and *Revolución*, 213–214,
216; and student movement, 182;
vagueness of, 178–181; and working
class in 1930's, 65
Prebisch, Raúl, 194
Prío Socarrás, Carlos, xviii, 109–111,
129, 146, 165, 250n.44, 253n.3;
Business Week on, 131; opposes
Batista, 151. *See also* Auténtico
party
"Problems of New Cuba," 39, 46

Radio Rebelde, 8, 196, 200
Radio Station "1010," 139
"Realists," 90, 124

Rebel army, 5–8, 22, 25, 170, 183–184, 189–190, 194–195, 200, 211, 213
Reciprocal Trade Agreement, xviii
Reed, John, 82
Report on Cuba (of International Bank), 102, 145; on labor competition between Auténticos and Communists, 130; and collective bargaining, 137
Republican party (Cuban), 91, 124
Republican period in Cuba, 56, 70, 82, 173. *See also* Cuban War of Independence; Martí, José
Revolución (newspaper), 208, 213, 216
Revolution of 1933, 90, 107, 111, 127, 128, 143, 146, 170, 171, 192, 202, 203, 211, 212, 220, 229; and anti-imperialism, 70–71; failures of, 39–40, 49–51, 77, 82–83; overview of, 235; versus revolution of 1959, 39–40, 202, 220; and revolutionaries in 1950's, 177–178; and working class, 38–39, 49, 64–65. *See also* General strike of 1935
Revolution of 1959, xi, xiv–xv, 3, 25, 71; Batista overthrown, 200–201; anti-Batista coalition, 23–24, 188–193, 205–206, 216, 236; class interpretations of, 4–7, 15, 16; Debray on, 7; Draper, Theodore, on, 14–16, 49, 71, 143, 165, 205–206; "La Sierra y el Llano" theory of, 7–10; as a middle class revolution, 14–16, 205–206; as a peasant revolution, 5–7; and populism, 178–181; and revolution of 1933, 40, 49, 52, 235–237; as a working class revolution, 5–7, 10–14; role of youth in, 52, 181–184, 255n.1; Zeitlin on, 10–14. *See also* Castro, Fidel; Rebel army; 26th of July Movement
Revolutionary Cuban Party. *See* Auténtico party
Revolutionary Directorate. *See* Directorio Revolucionario
Roca, Blas, 138, 162, 226, 229, 230, 232, 252n.39; on Communist party, 140–141
Rodríguez, Carlos Rafael, 232
Rodríguez, Conrado, 157

Rojas Pinillas, Gustavo, 173
Roosevelt, Franklin D., 36, 80–81, 122, 123, 250n.44
Russia. *See* U.S.S.R.
Russian Revolution, 15

Sagua la Grande, 158
Saladrigas, Carlos, 58, 108
Sánchez Arango, Aureliano, on student role in 1935 strike, 48–49
Santamaria, Haydée, 9, 198
Santiago de Chile, 185
Santiago de Cuba, 158, 159, 199
Santiago uprising, 189
Santovenia, Emeterio S., 21–22
SAR (Sociedad de Amigos de la República), 166–168, 174, 188
Sartre, Jean Paul, 199–200
Schulman, Iván E., 29
Seasonal workers, 13, 133
Second Front of Escambray, 197
Secretariat of Cuban Communist Party, 225.
Sergeants' revolt of 1933, 20, 21, 41, 75–76, 78; joint proclamation with students, 40–41; and old officer corps, 73; revolutionary government formed, 40, 242n.22. *See also* Batista, first regime of
Shelton, Raúl M., 22
Sierra Maestra, 5, 9, 15, 24, 35, 170, 184, 189, 190; 206
Smith, Robert F., 72
Society of Friends of the Republic. *See* SAR
Sorí Marin, Humberto, 9
Soviet Union. *See* U.S.S.R.
Spain, xvii, 45, 73, 103, 173, 241n.5; and "50 percent decree," 44; Ten Years' War (1868–1878), 28; Spanish Republic, 118, 123
Spanish Civil War, 82, 118, 123
Staley, Eugene, 103
Stalinism, xii, 251n.36
State and Revolution (Lenin), 124
State bureaucracy of Cuba: and ABC, 56; and Auténticos, 110; under Batista's first regime, 81; and capitalist development, 91–92, 112; and lower middle class, 63; and

State bureaucracy of Cuba (*cont.*)
trade unions, 136–137; after World
War II, 104–105
Stokes, William, 109–110, 119
Strike of April 1958, xviii, 158–159,
200
Strike of August 1957, 157
Student Directorate (Directorio Estudiantil), 50, 122, 244n.8, 245n.15;
ideology of, 40; and Sergeants' coup,
40, 242n.22; and Welles, 36–37, 60
Student Left Wing, 41, 66, 245n.15
Student movement in Cuba, 39, 66,
79, 160, 184, 188; and ABC, 50, 53,
56; Castro as product of, 23; Communist party influence in, 66; and
Directorio Revolucionario, 182–183;
and general strike of 1935, 48–49;
and Grau-student government,
40–43, 242n.22; isolation of, 182;
maintains revolutionary alternative,
176–177; opposes second Batista regime, 181–182; and political gangsterism, 119; and problems of student populism, 59–61, 245n.15; and
University Student Federation
(FEU), 169, 181; and U.S. imperialism, 13; Welles on his negotiations with, 60
Suárez, Andrés, 231
Sugar industry, xix, 13, 64, 103, 147,
212, 222; boom in mid-1940's,
101–102; *colonos*, 33–34, 91; decline
of, 1952–1954, 153; "factories in the
fields," 13, 132; and the Great Depression, 48, 64; Guerra, Ramiro,
on, 33–34; Ley de Coordinación
Azucarera, 91; a monoculture, 4, 40,
72, 132, 223–224, 234; after
Spanish-Cuban-American War,
98–99; effects on social structure,
32–36, 132–133, 242n.15; state regulation of, 91–92; sugar strike of 1955,
157, 163; U.S. sugar quota, 219–
220, 222, 223; post–World War I
prosperity, 35; mill workers, 25, 39,
44, 211, 242n.15
Sweezy, Paul M., 14, 15; theory of
Cuban revolution, 5–7
Switzerland, 111

Tammany Hall, 73
Ten Years' War (1868–1878), xvii, 28
*Tesis Económica del Movimiento Re-
volucionario 26 de Julio*, 194
Third Period of Communist Interna-
tional. *See* Communist party of
Cuba
Thomas, Hugh, on early Fidelistas,
9–10, 24
Thomson, Charles A., on general
strike of 1933, 37; on general strike
of 1935, 47
Trade Reciprocity Treaty (1934), 71–72
Trade union movement. *See* Labor
movement in Cuba
Tramway Workers' Union, 120
Treaty of Paris, 31
Trotsky, Leon, xii, 15, 19, 225
Trotskyism, 55, 67; influence on
Havana Federation of Labor, 65
26th of July Movement, 57, 163, 182,
183, 228, 256n.18; in anti-Batista coalition, 164, 188–193; Castro-
Chibás-Pazos document (Manifesto
of the Sierra Maestra), 190–191; role
in Cienfuegos rebellion, 170; and
Civic Resistance, 189, 212; and
Communist party, 229; disintegration of, 214; founded, 187, 254n.20
(*see also* Moncada barracks attack);
on imperialism, 207; "no strike
pledge," 230; Pact of Mexico, 169;
and populism, 179; after Revolution
of 1959, 203–204; on Revolution of
1933, 177; and SAR, 167; and strike
of April 1958, 158–159. *See also* Castro, Fidel, early regime of; Revolution of 1959

Union of Electricity Workers, 157
Union Insurreccional Revolucionaria
(UIR), 118–120
Union Nacionalista party, 94
United States, 29, 30, 44, 89, 99–104
passim, 108, 111, 115, 125, 144,
148, 156, 174–175, 206, 216, 224,
229, 231, 236; abolishes Platt
Amendment, 46–47; allies with
Batista, 20, 41–42; and Batista-
Communist alliance, 86; Batista on

United States (*cont.*)
Cuba's relationship to, 79; and Chibás, 123; and early Castro regime, 207, 217–218, 220–221; and Grau-student regime, 45; and "normalization" under Batista, 80–81; recognizes second Batista regime, 147; and revolution of 1933, 70–71; and student movement, 60; supports Mendieta regime, 45; trains Cuban officers, 22, 73, 171–172, 201, 255n.38. *See also* Economy of Cuba; Platt Amendment; United States imperialism; United States intervention
United States imperialism, xiii, 4, 115, 138, 145, 209, 224, 227, 239n.1, 250n.44; anti-imperialism of 1933 and 1959 compared, 220; and anti-imperialism of late 1950's, 208, 219–220; and Cuban economy, 72, 103–104, 200–201, 207, 219–220; and early Castro regime, 207, 217–218; and Cuban communism, 210–211; ignored by Auténticos, 89; new style of, after 1933, 70, 71, 83, 178–179, 246n.37; and second Batista regime, 201. *See also* Economy of Cuba.
United States intervention, xviii, 46, 71, 79, 200–201, 258n.15; Castro-Chibás-Pazos document on, 190; and communal lands system in Cuba, 32; in Guatemala (1954), 71, 208; Kennedy advocates, 219; and Platt Amendment, 30–32; and revolution of 1933, 49, 70–71, 246n.37; in Cuban War of Independence, 30, 241n.5; Welles and Caffery threaten, 41
United States Department of State, 147, 201, 217, 219, 234
University of Havana, xii, 82, 118, 126, 182, 184; autonomy decreed, 43; and political gangsterism, 121; provisions for in Constitution of 1940, 95–96; as source of political power, 119. *See also* Student movement
Upper class of Cuba, 21, 146, 189, 208; and armed forces, 21, 22, 73; and

Batista, 25, 80, 87, 147, 148; and Castro, 25, 191, 216–218; Desnoes on, 99–100; lack of ideology, 111–112, 135, 178; and middle class, 98–99; and SAR, 167; weakness of, 32–33, 77, 98–100, 102–104, 173, 215, 216, 235
Urrutia, Manuel, 199, 208, 212, 223
U.S.S.R., xiii, xiv, 89–90, 139, 162, 220, 229, 233, 234

Valdés, Ramiro, 9
Varona, Tony, 170
Velíz, Claudio, 114–115, 127
Venezuela, 234
Voltaire, 210

Weber, Max, 113
Welles, Benjamin Sumner, xvii, 70, 244n.5; and Batista, 40–42, 71–75; and Grau administration, 41, 44, 75; on Student Directorate, 60; as mediator of 1933 crisis, 36–39, 49, 50, 57, 65. *See also* Revolution of 1933; U.S. intervention
Williams, William A., on populism, 179
Women's rights and Constitution of 1940, 94
Working classes of Cuba, xiv, 64, 79, 106, 137, 166, 182, 235, 236, 245n.25; attitude toward upper classes, 100; and Auténticos, 61; and Batista-Mendieta regime, 45–46, 243n.32; and Batista-Mujal alliance, 147, 148, 156–157, 180; "class instinct" of, 12; and Communist party, 48, 64–65, 67–69, 130, 138–140, 157–159, 162; and early Castro regime, 218, 221–222, 225–226; and general strike of 1935, 47–49; and Grau-student government, 43–44, 243n.28; and Great Depression, 36, 40, 64, 93; Huberman and Sweezy on, 6–7; and job security, 135–136, 251n.34; and Joven Cuba, 63; lack of political training of, 142–144; and Ortodoxos, 127–128; and populism of 1950's, 180; and reformism of late 1940's and 1950's, 130–131, 134–

Working classes of Cuba (*cont.*)
135; and revolution of 1933, 37,
39–40, 50, 64–65; and second Batista
regime, 147, 154, 156–161; structure of, 13–14, 131–134; and sugar
industry, 35–36, 132; "typical Cuban
worker" characterized, 134; during
World War II, 100; Zeitlin's theory
of, 10–14, 142–144, 240n.13. *See*
also Economy of Cuba; Labor
movement

Yglesias, José, 142–143

Zeitlin, Maurice, 240n.13; theory of
working class revolution, 10–15,
142–144